Praise for *I Will Not Break*

I Will Not Break is a testament to the strength of a child's soul. Within the abyss of abuse, Judith Mattison finds beauty, refuge, and solace in nature. Her inner strength to experience profound harm, protect others, seemingly forget, remember, and ultimately heal is hopeful and astounding! She tells her story so that we as individuals, families, and communities commit to protecting and advocating for every child's sanctity.

—Julie Ellefson, executive director, Southside Family
  Nurturing Center, Minneapolis

An inspiring story of a woman's courageous confrontation with her horrific past. Readers struggling with the long-term effects of child abuse will find an honest, informed, and ultimately compassionate supporter in Judith Mattison's excellent memoir.

—Bill Percy, PhD, psychologist emeritus

Judith Mattison's memoir is an extraordinary testament to courage in the face of abuse and gratitude in the face of loss. By her candor and witness, she invites all of us to be more vigilant to the possibilities of abuse in our communities. More than that, she empowers us to seek help, offer comfort, support each other, and in all these ways be shaped more fully into a community of healing and grace.

—David Lose, senior pastor, Mt. Olivet Lutheran Church,
  Minneapolis

I WILL NOT BREAK

A MEMOIR

JUDITH MATTISON

I Will Not Break: A Memoir
Published by New Sun Press, Edina, Minnesota.

Author's note: I have changed the names of my family and of predators,
neighbors, and others who might prefer to be anonymous. The locations and
chronology of events are sometimes adapted.

Paperback ISBN 978-0-692-16397-9
E-book ISBN 978-0-692-17661-0

Cover design by Christian Fuenfhausen
Author photo by Julie Ho
Page design by Beth Wright, Wright for Writers LLC

The author is available to speak to audiences such as
abuse survivor groups, social work conferences, church
gatherings, and civic groups large and small. You may
contact her at judiematt@gmail.com.

CONTENTS

1

TRAIN TRIP

I didn't start to remember until I was thirty-six.

That was the year I took the train from Minneapolis to Milwaukee in the spring to visit my sister-in-law Sandy. Since I had two young sons, I joked that I was "running away from home." My husband, Eric, encouraged me to visit his sister. We were good companions.

The route was familiar. I had taken it with Mother and my sister, Sherri, several times before I was six. The sound of the conductor calling, "NEW Lisbon! Co-LUM-bus! LA Crosse!" rang in my mind. For years I had taken any opportunity to return to my Wisconsin childhood neighborhoods. I wanted to keep track of my memories, confirm the images that had stayed with me all those years. I could still find the building shaped like a giant cream pitcher where I used to beg to stop for ice cream. I knew where the Elks Lodge had a huge bronze statue of an elk looking out over the waters of Lake Michigan; it scared me, and I went there with caution. I wanted to verify my memories and make them concrete in my mind.

I always felt protected on the train—a long tube of cozy double seats facing each other and a wide window looking out on the passing countryside. In the old days we brought our lunches—sandwiches and an apple in a shoebox—and ate them as we traveled coach round-trip from Wisconsin to visit family in Minneapolis. Now, as an adult traveling alone, I savored my privacy in an individual compartment as the train skimmed over level countryside and gained speed, rocking back and forth, with clattering wheels and the heavy squeak of shock absorbers. Ahead, the train whistle blew, carried on the wind back to my car, a mysterious, comforting sound, day or night.

At a distance I saw a lone country tavern, red and yellow neon signs in the windows. As we drew closer, I saw a half dozen cars and pickups parked randomly in the gravel lot out front. Gradually I heard the old songs my father used to play in such places, "Margie" and "Waltzin' Matilda." And "Chloe." I didn't really understand it, but it was a song about searching in a swampland, trying to find a woman. It was a strange blues song that carried my emotions into darkness and sadness. I still had Dad's ragged 1927 copy of the sheet music. His mother, Grandma Libby, had given it to me. Suddenly the train passed into a tunnel with a *whoosh*; for a moment, everything was dark and quiet. I held my breath. Then, clear and bright again. But the sudden darkness had struck me with terror. Or was it the songs?

Always there were songs. Music shook the house in Shorewood as Dad played piano with his entire tall body, strong hands and nearly two hundred pounds, singing at the top of his voice. In our ten years in and around Milwaukee, the black Wurlitzer upright always went with us. Friends smiled as their highballs clinked in their hands or perched on top of the piano. The sound of the parties drew me in. Confident at three, I sang "Good Night, Ladies" for the grown-ups before I went to bed.

"She has her daddy's long legs," a woman said.

"Isn't she a pretty, talented little girl?" asked another. "All that nice long dark hair."

I basked in the attention. As a toddler, I sat beside Daddy, playing music with him. I looked up at him, and we both smiled as I pounded the keys aimlessly but sang notes impeccably. "Ah-ha-ha. You and me. Little brown jug, don't I love thee!" Me and Daddy, smiling and laughing. And my favorite color was royal blue.

The notes I didn't hear were the obbligato accompanying my chorus of memories—the descant that wove itself among events and rested deep inside my mind. It rose close to the surface from time to time, disturbing my daily life, but remained unidentified: events I had forgotten in order to survive.

Sandy's home was handsomely traditional: Colonial furniture from South Carolina, fine linens, well-crafted porcelain and artwork. She kept a tidy house and was skilled at entertaining friends and her husband's colleagues. I felt at ease there, even though I lived a more random and creative life in which clutter was familiar. We were drawn together by our relationship with Eric and easily confessed to each other the realities of our lives, different as they were. She was short and blonde in contrast to my tall, brunette countenance, and her practical candor was unlike my cautious and often quiet attitude, steeped with fearful perfectionism.

That first morning in Milwaukee, I asked Sandy, "Would you go with me to see my old houses where I grew up?"

"Sure."

"Look. I have graph layouts of them." I spread them on the table with pride.

"You're kidding," she said.

"I'm just so curious to see if I'm right about how things looked. I have a good idea of where the houses were. Maybe the owners will let us in to look around."

We drove across town and knocked on the door of one of my former homes, a stuccoed story and a half on a corner in the northern suburb called Shorewood. A forty-something man with a round face and body welcomed us.

"I grew up in this house," I told him. "That was during World War II. I was wondering if maybe we could see what it's like now."

"You bet you can!" he replied with a smile. "You just come right in. We love this house."

As I expected, I remembered it well: where the rooms were, the black and white hexagonal floor tiles of the bathroom, and the small stained-glass windows high in one of the living room walls. Even my memories of the room sizes were accurate.

We passed by a bedroom. "Look, Sandy. This was my room. I used to have a picture on the wall of a little lamb on its knees, praying." I didn't recall going to church in those early years, but I always said my prayers at night with my parents listening.

For years I had mentally seen the kitchen in Shorewood, a warm and welcoming melody of a fall evening. After I was married, I bought Fiestaware plates and bowls at an antique store, basking in the nostalgia of their colorful enchantment. The house held the memories of childhood.

"Judie Marie, will you help me set the table?" Mother asks, reaching for the Fiestaware.

"Can I have the big orange plate, for me?" I ask.

"You can choose whatever you like. You're a good helper!"

Sandy and I passed by my bedroom door, and the hall seemed suddenly dark. A glimpse of a memory stalked me. Another melody lingered deep inside, unknown.

I am three years old. I wake up in the middle of the night to the sound of arguing in Mommy and Daddy's bedroom.

"Walt!" Mother protests. Then there is a loud bump. It sounds like Mother fell to the floor.

"Walt!" I squeeze my eyes tight until I see black and gold. My body tightens up, and I lie very still.

Mother is hurt. I think she's crying. Maybe if I'm very good I can fix things.

Then everything is quiet, and I fall asleep.

"Look, Sandy," I said. "The only thing I'd forgotten was the pantry off the kitchen." My steps slowed as we walked down to the basement. What would I find? It smelled clean and felt cool. Suddenly I recalled my first trike, red with pedal covers. I had ridden it in the basement while Mother hung up clothes. I smiled and breathed in a happy, familiar remembrance.

"Do you ladies want to see the garage?" the owner offered.

Startled, I said, "Oh yes, of course," but I was hesitant.

As Sandy and I walked behind him to the garage side door, I felt a strange chill. I walked cautiously, expecting to enter a dark wood garage. My hands trembled. I put them behind me so no one would notice.

There was a photo I had seen once. A picture of a dark garage with unpainted brown wood. Me, three or four years old, in a snowsuit jacket and a square-topped hat tied beneath my chin, standing near the front of the garage. It's nighttime. I've been crying. Mother is behind me, looking cold in her apron and sweater. I'm reaching my arms up, holding my mother's hands. Why was I crying?

And a second picture. The big shadowy deer hanging by its antlers at the back of the garage. The single lightbulb casts strange shadows on its face.

The owner said, "We fixed it up a little. Sheetrock. And we have a garage door opener now."

The garage walls were white. No dark shadows or dark brown wood. I forced a stiff smile and said, "You've kept up the house very well." Then quickly, "But I suppose we'd better get going."

With a questioning frown, Sandy nodded, and we headed back to the kitchen. "I can't thank you enough," I said. "This was such a treat to see the house again."

"You ladies come anytime," our host enthused. "It's been a real pleasure."

Back in the car, I gazed out the window at the houses passing by. Trees arched over the street of the aging neighborhood. Only the sound of the motor filled the silence.

"I was surprised you wanted to leave so soon. Are you glad you went, Judie?"

I set aside my pensiveness. "I sure am. My memory of how it looked when I was small was really good, wasn't it?" I had verified my memories and drawings.

Sandy smiled. "You're remarkable. But I think it's time to plan a nice evening at a good restaurant."

It would be a helpful diversion. I needed to shake my unease.

Night had settled in, and the air was damp and chilly. The gold pressed-glass door to the restaurant radiated warmth from the lights inside and drew us in. Sandy and I stepped into the comfort of the narrow foyer. The smell of pork enveloped us. I was hungry for spaetzle.

Suddenly dread came over me, and I stopped. "What's in here?" I asked her.

"What do you mean?" She slipped out of her raincoat.

"I have a bad feeling about this place. What does it look like?" My diaphragm trembled, and I was scarcely breathing. I stood still with my coat and gloves on.

"I don't get what you mean," Sandy said.

"I think there are hunting trophies in there."

"Sure—it's kind of a German hunting lodge atmosphere. This is Milwaukee."

I peeked around the corner and saw the outer edge of a spread of pointed elk antlers.

My legs buckled, and I froze. "I don't know if I can go in," I stammered. The host tapped his pen, waiting for us to enter the main room. "I'm so afraid of them." I squeezed my eyes shut and began to wring my hands. A cold breeze blew over me. "I may have to leave."

Sandy's eyes opened wide. She had just remembered my phobia of deer trophies. I'd had it since I was a toddler. I was shaken with fear whenever I saw one. Countless times I'd had to turn away or be led from a room. Struck by my paralyzing reluctance, Sandy said, "Do you want me to go in and look around?"

I closed my teal raincoat tighter around me. "Would you?" I asked.

Sandy confidently approached the host. "Do you mind if I go in and look around?" He frowned but graciously gestured for her to move in. I turned away, embarrassed, and tried to look through the opaque windows, unable to see anything clearly.

Sandy returned to say, "There are three deer, and I think the other two are elk. And a couple of antlers. What do you think you want to do? We can leave."

"Well, just tell me where they are. Maybe I can avoid seeing them."

After identifying the locations of the trophies, she led the way into the restaurant with all its dark wood beams and peasant paintings. The lights were low, which increased my growing sense of terror. I knew those heads were looking at me from someplace. I kept my eyes down and took a seat that faced out the window into the darkness. The sounds of china and tableware became muffled by my intent focus. The animals lurked behind me like death, watching, but I hoped to forget about them.

"I'm sorry, Sandy. I'm so embarrassed. I hate this part of me. I've had this fear my whole life, and I can't get over it. It's like a shock wave that goes through me when I see one of those heads." I twisted my hands in my lap. "I've even tried to just sit in a room and gradually stare at a deer head for a long time, but it doesn't do a thing to help. The next time I see one, I'm terrified all over again. I hate it."

"We all have our fears. I would've warned you before we got here, but I forgot about it. Thank goodness it's just an occasional problem."

"No. That's the point. There are heads in restaurants and gas stations and hardware stores and grocery stores and on and on. This is the Midwest. They're everywhere. I'm on guard all the time." I was close to tears.

"Well, we're going to make this a nice evening in spite of it," she said. "Let's order some Mosel wine." She smiled and touched my hand.

Practical Sandy, who sometimes had a short temper, was loyal. She made no judgments of what I considered a flaw. I loved how she accepted me.

When I was four years old, our family had moved away from Shorewood and rented a suburban half bungalow in Wauwatosa. It happened to be close to Sandy's present-day house, so two days later, as she drove me to the train station to go home, we passed by the white-frame double bungalow. Sandy stopped the car so I could gaze at the house and reminisce.

I could almost hear the whisper sound of Bromo-Seltzer pellets falling into a glass from their cobalt-blue bottle. In those young days, I would look up at Daddy as he poured the fizzing water back and forth between glasses and then drank it down. When he let me try it, I didn't like the way it fizzed in my face. It tasted salty stale. Daddy drank it in the morning after parties.

I turned to Sandy and said, "This is where I started kindergarten. I remember one day I walked to school with a neighbor girl, Sheila. She came up with a new way for us to get to school. We took a detour through the train depot area. I was all for it. But when we got to class we were late.

"Our teacher, Miss Grady, asked us where we'd been. Sheila immediately pulled out a story about our being chased by 'big boys.' I went along with it, but Miss Grady looked skeptical. She said we needed to learn to be on time. And then: 'Let's get back to our story about the steam shovel.'

"When I got home, Mother confronted me. Miss Grady had called her. Mother gave me a good talking-to about always telling the truth. And I had to stay in the yard for a week and not play with Sheila anymore. I was ashamed. I disappointed Mother, and in our family we were not supposed to tell lies. I felt terrible."

Sandy smiled with compassion. I pointed to the left side of the house. "Sherri and I slept upstairs in the large back bedroom. There was a porch just off it. It had French doors. I thought that was magical. And I had a place where I could hide." A slight shiver went through me.

"Hide?" said Sandy.

"Oh you know. That's what kids do."

Sandy drove to the station as I mused. Different homes, different memories.

A mystery of Shorewood lingered in my psyche. It had been dislodged when I walked into the garage and erupted again at the restaurant. But I had long ago learned how to tamp down those vague, unconscious memories. Even the most disturbing events were strangely wrapped up in songs, and I found the songs comforting—they were my past, my life. The songs drew me back, and I never gave up hope that things would get better.

On the train ride home, the track wound along the Mississippi in Minnesota. The cars moved slowly beside the overflowing river, trees up to their midsections in standing water. Clouds hung low overhead. Still unsettled by my visit, I had no energy to concentrate. I just sat, unmoving, staring at the gray and muddy water coming nearly to the bed of the tracks. It was twilight, and the few small homes on the river's edge were near drowning. Small lights of evening began to blink on in the houses as darkness increased.

The blues song "Chloe" returned. Swamplands, searching, darkness. I heard my own heavy sigh as I longed for night to come and hide it all. It would be good to be home with Eric and the boys.

2

PIANO DEBT

Both of our sons were at the breakfast table, dressed and ready for school. I smiled. "Who'd like a cup of hot chocolate with your cereal?" Both called out, "Me!"

"How come we get special breakfast today?" ten-year-old Danny asked. Seven-year-old Andy was already eating his cereal.

"Just because I'm happy to be home and I thought you'd like a treat," I said.

My husband, Eric—a pastor—had an early meeting, so he was helping get milk out. "Pretty special, boys. Aren't you glad Mom's home?"

The room was warm with sunlight and reunion as we all ate.

"Don't forget to brush your teeth," Eric reminded the boys as they headed for the bathroom. I could hear them jostling in competition for the sink, and soon after they got their jackets.

"Bye, Mom! Dad!" and they were out the door.

"Don't slam the screen door," Eric called.

"Have a good day," I said and walked to the refrigerator to get butter for my English muffin.

Eric lingered after breakfast, which he seldom did. "While you were gone, you got a phone call that I need to tell you about. It was from a piano store."

I buttered my muffin and sat down with some juice and marmalade. "We already have a piano."

"Well, it seems your dad bought a new one for himself and used you as his backup person."

"What do you mean, 'backup'?"

"A reference. He hasn't made the payments, and they're calling you about them."

A shock went through me as I grabbed the tabletop. "I can't believe that. I never, *ever* talked to him about that. What did he think he was doing?"

It was as if I were cast back into the house in Shorewood. There was a lingering presence of mystery and a faint smell of bourbon. Dad was undependable and crossed my boundaries without a moment's consideration.

I called the store and explained that I knew nothing about the situation and gave them Dad's phone number. I turned to Eric, who was preparing to leave. "How could Dad do that to me? He's an alcoholic, plain and simple. And he takes advantage of me."

"You're pretty hard on him, Judie."

"How do you stay so calm? He was dishonest! I've got to do something about him and his drinking." I had read about alcoholism for years. "I've lived with this for my whole life. Now he takes advantage of my good credit without even asking me."

He gave me a half hug as he rose. "I'm sorry. Give yourself some time to think about this. We'll figure it out." He gathered up his briefcase and papers and prepared to leave. "I really have to get to the office. I'll call you later."

I was stunned by Dad's audacity. Washing dishes, I dropped a cereal bowl and broke it. "Damn!"

I did my morning chores, snapping the sheets on the bed and smoothing the bedspread while stewing about Dad's latest stunt. I'd never had the courage to confront him face-to-face, but I argued with him in my thoughts.

I had years of saved memories: the smell of Dad coming home after "a few beers" or a night of highballs. Just the hint of alcohol on someone's breath or clothes brought back those times when I leaned away from his unsteady walk or quaked as I wondered what he might do next. I once found him passed out beside the couch. And I never knew when he might be super sweet or in a sudden rage after drinking. Such sights and sounds formed a heavy cloud over me as a child, settling like smoke, stealing breath, and leaving an unending feeling of insecurity. *My life is scary. What will happen next?* It never went away.

I eventually settled down that day, but I felt a sinking sense of abandonment that I seldom let in. *My dad doesn't love me. He uses me. I can't count on him for anything. If only he didn't drink.* I saw in my mind the image of me sitting beside him on the piano bench and heard my toddler voice singing. *"Ah-ha-ha. You and me. Little brown jug, don't I love thee?"*

The next night I had a dream. A dining room. It was dark brown wood. A huge moose head hung above the built-in buffet. It grew larger and larger, filling the room, terrifying me. Then the dream switched to a bedroom. I was young, perhaps four, and about to go into the room in my bare feet and long mint-green nightgown. I held back. There might be a deer head in there. I wouldn't dare sleep in a room with one of those on the wall. I was resisting going in, but some grown-up was pressing me to go in and go to bed.

"Oh!" I woke up, shaken. I searched for the beam of the night-light to steady myself. I hated how those animal trophy dreams disturbed me. Such vivid dreams. *Am I crazy or what?* Maybe the restaurant in Milwaukee caused it.

In the morning, lying in bed, I told Eric, "I dreamed about a big moose head last night. It was awful. I can't go on like this. It's worse since I went to Milwaukee. Maybe I should talk with someone about it."

He paused. "Who could you talk with?"

"I don't want to go to a pastor. I wonder if I could find a counselor someplace?"

Silence again. "Maybe if you just talk it over with your friends."

That was so like Eric. He knew professional counseling was worthwhile but avoided admitting when we might need it ourselves. I suspected he hated to spend the money. Maybe that wasn't fair, I thought—but it was typical. Money first.

My intent became stronger. "I think I'll talk to Karen about it. She's smart about this stuff. Maybe that'll be enough."

Karen had been in college with me. Back then we had good talks about boys and classes. She had a keen sensibility about people. She noticed how they expressed themselves and what they didn't say. She went on to get a master's degree in social work, and we stayed in touch. She was tall and willowy, a brunette with a carefully coiffed French twist, and had never married. She carried herself with poise and watched others with her piercing green eyes. I decided to call her that day. It would feel less scary to talk with someone who knew me.

"Hi," I said into the phone. "Got some time to talk?

"What's going on?" she asked.

"Oh, it's the same old stuff. You know—Dad. He's drinking all the time. And I get those deer nightmares for no reason." I told her about the piano debt. "Really I don't know what to do."

For years Karen had heard me talk about my father's alcoholic incidents, like the night when I was in college and he came home so drunk he passed out in the living room rocker. Sherri had to break her piggy bank to pay the driver. Dad had his favorite bars, and I could smell when he'd been to one of them even before I saw his glazed eyes.

Some time ago Karen had advised me to see my father less because it was so upsetting to me. "Have you seen him lately?" she asked.

I noticed a crooked curtain and went to straighten it. "I went to their apartment about a month ago. He's friendly and glad to see me. But I always take the kids and Eric with me, because—I guess I'm afraid of him. But the truth is, I really don't want my children to be around him and all his drinking. Lately, I don't want to see him at all."

"Is there anything I can do?" Karen's voice was matter of fact, but I could hear compassion woven in between the words.

"No. That's okay. I just wanted to talk to somebody. Maybe I can be more intentional about seeing him less. I feel guilty when I pull away, though."

"Trust your instincts, Judie. When you don't feel like spending time with him, you can pull away gracefully."

I was silent, then took a deep breath. "Do you have any ideas about a counselor I could see? You know, about Dad and the deer heads? We don't have a lot of money."

"Insurance may help with that. I know a good guy for family therapy issues. Do you think you could work with a man?"

"I think so. Why not?"

"Well, some people prefer their own gender."

"I don't think it would make any difference," I said.

"His name is Dr. Chris Hayes. Why don't you call and tell him I referred you? Then go for your first appointment and see how you feel about him. If it doesn't feel right, call me back, and I'll give you another suggestion."

"Thanks, Karen. I can always count on you."

I sank back in my chair, relieved to have an option for managing my growing unease.

"How do you do, Mrs. Strom?" Dr. Hayes was a gentle-spoken man, shorter than Eric, and about fifty years old. He had a well-trimmed, sandy beard and blue eyes, and he looked like a runner. I immediately liked him.

"Tell me a little about yourself," he said.

He seemed approachable, nonjudgmental. I freely shared my basic story: my husband and children, my parents and two siblings, a glimpse of the chaos of moving every couple of years as a girl, and, of course, the drinking. He gave me his full and compassionate attention and did not take notes.

"Your parents are alive?"

"Oh, no. My mom died when I was a freshman in college." I sighed, and he waited.

I could feel my whole body tense up. "Life got worse after that. I got married to Eric a year after I graduated. My dad quit drinking for about six years before Mom died, but now he's back to heavy drinking, despite getting diabetes. And things seem to be all mixed up. I've been quite depressed lately—I just can't get myself to be positive. I'm sort of tired of living."

"Is life worth living?"

"Oh, sure. Not *that* depressed. But I have these dreams all the time." His brow wrinkled slightly. "They're nightmares, really. And then I can't go back to sleep."

"Is that the main concern that brought you here?"

"I'd love not to have those dreams. It's what they're about that's the problem." Dr. Hayes kept his eyes on me. "I have this odd phobia."

"Phobia?" He tilted his head with concerned curiosity.

"Yes. It's embarrassing, really." I looked away from his gaze, noticing how tidy his office was. "I can't stand to be around deer heads and animal trophies, or antlers, either. I get scared to death. I've had so many times when I had to leave a barn dance or sit in a different place in a restaurant just to get away."

I felt relieved when he didn't laugh. All my life, children and even adults made fun of me when I told them about my fear of deer heads. More than one child intentionally dragged out some antlers to find out if it was true that I was scared. I hated those kids when they did that.

"It's awful to admit. People must think I'm crazy. Eric is good about it. Well, he sometimes forgets to warn me that there's a head in a room, but he's patient. And he doesn't judge me. I'd just love to get over that phobia."

"Would you like to work on some of those issues for a while?" He spoke quietly.

I looked away, reconsidering—should I take the risk with this new person? He sat, calm.

"Would it take a long time?" I asked, frowning. I knew it would not be cheap.

"I don't know. But we can see how it goes, and you can make a decision as we go along." He wasn't pressuring me. I liked that. And maybe insurance would help with the bills.

I had to try something. I decided I could always back out. We set up three appointments, a week apart. "If you want to, you can stop appointments any time. What would you like me to call you? Mrs. Strom?"

"I'd rather be called Judie."

"If you like, you may call me Chris."

I left, and as I walked down the sidewalk of the Dutch Colonial house where he had his office, I noticed that the sun had come out. Then, from a nearby cedar tree, I heard the uplifting call of a cardinal. I could tell that Dr. Hayes—I wasn't ready to call him Chris—was both confident and compassionate. And my intuition said he was trustworthy. *Please let him be trustworthy.*

"How'd it go today?" Eric asked when he arrived home.

"Oh, fine. He seems nice, and I think I can trust him." I wasn't ready to talk about it. I kept working on frying pork chops for dinner, and Eric proceeded into the living room. A wave of determination went through me; I had taken charge of a part of my life I didn't understand. I didn't want to look ahead, afraid to speculate what might be coming. I sighed. This would have to be my own struggle.

3

GRANDMA LIBBY

I had promised Grandma Libby, Dad's mother, that I would drop by after I returned from Milwaukee. She lived alone in the big duplex her parents had built for her when she was first married to Grandpa Paul—right next door to them. The house was the queen of the block, and Grandma lived upstairs and collected rent from the couple downstairs. Going to Grandma's had always been a treat, especially when Dad and Mom first returned from Wisconsin with the three of us kids, when we lived in a small, cheap rental house on the low-income Northside.

Grandma's house had dark, polished oak doors and woodwork, with a fine dining room and a table that seated ten. Beautiful cut-glass pieces sat on the sideboard: a large pitcher, a vase, bowls, and a complete set of water glasses gleaming in the sun. In the cupboards below was a full set of gold-rimmed Haviland Limoges china on which Grandma served cake at the birthday parties she loved to host. The buffet held elaborate engraved silver tableware. I thought Grandma Libby was probably rich. She always gave us quarters when we came to visit, and in high school and college it became a dollar or two.

The sound of the heavy glass door closing resounded behind us as we climbed elegant wood stairs toward the upper foyer. The royal purple carpet was held in place on each stair with brass rods, and on the left at the landing was a magnificent stained-glass window featuring a multicolored, long-plumed bird in yellows and bright red and purple.

Grandma Libby would invite me or one of my siblings to stay overnight periodically. We liked that. I was a reliable and compliant child, and Libby had a television set, so it was a treat to set up a card table and watch *Make Room for Daddy* and *Hopalong Cassidy* on Saturday mornings. Grandma gave me old greeting cards, which I cut apart to paste the pictures into paper-cover scrapbooks. Grandma took the scrapbooks to people at the old folks' home to look at. I thought it was a nice thing to do for the old people. Grandma often visited people in rest homes, and she also played piano for the Ladies' Aid meetings at her Lutheran church. Sundays, she attended Grandpa Paul's proper Methodist church downtown, but she maintained her membership at the Swedish church in the neighborhood. I sometimes went to the women's meetings with her. We walked the six blocks to church, and I sat quietly on a folding chair, my toes just touching the floor, singing when I could.

Grandma served me Cream of Wheat in a small yellow Fiestaware baking dish that had a cover. To while away time, I sometimes went to the four-shelf stand in the hallway between the bedrooms and the kitchen. I pulled open the bright pink cloth curtain and rearranged the small treasures that resided there: a small glass, a covered dish, miniature animals, pads of paper, pencils—the accumulation of many years of junk. It kept me busy for half an hour. Some days I would help Grandma by hooking her full-torso corset hooks. It was an effort, but Grandma wanted to look shapely. She still had slim, strong legs and a round body on her small frame.

I usually slept on the couch in the front room, where I heard the big clock bong throughout the night, accompanied by the smaller clocks on the dining room sideboard. Occasionally I would sleep with Grandma in her double bed, but Grandma said I kicked a lot. On the massive dresser with a mirror was Grandma's round, silver hand mirror, engraved with her initials, O.T., for Olivia Thorsen. There was a framed picture of Grandma when she was four years old, taken in Escanaba. She wore a long plaid wool coat with a matching black hat and a black muff with a decorative appliquéd flower. Snowflakes dotted the picture, and a Swedish-style farm home was visible in the background. She had a shy, suspicious look, her round face unsmiling, her head cocked slightly to the left.

On the dresser's white linen scarf sat two hobnail perfume bottles and a small yellow china Dutch clog, decorated in red and just my size—until the day it broke because I had grown. I was afraid to tell Grandma, but she didn't scold me, and Grandpa glued it back together without comment. Grandpa slept in the bedroom off the porch, where Dad had once slept, in the big brass bed.

At night, as I prepared to get into bed on the couch, I saw Grandma on her knees, saying her prayers with her hands folded on the bed.

Grandma had routines: humming as she dusted, watering the plants, filling the radiator pans to keep moisture in the winter air, hanging clothes in the attic. In summer we went out into the small backyard, where Grandma had her garden. She grew flowers—pansies—and sweet peas, which she strung on strings for support. The pansy faces pleased us both, soft browns and yellows, deep purples, white for contrast. Grandma's garden was very tidy. She didn't grow vegetables, only flowers, and it was a place of beauty for a small girl who noticed such things.

Grandma loved company, so friends and family came by for coffee and cake for various parties and gatherings. Some were jealous of her perceived wealth. Everyone called her Libby. Some relatives of long standing were called by their first names—Karin, Mae, Pearl, Lois, Celeste, and Elsa. Some friends, like Mrs. Cutglass Ohleen or Mrs. Helvig, had more formal names. The chatter was happy and the Swedish coffee clear, served on the fine gold-edged plates with the ornate silver tableware. Mother's mother, Grandma Trina, would come to some of these parties, noticeably pretty with her dark hair and perfect narrow eyebrows. She was charming in her unpretentious way, open-hearted and appreciative.

Grandma Libby, on the other hand, wanted to be proper. I could tell she didn't approve that Grandma Trina was divorced. Trina had a very modest home, and to treat us she baked cookies and sewed clothes. To show her interest in her grandchildren, Grandma Libby gave us quarters and candy, bought us gifts, and sang songs with us. Between them I had a cache of good memories; I felt loved.

We were friends, Grandma Libby and I—a bond of a grandmother and her accomplished, accommodating granddaughter. We shared music and flowers, service and sociability. And secrets—secrets that held us together and secrets that separated us.

Grandma Libby had left the entry door open for me. "Yoo-hoo!" she called from the top of the stairs. I needed her cheery voice after my disappointment with Dad.

"Hi, Grandma!" Unlike my father, she was short and plump. She wore a pink print dress and customary full apron in blue.

I hurried up the dark, shiny stairs. Grandma Libby waited at the open dining room door alongside what I called the "shaking machine." It looked like a stand-up scale but had a wide leather belt that shook one's body at the waist. It was designed to help people lose weight. Years earlier Grandma had been very heavy, but now she was trim.

We seldom hugged, but with ease and comfort I headed straight to the big square kitchen where egg coffee was brewing. It was a Swedish tradition: mixing a fresh egg with coffee grounds, then pouring them into a boiling kettle of water. The egg gathered together all the grounds, and the coffee was crystal clear when it poured from the pot over the strainer. Grandma Libby's blue parakeet, Petey, screeched as we sat at the white enamel-topped table, a remnant of the 1920s. Humming as she walked, Grandma brought a plate of shortbread for us to eat. I had sat at that table since my feet couldn't touch the floor, looking out at the house next door—Great-Grandma Marin's house—where Grandma had grown up.

"How's the family? she asked. "The boys grow so fast." She reached under the table extension for the silverware drawer, which clattered as she took out two spoons. The room smelled like good food and hot coffee.

I nodded. "It's amazing how much they grow and learn."

"How was your trip to Milwaukee?" she asked with a singing voice.

"Oh, it was fine," I fibbed. "I always have fun with Sandy." My monotone quarreled with my words and stirred up my anxieties.

I changed the subject. "Have you heard from Mona?" I asked. Aunt Ramona was three years younger than Dad. She seemed so much more accomplished than her brother, responsible to a fault and hardworking. I admired her. She had traveled throughout the world, even in the 1940s, ambitious for a woman. As a child I'd seen photos of her high in the hills around Rio de Janeiro. *Maybe I'll do that someday,* I thought.

"Ramona writes every week with the news," Grandma said.

I twisted my cloth napkin. "I wish Dad were as dependable as Mona is." I hesitated. "He's been drinking too much again," I said, afraid to be reprimanded for my honesty. We seldom talked about problems among family members.

To my surprise, Grandma was straightforward. "A little wine now and then would be all right, but he doesn't know when to stop." I said nothing, my teeth clenched. I knew Grandma enjoyed a little glass of wine at celebrations, especially sweet wines. The squatty bottle of Mogen David was usually on the sideboard. I had small tastes when I was a girl, but my nose always wrinkled at its flavor.

"I feel sorry for Walt," Grandma added and sighed. "It was hard to support a family."

"We just have to leave it in the Lord's hands." "Things work out for the best." Grandma often summarized life in aphorisms. It was as if I had Pollyanna sitting beside me. A catchy saying was a good way to sidestep a difficult reality. I wanted to roll my eyes, but kept a steady gaze.

"I worry about him," I said. She preferred avoiding the issue and said nothing more. *Go along to get along,* I thought. *Don't raise any dust.* The only sound was the clinking of her spoon stirring in her yellow china cup.

Over the years I'd come to call her Soft Grandma. Not bruised by poverty or divorce like Trina, but with short, fleshy fingers, pale mauve nail polish, a weekly hair appointment, and a once large, soft body that felt warm for a young girl to lean into—though she usually stood at a distance. She was afraid to ride in boats on the lake and of unknown places far away. Her friendly welcome had an invisible guardedness. Grandma Libby was kind, but an occasional tremor in her hands revealed caution.

"Well, let's you and I go into the parlor and play the piano," Grandma said. "We need to brighten up."

Not wanting to dampen her day, I took a last sip of tea and helped clear the table, taking dishes to the freestanding sink in the middle of the long wall across the room. I had to bend low to use it. I followed her to the parlor to her upright Brazilian rosewood player piano by Steck. The instrument commanded the room, heavy and large, with an additional mechanism to play rolls of music, cutouts stamped in paper. Her parents gave her the piano shortly after she and Paul moved into the house. Player pianos were deluxe in those days of Woodrow Wilson, and it remained highly polished and beautiful with its reddish-brown colors. I had stood beside its bench with her for years and years.

"Sing a little something with me," she said. We sang "Three O'Clock in the Morning" and some ditties she had taught me as a child. I admired how, in contrast to my father, whose strong hands pounded the blues into my very soul, she was as proficient and happy as ever, lightly tripping her fingers over the keys. I smiled, enveloped in reminiscence.

From the time I was a small child, piano music filled my memories. In the middle of the night in our house in Wauwatosa, I used to creep onto the landing above the stairs, where I could lie and listen to Daddy playing songs and singing with friends who had drinks in their hands. He even had a record of himself playing at a Milwaukee bar with patrons joining in. When we moved back to Minneapolis, Grandma saw that I was interested in learning to play, and for years she paid her friend Evelyn, who was an organist at the Lutheran church, to teach me.

Happily, I joined her to sing "Waves and Nightcaps" and "Monkey Town." I glanced at the familiar painting hanging on the west wall of the adjacent living room just above the radiator. It had a dull gold frame. For the first time ever, I was conscious that it was a picture of a hunter in bronze-gold clothes, gun under his arm, pursuing a deer that stood observing him from a distance at the edge of a snowy woods. An armed predator. With a slight shudder, my mind blanked, and I looked away quickly, my thoughts rejoining the music.

After fifteen minutes, Grandma paused for a moment, and I said, "I'd better get going before those sons of mine get home from school."

She rose from the piano bench and walked to the dining room with me. "You just say hello to those little lads," she said. "Bring them over some day."

She walked over to a candy dish on the dining room buffet and dug her short fingers into the wrapped jewels. "Here. A few pieces of candy for them." She dropped them into my hand. Then she reached into her apron pocket and handed me a five-dollar bill.

"Grandma! You don't have to do that."

"Buy yourself a little something that you like."

Shaking my head in resignation, I took the money and stuffed it with the candy into my jeans pocket.

"Gosh! I'm late!" I didn't want to keep the boys waiting after school. I headed for the door. The feelings of worry about Dad had dissipated, moved to the back of my consciousness.

As I walked down the front stairs, she called out with a smile, "Remember! It's a great life if you don't weaken!"

I smiled and yelled, "Take care, Grandma! Thanks!"

4

MOTEL

A few weeks later, I attended a national church meeting in Chicago. I had decided to drive there the day before the meeting and made reservations at a nearby motel in advance. It looked safe and pleasant in the advertisement and had its own dining room. When I arrived, tired from the four-hundred-mile journey, I wanted to have some dinner, watch a little television, and turn in early.

The friendly male clerk in his taupe uniform handed me my key card. I looked around to see if anyone was watching or listening as he gave it to me. The reception area was empty. There were a couple of businessmen in the nearby sitting area, talking and having a drink. I missed the protected feeling of being in the car. I was exposed, a woman alone. I was accustomed to Eric checking us in at motels. Was I safe?

I looked around the check-in area. There were a few shelves of notions—aspirin and toothpaste—and a refrigerator with bottles of pop. Nothing spectacular. Soft music played in the background, and I caught a glimpse of myself in the lobby mirror. I looked tired.

"Do you want help with your luggage, ma'am?"

"No," I responded too quickly. "I'll do it myself." I put on a smile to hide my unexpected unease. "Thank you very much." Why was I feeling apprehensive?

"Have a good evening, ma'am."

The door to my room was at the far end of the third-floor hall. I didn't see or hear anyone nearby. The dark green carpet and beige walls were pleasant, and large commercial prints hung on the walls. It was all very predictable.

My luggage was heavy; suitcases didn't have wheels yet. As I walked down the hall, a door closed behind me. I jolted a bit and surreptitiously looked back, wondering who I would see. A businessman. He turned the other way and headed for the elevator area. I breathed again. I hastened my step, looking for my room number. Finally. Three twenty-nine.

My door card didn't work. "Damn!" I whispered. I tried several times before it functioned, and just as it opened, a couple came out from their room several doors away, laughing. It startled me.

I hurried to drag my suitcase inside and put the double lock on the metal door after it slammed shut. I looked ahead to the windows. The room backed up to a hill with scraggly brush and trees. So much for aesthetics. I closed the double curtain so I could not be observed, or awakened by the sunrise.

I turned to observe the room. Beige. Two double beds with green-and-gold quilted spreads, a small table and a brown faux leather chair on casters, a bank of drawers, a desk, a television, and a small brown refrigerator. A dark room, but clean and in good repair. I hung my jacket in the closet. Peeking into the bathroom, I saw that it, too, was beige. A warm shower would feel good, but I didn't want the water running to attract attention in the early evening. I'd wait until morning. I felt simultaneously alone and watched.

I called Eric. It was the middle of dinner, so he couldn't talk long, and he didn't put the boys on the phone. Long distance was costly, and besides, it might make them lonesome for me. I wanted to feel independent for a change. After we hung up, I gathered my purse and room key and headed to the restaurant. No one else was in the hall or elevator.

As I approached the entryway of the restaurant, cooking odors from the kitchen reminded me of how hungry I was. Then it occurred to me. It looked like Western decor. How many deer heads was I going to find there? They would spoil my dinner. Maybe I could leave and just order room service. I took a deep breath and surveyed the walls. I was in luck.

No trophies. Just wagon wheels and pictures of cowboys and horses. The greeter ushered me toward a table off to the side in a dark, isolated corner.

"Could we find something in better light?" I asked. He accommodated me. I slipped into the captain's chair at the round table facing the bar and began to scan the menu.

The server came to pour water. He was handsome, with curly black hair and a ready smile. I smiled back. "May I get you a drink, ma'am?"

I weighed the choice. A drink would help me relax. But I was alone.

"I'll have a gin and tonic," I said. That would be tame enough.

Waiting for my drink, I realized I had nothing to read. What's worse than eating alone in a big place with nothing to distract me? I peered around for a newspaper. No luck. Trying not to look nosy, I watched the people around me. There were several couples, including an interesting-looking pair: a young, chic woman and an older man. There were individual men, no doubt on the road for their work. It reminded me of how Dad had spent weeks at a time in cheap hotels, likely eating inexpensive meals in boring restaurants. He no doubt had a drink at the bar—or several. He liked bourbon.

My reverie was broken as the waiter brought my drink. "Oh, thank you. I can order now."

Comfort food looked good; nothing too extravagant. I ordered meatloaf. As I sipped my drink, I glanced in the direction of the bar. A man about fifty was there, and he looked my way with a double take. He was handsome, blonde, and tall. He had a good tan and gray eyes. I looked away quickly.

The music was annoying easy listening. *Is he watching me?* I wondered. I tried to see him without staring. Yes, I was sure he was watching. I arranged my silverware and took a sip of water. If only I had my book.

A group of four burst into laughter across the room and alarmed me. How long would I have to wait for my meal? I was starving, but my eyes darted around the room, wondering how soon I could leave. I focused on an old-fashioned wooden statue of an American Indian standing off by itself near the entrance.

At last my salad was served, and I wolfed it down. *Not very graceful,* I thought. But soon the entrée arrived and distracted me. As I began to eat, I became uneasy again. Was the man at the bar looking at me? Could he tell I was alone? Why in the world did I want to do this—stay alone in a motel? And it would be such a long walk down that hall back to my room.

I dropped my knife as I buttered my roll. I looked out from under my lashes to see if anyone had noticed. Nobody. I ate as fast as possible.

"Dessert, ma'am?"

I smiled without looking at the server. "No, not tonight."

"Perhaps some coffee?"

Hastily I added, "No. No coffee tonight. I have to get some good sleep." I second-guessed my response. Was anyone listening? Oh, of course not. People don't watch or listen to other random people.

"Just bring the check."

I paid the bill, confounded about how much tip to leave. *Foolish,* I thought. Was the man at the bar still there?

He had slipped away, replaced by a noisy drinker already well past sobriety. His broad gestures were loose from his shoulders, his hands moving as if numb. He spoke too loudly to the bartender and turned to look my way. I couldn't get out of there soon enough. *Nothing worse than an unpredictable drunk,* I thought. It gave me the chills. I avoided looking his way as I left the restaurant.

I walked toward the elevator. My hands were clammy. What if I met someone on the elevator? Or if there was someone on the third floor when I arrived? There were places where someone could hide—the alcove where the ice machine was, the corner where the hall turned to the right.

I pleaded with myself, *Judie, stop it! This is crazy. You're in a perfectly safe place. You've traveled for years. No one is after you. The drunk stayed at the bar talking to the bartender. You're fine.*

I got a grip on myself and breathed steadily as I walked to the room. I checked the hall before using the key card, which worked perfectly. I squeezed through the narrow opening of the door, double-locked it, and brusquely turned around. No one else in there. My heart began to pound again, and I burst into tears.

It occurred to me that I hadn't always been timid the way I was that night. Two years earlier, Eric and I were in the car with the boys, headed into a hot, dusty parking lot near the local barbershop. Two figures emerged from the makeshift roller garden next door in the strip mall. One was a dark-haired girl of about thirteen, tall, with a large belly, and carrying her skates. Behind her was what appeared to be her older brother. He wore a white muscle shirt and jeans. He pushed her, and she stumbled into the wall. He pushed again. She swung her arm to push him away, but he caught it and pulled it back, shoving her into a support post.

"Stop the car," I shouted. In a flash I was out the car door, striding toward the pair. Eric called through the open car door, "Be careful, Judie." My rage blocked my caution as I moved forward.

I shouted at the boy. "Let her go. You have no business hurting her."

The boy let go of the girl with a grunt. They went over to his truck and got in.

I climbed back into the car, trembling. The boys sat wide-eyed and silent. "I couldn't let him do that."

"That was dangerous," Eric said.

"I couldn't help it. I had to stop him." I took deep breaths; I shook inside. We didn't speak of it again. Why had I done that?

I opened the motel bathroom door a few inches and left a light on to help me relax. After climbing into bed and watching the news, I tried to sleep. I rearranged my pillows and adjusted my blanket over and over. Finally I let go of my tension and fell asleep. Within about twenty minutes I woke up with a start. Had there been a noise? I lay perfectly still. Nothing. No shadows, no noise.

I closed my eyes, and in moments I was dreaming. I was standing at a motel window, looking out at the dark, calling, "Help! Help!" But no sound would come out of my mouth. I kept trying to scream, but I made no sound. Desperately I tried to open the window so I could climb out—

and then I woke up. I sighed and turned on the television until I was so drowsy I fell asleep for the night.

Although I had impulsively fought to protect the young girl that day at the roller rink, now I found myself awake at night, reliving recent fears. The motel, the deer at the restaurant, the unexplained chill of the Shorewood garage. A strange weak trembling built within me, a quivering in my abdomen, unspoken, unidentified.

5

ONLY A CHILD

One early summer morning, shortly after returning from Chicago, I went shopping at Dayton's downtown store. The Dayton Company was the dignified, respected department store in the heart of downtown Minneapolis, founded at the turn of the century and led by a community-minded family. One dressed up to go shopping in those days, and Dayton's had sixteen-foot cream-painted ceilings with lush decorations for each season. The counters were made of well-shined wood with round corners, and enclosed displays shone under hidden lighting.

I was on the main floor, steps away from the aisle most shoppers used to go to the escalator. A clearance sign caught my eye, and I looked through a few skirts on a rack. Suddenly a woman's strong voice caught my attention.

"Stop it!" a large woman growled at a three-year-old boy, who must have been her son. She was dressed neatly but in casual shoes, her hair in a ponytail and her lipstick worn off. A busy mother. Her son looked up from crawling under the rack; she grabbed him by the arm, dragged him to an adjacent clothes rack, and shoved him to the floor. A slightly older girl in her care ducked out of sight behind the rack. The small boy whimpered a bit, and when she looked away, he crawled over to sit on the terrazzo floor against a counter in the main aisle. The lights from the display case shone down on his frightened face.

A man in a business suit passed by, avoiding him by walking stiffly outside the pathway. He glanced quickly around the area, as if to search for a parent, and then continued on his way.

My stomach tight, I went back to my shopping. Then I saw the large woman again as she abandoned her shopping and stalked over to the boy, her ponytail flapping. "You cut that out!" She slapped him. He ducked his head to avoid her blow, still crouching alongside the wood counter. He started to cry. People passing by in the aisle slowed their step, avoiding the confrontation, wary, glancing at the mother and child. I looked away, my face grimacing and eyes nearly closed. I longed to slip away but felt compelled to stay. The familiar din of the busy upscale store faded, and my whole body, in silence, focused on the child.

She pulled him up and shook him by one shoulder. "Stop that crying," she demanded.

My stomach trembled. *Should I say something to defend the child? Should I keep quiet because my words might get him in more trouble later? Or is it more important for the boy to know he has an adult advocate?*

I walked nearer to her. "He's just a little boy," I pleaded.

She turned to me, blue eyes squinting and her mouth set firm. "Mind your own business." She yanked him away, his feet running double-time, and left the clearance area. Three women stopped, staring at the scene. One turned to hurry toward the escalator, while the other two frowned. One in a navy beret said, "Really!" They commenced their shopping. I lost sight of the mother and her two children near the entry door.

I walked away toward another nearby counter and stood looking at the gloves displayed in the lighted glass case. I saw only a small boy being dragged away. The clerk, in a black skirt and crisp white blouse, waited, saying nothing. Then my shoulders caved and my hands pressed on the countertop for balance as I melted into tears. I shook with sobs.

I grabbed my purse and dug for tissues, pressing to regain my composure.

"I'm sorry," I said to the clerk. "I just saw something that upset me." It was all I could say. She nodded and turned away to work with a stack of gloves behind her. I took deep breaths and wiped my cheeks dry. I walked away slowly, pondering what I had experienced. I didn't feel like shopping.

I told Eric about the woman. "I feel sorry for that little boy," he said.

That night, I spent extra time singing to Danny and Andy before they fell asleep.

I couldn't shake the image of the mother and child in Dayton's. My eyes welled up each time I thought about it. Why did I feel so vulnerable? The next week at therapy I recounted the story of the little boy to Dr. Hayes.

"It has unnerved me terribly. He was just a little boy." Then, before I had time to continue, I was flooded with a memory. My mind was racing and could not settle. It was as if a movie had sped up, its images conflated in a wild jumble.

"Something's happening to me. I'm remembering when I was about the size of that little boy. Maybe three or four." I reached down and for some reason took off my shoes, which would become a ritual of therapy memories, one I never understood. I closed my eyes as if to retrieve something from deep within. In an even, distant tone I began to speak slowly.

> It's fall. It's cold outside. We live in Shorewood. Daddy went hunting for a deer again. The phone rings, and Mommy talks to someone. Then she comes to find me in my bedroom.
>
> "Daddy got a deer, Judie Marie. He'll be home by four o'clock."
>
> I watch at the dining room side window until I see Daddy drive up in his maroon Packard with its fancy hood ornament of the god Mercury. It's getting dark outside. I see the big deer tied to the fender. Its eyes are open, and its head and antlers droop toward the bumper. I turn away.
>
> "Should we go out and meet Daddy?" Mother asks. I shake my head no and go into my room where my big doll, Betty Jane, is sitting on my bed.
>
> "It's getting dark, Betty Jane. Pretty soon you'll have to go to sleep. I'll cover you up with the blanket." I fix her blanket tight around her.
>
> Later, I hear Daddy throw open the back kitchen door, letting in the November cold from the dark night outside.

"I've got it strung up. Bring Judie Marie and come out and see. He's a dandy, Jeanne!" Jeanne Marie is my mommy's name. It's almost the same as mine.

"C'mon, Judie Marie. Let's go see Daddy's deer," Mother says. I don't leave my room. I don't like dead deer.

Mother comes to the bedroom door. "Don't be silly, now. I'll go with you." I go into the kitchen as slow as I can.

"Here, I'll help you put on your snowsuit jacket and hat." I try not to cooperate, but she ties the hat under my chin. Mother opens the door to the outside, and I walk slowly behind her. She's wearing a sweater with her housedress. As we get closer, I hurry to take her hand. Daddy meets us at the garage side door. "Look at that! Ten points!"

The animal is huge, hanging by its antlers from the dark and shadowy rafters and looking down at me. The single lightbulb in the garage casts strange shadows on its face. I look away and stand by the garage door, far away. "Here, let's take your picture with the deer," Daddy says.

I don't move.

"She doesn't like deer, Walt. You know that."

"Foolishness! C'mon over here, and we'll get a good picture next to Daddy's big buck!"

I just stand there. I don't look at the deer. I don't move.

"This is ridiculous," Daddy says. "She's always afraid of deer!" Daddy grabs my arm real hard, and I feel weak all over. I begin to cry.

"You come with me, young lady!" He drags me by the arm, my feet stumbling to keep up, over to the deer. "This will teach you to mind me!" He thrusts my head into the big hole in the deer's stomach.

I gag and cry into the messy opening. It smells like salty leather and dried blood, and I cry and cry. He shakes my shoulders and then pushes me toward my mother near the garage front door. "Get over there!" I stumble toward Mother.

"Walt! She's just a child!" Mother holds me close to her, and I hide my face in her dress and sweater.

"Jeanne, just stand there, the two of you, and we're gonna take this picture." Then, in a sweet voice, he says, "Smile, Judie Marie!" I try to smile, but my cheeks are red and swollen, and I am still heaving short after-sobs.

Daddy takes the picture, then stalks out of the garage, leaving us girls behind.

Mother holds my hand, and we go inside the house. She gently takes off my jacket and hat and I go alone into my bedroom. I find a paisley blue headscarf on the floor of my closet. Carefully I spread it open on the floor. I take my favorite tiny porcelain doll, a small ball, and two playing cards with pretty scenery on them and put them all into the middle of the scarf. Then I fold in the corners as best I can and carefully tuck it under my mattress, where it will be safe. I crawl into my double bed with my clothes on and fall asleep. Later when it's very dark, Mother finds me and wakes me up.

"Do you want some supper, Judie Marie?"

I shake my head no. She dresses me in my pajamas real nice so I can go back to sleep.

I am learning how to not let myself feel emotions. They hurt too much. I go to sleep.

I opened my eyes and gradually adapted to the light of Dr. Hayes's office. Tears brimmed in my eyes. My hands were calming each other, fingers rubbing over the backs of my hands. I felt as if I needed someone to hold me. My voice was adult but soft.

"It was hard to be a little girl," I murmured.

"Why do you suppose your mother didn't help you afterward?"

"I don't know. Maybe she was afraid. I'm pretty sure he knocked her down that one time at the Shorewood house. He was really big."

The image of Dad's big hands with dark hair on the knuckles made me shiver. Did I love him or hate him? Did he ever really care about me?

"You were on your own."

"Yes. And so small. So small." My voice faded. I sat looking at my hands. "See, I still have very slender fingers, sort of delicate hands." I sighed.

"Hands like your mother's?" he asked.

"No. Her hands were less slender." I didn't want to think about Mother.

"How are you feeling?"

"Worn out," I said. "He was so insensitive. I was just a little girl."

"He was cruel and thinking about himself," Dr. Hayes added.

I shook my head from side to side as a tear ran down my cheek. "I know. It wasn't right."

"Exactly. It wasn't right. How do you feel about this memory?"

I shrugged my shoulders. I was too numb to feel. I wanted to quit thinking about it. The experience of that little boy must have reminded me of my scary garage experience. Was that why I wanted to visit the Shorewood house so badly? Why at this time in my life? Were there other memories inside me? I felt simultaneously curious and afraid. I stared out the office window.

"Judie?" Dr. Hayes gently entered my reverie.

I was drawn from my thoughts back into the neat office. "I'm sorry. I was just thinking—do I have more memories like that somewhere inside me? I've been so unsettled lately. So much fear—at the garage, at the restaurant in Milwaukee. I even had a battle with fear of deer heads and strangers when I was staying at a motel recently."

"It's hard to know how it all fits together. Let's just take it a little at a time. Next week we can talk about this Shorewood garage story—and the woman at Dayton's."

I sighed. "Yeah. I guess it's just a surprise to discover I could forget something so powerful and dramatic." A shiver ran through me, sparking a sense of dread. I'd have to trust that Dr. Hayes could lead the way and help me feel better.

As I continued my appointments with Dr. Hayes, I started to dig up other forgotten memories, buried even deeper. There was a memory from when I was two years old. I was sad when Mother left for a luncheon. Standing at the living room window, barely able to see over the edge of the dark wood sill, I cried.

"Don't cry, Judie Marie," said Daddy. "Mommy's only gone for a little while for lunch. Come play piano with Daddy." Daddy walked over to the piano bench.

I kept crying. I didn't understand that Mother would come back. I missed her. I cried. Daddy pleaded with me and tried to appease me with a doll, which I cast onto the floor.

"Stop it, Judie Marie!" Daddy picked me up under his arm and carried me into the kitchen, my legs flailing behind him. He hoisted me up more securely under his arm and turned on the stove, then took my hand and held it over the flame. I screamed and tried to wriggle away. Firmly he set me back down on the floor. I was unsteady on my legs. I wanted to run away and not fall down.

"That'll teach you a lesson!"

It did. I stopped crying and went into my room, where I crawled under the crib to hide. My hand felt sore. I was scared, but I blocked my fear. I forgot about it. The moment was hidden away, saved where it could not hurt me again and again.

Each week in therapy we talked about facets of the garage memory: my mother, my father, the deer, the photos. I felt confused and numb, with an aching disbelief. I wondered, *Did these things happen to me?* I was disappointed with my parents, which left me feeling guilty. I remained cautious and fearful. Where was all this leading me?

"Why don't you do this?" Dr. Hayes said. "When you go to the lake next week, just write down in a notebook any thoughts or events you remember from your childhood. Nothing too dramatic. Phrases, images—just whatever comes to mind. When you get back, we can talk about them."

I welcomed having a concrete task and put a steno notebook into my suitcase as Eric, the boys, and I left for Lake Vermilion.

Our usual eighteen days of family vacation at Lake Vermilion got off to an ugly start. The four-and-a-half-hour drive north was full of irritation. Eric was compulsive about not leaving until the kitchen was perfectly tidy, and he complained about city drivers until we reached the freeway, with its tall stands of birch and pine. The grass along the road beside the shoulder was fading to gold, thirsty for rain, and traffic spread out to a more manageable pace. After two hours, we took the narrower state and county roads into hunting and fishing country. The air became cooler and fresh with the smell of newly cut logs and pine sap. I took a deep breath with pleasure.

Eric lamented the time it took to get through a small town, with its single stoplight and slow traffic. He didn't want to spend money for donuts at the truck stop. The boys got into a back-seat scuffle and then withdrew into their stacks of books. When we took the final ten miles of gravel road to the lakeshore, Eric whined and complained at the inevitable sound of rocks hitting the undercarriage of the car. I was sullen at the end of a long ride and after having organized the camp equipment almost entirely alone. My temples were pulsing.

There were no roads to our cabin—only a lake crossing. We parked on the roadside with other cars and boat trailers, a block from the lodge and marina called Timbuktu. Eric retrieved the boat from its slip and drove it up to the huge landing dock. The boys and I carried all our bags and boxes from the car to the boat, while Eric spent the entire time fussing with the backseat and trunk of the car, arranging and rearranging the blankets and jumper cables and small equipment. My jaw was set.

Finally, the sun bright over the channel by the marina, we took off from the landing, our small aluminum fishing boat low in the water, pointed east toward the cabin with a shallow wake trailing behind us. The water was still, with only occasional thumps of water against the boat. The air was northern—crisp, pine-scented, with a fresh light breeze.

From the lake we could barely see the A-frame wood cabin, set back and hidden by trees. Secured on a gigantic granite outcropping high above our small makeshift dock, it was surrounded by aspen and pine. No structures were visible around us except for a small log cabin on the island across from our dock. This was quiet territory, where neighbors were a good distance apart—friendly, but isolated.

Although it had been a week since I had worked it through with Dr. Hayes, I was carrying the garage memory close to the surface of my consciousness. The deer hanging there, bloody and smelly. Being only three. Daddy so angry when I was afraid. After years of repressing the memory, I had cried and talked it out. But the remainder of the pain hung heavy, poking at me. I was easily annoyed and tense. I needed some peace, some soothing. Somehow, being in the Northwoods awakened the past. I couldn't shake the feeling of being powerless and small—and the fear I might have more terrible memories to come.

I dug out my steno notebook and put it on the bookshelf. I wanted to have it handy if I remembered anything. The idea was at once tantalizing and scary. For months I had felt driven to return to early childhood memories. It would feel good to think about fun times, about Milwaukee and its mysteries in the eyes of a child. But the garage memory had been filled with such terror that it spoiled any happy anticipation. Into what past wilderness was I headed? I looked across the lake at the island and tried to calm myself.

My steno notebook rapidly filled with fragments of events: my doll Betty Jane, the violets on the hill at our home in the country, the time Dad covered up the moose head and deer heads in his buddy's exotic basement so I could walk through the room. Aunt Mona teaching me about Paris. Dad's loud laugh as he played the piano. The colorful profusion of zinnias at a neighbor's house. A strange wisp of a thought: Was I left behind at a beach when I was two? Where did Daddy go? Bits and pieces of experiences. They piled on each other, melting together, creating a list.

Our beds were in the loft, which was connected to the first floor by a metal spiral staircase. The second night I had a dream. I was in a bright red chiffon dress. I was running, running along the ledge of the cliff near where our cabin stood. Running. Then I jumped into the air, falling toward the rocky water below, my red dress billowing around me.

I started awake, breathing heavily, eyes wide open. *What was that dream about? Why was I running away? Why a red dress?* I lay there, listening to branches brushing across the roof and welcoming the breeze stealing into the loft. I didn't understand the dream. I wrote it down the next morning.

At the end of the first week Karen arrived to visit for the weekend. By then Eric had settled down from his usual travel anxieties and neurotic fussing, and things were running smoothly. We divided tasks, including him spending time in the water or fishing with the boys. He took them with him to pick up Karen at the marina. Seeing her, I was happier than I had been for months. She was outfitted in hiking boots and jeans, her usual French twist covered by a wide-brimmed leather hat. She was accustomed to the Northland and settled in energetically. We had a cot for her in the living area downstairs.

After a few hours the two of us went outside and sat on camp chairs under the trees. The white pines were especially tall there, whispering as they do in the breeze, and fragrant.

"Dr. Hayes asked me to take notes while I'm here, about whatever I think of from my childhood," I told her. "I have a huge list already."

"What's your list like?" Karen asked. She never pushed me for therapy details. I offered them freely.

"Lots of little things. You know, my dolls and the time we went sliding at the park. And some scary ones. Like deer heads and Dad drinking." I rubbed my palms on my thighs. "I don't know what I'm going to remember next," I said. "I'm afraid."

I described the dream of jumping off the cliff. "I don't understand it. A red chiffon dress. Falling to my death."

"Red can be a sexual symbol," she mused, her therapist background surfacing.

I turned my gaze from her to the rocky ground with its low brush, but I knew she was looking at me.

Staring ahead, I told her about the glimpses of Dad burning my hand and the garage deer. As I looked up at her, she grimaced. I realized she was crying. It was so unlike her. "Why are you crying?"

"I know a little about what might be ahead," she said softly. "I think Dr. Hayes will be a good one to work with." She brushed her tears away. "It might be a hard time."

Faced with such honesty, I frowned and crossed my legs tight against dread.

"You may not be able to share much of this with Eric. It may make him angry."

My tension doubled. What was she hinting at?

"I'll be here for you," she said. Her words calmed me, even though they scared me to death. The breeze blew my hair as she reached to give my hand a squeeze.

I smiled, paused, and then said, "Well, let's go sit on the deck in the sun. I'll show you the weaving I've been trying to make. I'm using small sticks as a border." I needed a change of subject.

That weekend Karen was open to hearing my lists, but we chose not to focus on them and instead just enjoyed the woods and water. With full sun above, the shadows of aspen leaves blowing in the breeze danced on the deck and entertained me, building distance between the woods and the pressures of therapy. I relaxed. I felt safe.

On Tuesday Karen left. Eric was in a playful mood, so he took the boys to the marina to get minnows when they dropped her off. I stayed back, alone.

Since our cabin was separated from most settled areas, I could see no people nearby. As familiar as the land was, for that hour I felt a growing anxiety. What if someone came to hurt me while they were gone? The movie *Deliverance* swept through my mind. I imagined I heard the film's soundtrack of banjos playing. I shook inside. Was I safe? Images from the movie flashed: an attack by rugged men in camping clothes, chasing someone. Then they were chasing me in their hunting boots. It unnerved me, so I went indoors, my hands shaking as I locked the doors despite the warm afternoon. I couldn't wait for our boat to come into view. Even my young sons would seem like protection. The fear drifted deep into my psyche, barely part of my consciousness. Was I also depressed?

In the days that followed I tried to stay busy, clearing rocks in the beach, rearranging the tool closet, washing clothes, scrubbing the deck floor. There was always plenty of housework to do, since we tracked in sand and had to keep on top of clutter in the small cabin. We had popcorn some nights and huddled one day as a rainstorm passed over at noon.

Ultimately, we left four days early. We had only the small boat, so we didn't water ski. Nor did we hike except to hunt for blueberries, which that year were sparse. The weather had been cool and windy for three days, limiting our water activities and preventing travel to other areas of the lake—the river entry, the state park. I ran out of creative ideas for activities for the boys when we were indoors, and everyone was tired of reading. The boys wanted to play ball at the city park. We talked it over. Then we packed up, eager to go home. I wanted to see Dr. Hayes.

6

POSTER

I started awake at 3:00 a.m. I didn't move. What was it? My hearing was heightened—had there been a noise in the house? No. It was quiet. I struggled to remember. Had there been a dream? It was gone, but it took almost an hour before I fell back asleep. Were my garage memories causing my anxiety? My demons were back.

In the morning, my mind felt heavy, my body uneasy. *What is it?* I wondered as I hung up the towels Andy and Dan had left askew in the bathroom. The day's chores pulled me away from my musing, and I set it aside.

I had some time in the afternoon, and the next day I was to meet with Dr. Hayes, whom I had begun to think of as Chris. I gathered some magazines together and sat with a cup of sweet-smelling jasmine tea in the family room. It was a comfortable place, with wood paneling and red and tan decor. The sun was steady through the windowpanes and warmed my stocking feet. I began paging through a copy of *Life*, and I was captured by an advertisement for Jim Beam bourbon. I hastily tore out the ad and set it aside on the end table. Then I pored through the entire magazine and three others, tearing out advertisements. Beer. Bourbon. Scotch. I was driven but not sure why. I knew it was important somehow. By the time I finished my search, my tea stood cold. I gathered together a pile of ragged pages and put them in a manila folder to bring with me to therapy.

"I don't know why I did this. They're all about alcohol. It's probably about my dad's drinking."

"Do you want to talk about that?" asked Chris.

Stories poured out. "There were always Christmases at Grandma Libby's when Dad arrived with liquor on his breath. Grandpa Paul didn't like it. He was a teetotaler.

"After I got married, my brother, Eddie, who was in high school, told me he would get calls from Dad after the bars closed. Dad couldn't drive home, so Ed had to wake up a friend to get a ride to the bar and drive Dad home in our car. How embarrassing!" My voice intensified. "It was so unfair—waking Ed up on a school night."

I remembered the sound of his heavy body bumping against the walls in the dark night when I was a kid. I would escape to our bedroom. I didn't want to be around the smell of his breath. He'd just fall into his bed and pass out. My fists squeezed out my recollections. "During the years when he quit, he was still petulant and critical of everyone in the family."

"The magazine pictures remind you." Chris nodded his head.

"The pictures are *my life!*"

"How did you feel in those drinking days?"

I stopped cold. I didn't know how I had felt. I paused for a long time, wrinkling my forehead intensely.

"Fear. Mostly fear." I shifted in my chair. "And the older I got, the more disgusted I was. I detested how he interfered with all our lives. He was selfish."

"This week, just notice what you feel and remember," he told me. "If it helps, why don't you write down whatever comes to mind, including any anger?"

I hesitated. I would not like admitting I felt angry. It made me uncomfortable to sound harsh. I wanted to look like a nice person. And what if I lost control of my anger?

The third day after therapy I looked through some family photographs and found one of Dad. He was holding a work sample, a plush toy rabbit. I took the picture to a nearby photo shop and had it made into a three-foot-tall poster. Even though he was smiling, the full image of him was scary. I realized how large a person he was, especially to a child. I gathered together a packet of potential tools: red and black markers, a pointed wooden letter opener, and a small silver vase that Grandma Libby had given us.

At the evening appointment I unrolled the poster for Chris. "Here's what my dad looked like when I was about thirteen."

"What would you like to do with the picture?" he asked.

My voice dropped, along with my head, as I looked at the carpet. "Well—I thought maybe I could sort of talk to him. Tell him what I've been thinking about."

"A good idea. Go right ahead. You can sit where you are, and I'll hold the poster so you can look at it." He moved over to stand about four feet in front of me so I looked directly at my father.

At first, I was speechless, and then I stuttered a few words, talking to the picture. "Dad, I've, I've been think . . . been thinking . . ." *Are people staring at me? Can they hear me?*

I looked right at the picture with its toy bunny, just like the one he'd given us for Easter one year.

"Daddy, I tried to be a good girl and make you happy. Remember how we used to play piano together? You took me skating for the first time," I said, almost pleading, in the voice of a four-year-old.

My shoulders stiffened. "But I could never please you. No matter what I did, you found a way to criticize me, or you had to be smarter or stronger." I spit out my words. "What was the matter with you? You were the grown-up. I am the child." Suddenly I rose to my feet and moved closer to the poster.

My shoulders folded, and my legs felt unsteady. "I'm a little girl, Daddy! Why don't you like me?" I began to cry. "Why . . ." I cried harder. Then I was angry. I picked up a marker and scribbled on the poster. Chris held it firmly against my attack.

"You were selfish! Everything was about *you!* You bossed everyone around when you were home. You drank and drank! I hated when you came home smelling like booze and rocking on your heels! Stand up!" I struck the poster. Chris stepped back, surprised by the sudden move.

"You didn't care about us. Mother had to do everything. You picked on Sherri. Eddie was afraid of you. You made him pick you up at the bars. You, you, you! It was all about *you*. And you drank away all the family money and, and . . ."

I sobbed, flailing my fists, hitting the poster again and again until I smashed a hole in it. Chris had to strain hard to hold the poster firm against my assault.

My breathing was heavy as I reached for a weapon. I struck Dad's picture with the letter opener. I castrated him.

"There!" I growled. "It's your turn to be hurt." I dropped the silver vase on the floor and stamped on it, denting it. I fell back into my chair. I took deep breaths, gradually calming myself. My hands shook in my lap.

Had anyone heard me? No, it was quiet at the office at night. Any staff were far down the hall.

I took a tissue and sighed. "That felt good." I smiled faintly. "I didn't know how angry I was." I rubbed my cheeks and forehead.

"You did a good job expressing yourself. I wonder how long you've felt that way?" Chris asked.

"Forever, I think—I don't know. A long time. It seems like since I was really small."

"You sounded very young at times. That probably tells us how young you were when your anger started. And you held it back all these years."

"I had to." I paused. "You know, Eric doesn't get that. He thinks I should've stood up to Dad. He doesn't realize what would have happened to me if I'd fought back. Do you know what would've happened? I'll tell you what. I would've been killed—emotionally or physically. I didn't have a chance."

I paused for a few moments to look across the room and out the window into the dark night. "I'm so glad I have you to tell."

"I'm glad I can be here for you."

As if a clock had chimed, I said, "Oh! What time is it? Have I stayed past my time?" I hastily picked up the markers and the letter opener.

"No, not yet. Are you feeling like you can leave and drive? You can always stay in the lounge for a while."

"Look. I dented the vase. It's wrecked. I shouldn't have done that."

"Expressing your anger is more important than an old vase."

I took the poster and crushed it as I carried it to the wastebasket. "I think I'm okay to leave. I'm tired, but I feel sort of good, too. Thank you."

"If you have some hard moments this week, you can always call and leave a message for me. I'll call back as soon as possible."

"Okay." I glanced around the neat, composed office. Everything was in its place, and a Tiffany-style lamp on a desk gave calm light. I sensed that Chris was not only trustworthy but also very competent. It diminished some of my fears of looking back at my earlier life.

I sighed. "I think I'm ready to go."

I left the quiet building and followed a slow traffic route. I hardly noticed where I drove, welcoming the chance to wind down. I didn't tell Eric what happened—I didn't know if he would think it odd to act out my feelings in that way. But I slept soundly that night.

7

HOME MOVIES

Six weeks later, I went into our storage room downstairs, where there was always a collection of memorabilia: manila envelopes with the boys' first drawings and papers, an assortment of our slides from trips to Europe, toys saved for hoped-for grandchildren in the far future. Eric was having coffee at the kitchen table after work that late afternoon when I hurried up the basement stairs and puffed through the door of the kitchen, carrying an old winter boots box.

"Look what I found in the storeroom," I said.

I nearly tripped over one of the boys' chairs, which hadn't been pushed back under the table. Eric looked up from his newspaper. "Careful, Judie."

"These are all the home movies Dad made when Eddie and Sherri and I were kids." I put the box down on the table with a thud and hastily tugged at the knotted sisal twine.

I lifted the lid. There they were: a dozen or so three-inch gray plastic reels, still in the gold cardboard mailing boxes in which they had been sent. Under them were two oversize metal reels in brown metal canisters. When I was about thirteen, I had been the one assigned to combine some of the smaller reels onto the larger ones. I had sat at Grandma Libby's dining room table, carefully matching the pieces of film and splicing them together with clear tape.

"I can't wait to see them," I told Eric. "I'm pretty sure there should be one with Grandma Libby holding about six parrots on her outstretched arms and one on her head. You'll never believe it."

"What will you do with them?"

"I'll have to rent some sort of projector so we can watch them. I think even the boys will get a kick out of them."

I put the lid back on the box and carried it over to the kitchen closet, where I set it on the floor for later use. Those movies from the 1950s were priceless. In those early days of home movies, family photographers used a pair of giant spotlights on a metal strip that had to be held in the air or attached to the camera. Everyone was always squinting in the indoor shots. Pictures of the old days. This was going to be fun.

A few days later I was all set. "Okay, everyone," I called. "The projector is all set up. Better turn off the lights because the pictures may be hard to see sometimes. They're pretty old."

Eric and the boys sat on the couch, and I took my place by the projector. The quiet, rhythmic rattle of the machine began, and images appeared on the screen. The first films were of Grandma Libby and Grandpa Paul and their friends on a trip to Florida. Probably 1952 or so. They were all unaccustomed to being filmed; they walked in a stiff line from one location to another, self-conscious, sometimes giving a little wave, often unsmiling. We laughed at them.

Then we saw Grandma Libby, looking nervous, slowly turning in a circle with big, colorful birds perched on her arms and head—red, gold, blue. The boys squealed. "Show that again, Mom! Show that again."

The stories on film unfolded. I took a long breath to see a party at Grandma Libby's house with everyone passing by the dining room table, where Mother pours their coffee into china teacups. It had been so long since I last saw her. She looked beautiful, with graceful movements and a full smile. As a child, I'd hoped I would someday be like her.

Then we saw a parade of people walking through Grandma Libby's sitting room, each pausing to show to the camera a dish they are carrying: mashed potatoes, gravy, a big turkey, sweet potatoes, buttered carrots. Behind them is a giant shadow, and each person blinks under the camera's intense light.

The films replayed my sister Sherri's trip to camp in seventh grade and Eddie playing catch in the backyard. But the scenes lasted too long, so the boys grew restless and started wrestling. "Watch, guys," Eric intervened. "These are pictures of when your mom grew up. Can you find her in the pictures?"

I switched to the larger metal reel and started the projector again. There are scenes from a holiday party when I am in high school, after we've moved to a former farmhouse in Minneapolis: Dad hasn't been drinking since we moved to Parkland, but he still wants to give everyone a highball. The film catches glimpses of the dark green room with its high ceilings. Christmas tree icicles glisten in the camera lights, and Dad sits at the piano with friends, singing. Two men put on nine-year-old Eddie's brand-new football shoulder pads and helmet and pretend to block each other in an imaginary game, looking ridiculous and laughing madly. *Grow up, you guys!* Eddie watches from the couch, his face frowning with cautious discomfort. Those are his new pads. They are big men. Will they ruin his equipment?

The camera panned to the left. I relaxed when I recognized Sid, Dad's childhood friend, with a kind face and full grin. I smiled.

"Who were all those people?" Danny complained.

"Those were my father's friends," I said.

The tradition of kisses under the mistletoe begins. Dad passionately kisses Vern's wife. I wince. Every adult in the movie is laughing. Now comes a sequence of Mother standing, looking very coy, waiting to be kissed. I regress to a teenager, embarrassed to be a witness.

Sherri is usually in the background, squinting against the lights in her coral cotton dress and pigtails, trying not to be noticed. Eddie's eyes open wide in a curious look, watching adults on a caper. I appear in the pictures, now here, now there, joining Mother with hospitality, smiling uncomfortably in my black wool sheath dress from the sophomore home-coming dance. Dad had been drinking only ginger ale for about three years by then, but we never knew what might happen—anger, irritation, laughter, criticism. He was larger than life to his children, who hoped he would never drink again.

Now come close-ups of the faces of Vern and Dad's friend Lotty. They're laughing. Their teeth and wide eyes dominate the picture. The film rolls, and my stomach rolls as well. Vern's wide grin always disturbed me. He looked at me differently than other people. I used to steer away from all those men, making sure we weren't alone and that there was ample space between me and each of them. Sid was different. He was nice. I trusted him.

My mind traveled back to one party, recorded only in my memory.

> Vern sidles over toward me as I stand near the door to the basement. He speaks with a strange lisp. "You're growing up fast these days," he says, grinning. Is he looking at my breasts?
>
> I edge away toward the nearby stairs to the second floor, smiling faintly. He leans on the doorway, his outstretched arm blocking my path.
>
> "How are the boys?" I ask him, changing his attention to his three sons, who are all older than I am.
>
> "Too bad they aren't here," he says. "You'd be just right for one of them." His smile widens, and his eyes twinkle.
>
> Changing the subject to his sons gives me the impetus to duck under his arm and head for the living room to join the partygoers. I can't stand him, but I have to be friendly to company.

The movie kept running as I gazed away into our living room, looking at dust moving across the light beam, lost in the heat and smell of cinema, in another world. Parties. Men. Family friends.

The boys had lost interest altogether. They were wrestling again, and Andy hollered when he was punched. It shook off my reverie, and I turned my eyes back to the screen as they scrambled away to their rooms, bored by all the strangers in the movies.

"Let's watch the rest later," Eric suggested. "This reel is over."

I agreed eagerly. I uncurled my tightly clamped legs and rose to stop the film.

Throughout the week, as I drove to the store or straightened the house, I replayed the movies in my mind. Recalling the chill of Vern's approach made my stomach tighten. I didn't want to watch them again, yet I was drawn to the films. There were still several more for me to look at. Finally, I set up and viewed all the movies again, alone in the living room. I drew the tan drapes for privacy and stepped back into that forgotten dark period of my life, unaware of why I felt such foreboding when the films started to run. I began with the reels of the sad days when I was about to enter high school and we moved.

I don't want to move again. I'm sick of moving, I'd thought. But the Parkland schools were overcrowded, and Mom and Dad wanted to buy their own home in Minneapolis. I was in ninth grade. Skinny and self-conscious, I set out to make all new friends. Gym was miserable, but not because I didn't like sports—I did. But I raced to claim a curtained cubby where I could hide my body, shy, surrounded by girls wearing large bras. I still wore cotton T-shirts. Mom said I wasn't ready for a bra yet. One of the older girls made fun of me. I didn't want people staring at my body.

When Dad found out I missed Parkland, he boasted, "You live in a better part of town now. Not everyone can live by the lakes." I grimaced and watched other kids go for hamburgers I couldn't afford. I wanted to get a job.

"My daughter is not going to work. You can always do that when you're grown up," Dad said. So I wore relatives' outmoded hand-me-downs and had to skip the costly church choir trip to Banff. He still wasn't drinking, but his grandiose ways affected and embarrassed us all.

The movies wound around their take-up reel and drew me back. We bought an 1895 former farmhouse with an extra lot, set on a hill on a corner. It was white-painted brick, with narrow first-floor windows that were eight feet high. The house stood out among the modest stucco homes on the block. We never shoveled the two long sidewalks, and the cumbersome grapevines that grew along the fence on the front retaining wall yielded sour grapes. I loved the Japanese irises that grew untended along the inside of the front wire fence, and Dad wanted to plant tulips in place of the wild asparagus along the alley snow fence. The old house's stone foundation walls were a foot thick, and Mother promised that someday we'd have a recreation room in the basement.

At my new school, I kept my feelings to myself. If anyone knew how I felt about life, I would be exposed. Every year I had a secret crush on a boy. I would talk about him to my best friend, Deanne, but I was quiet around boys and found my place as a good student and in music. I was admitted into the prestigious high school choir, and by the time I was a junior I was selected as the student director. Achievements like playing the lead in the class play concealed my lack of self-confidence, especially with boys.

When I was sixteen, I was infatuated with a boy a year younger than I named Hal. For my birthday Mom and Dad gave me one of Dad's work samples, a pink plush puppy for my bed. I took off its pink ribbon, wrote *Hal* on the underside, and put it back on the puppy's neck. I didn't want anyone in the family to know. It was the puppy's and my secret.

We were used to secrets at our house. My junior year, when Dad picked me up from a meeting, he mentioned to me that Mom had never finished high school.

"I didn't know you didn't finish high school," I said to her when I got home.

Her face dropped with disappointment. "I told him never to tell you that," she said. I think she was ashamed and wanted me to do better than she had, so she had kept it a secret. I was almost fifty years old before I heard that Grandma Libby was adopted by her aunt and uncle, Marin and Peter, who I had always thought were my great-grandparents.

In the movies of Eddie playing ball, I noticed our old navy-and-white Buick on the side street by our big yard. Shortly after I got my driver's license, Dad suggested I go along on a trip to the drugstore for his cigarettes. It was winter, and behind our house the alley had a short hill, with retaining walls on both sides. "Why don't you drive?" Dad asked.

I looked at the small hill. The moonlight revealed some ice on it. I hesitated. "I'm afraid of the ice."

"Just don't brake if you start to slip," he said confidently. So I got behind the wheel.

The large Roadmaster inched down the hill. Then, predictably, it began to slide to the right, closer and closer to the retaining wall. Instinctively I braked.

"Don't brake, don't brake," Dad corrected.

It was too late. I scraped the side of the retaining wall and then veered left, clipping the telephone pole at the edge of the street with the left fender. The car clunked over the curb and came to a stop. My heart sank.

I started to cry.

"Don't worry about it. It'll be all right," Dad said. "Do you want me to drive to the store?"

I nodded eagerly and traded places with him.

After the stop at the drugstore, Dad said, "Now I want you to drive home."

"Oh, I can't. I don't want to," I pleaded.

"I think it's important for you to drive. You're a good driver, and you just have to try again right away."

My hands felt cold, and my body was tense, but I got behind the wheel once more. The return trip on mostly cleared streets was uneventful, and we entered the alley from the level end, as we always did, so I avoided the hill.

"We won't say anything to Mother," Dad said.

"Okay," I agreed with relief.

The next day Dad left early for work, and when he came home about suppertime, the Buick was repainted a salmon color and showed no dents.

"I just thought we needed a new color," Dad told all of us.

I didn't much care for the color, but I didn't say a word. It was our secret.

Watching the home movies stirred up a heavy sense of loss. What was it I was missing? Was I just feeling the residue of the usual high school insecurities? The internal quarrels of a young girl feeling left out and unpopular? What secrets had I forgotten?

I had relied on the girls of our high school Girl Scout troop for support and acceptance. We seldom wore our uniforms to school because we felt the disdain of our classmates when we did. We were busy with canoe trips, being assistants in hospitals or schools, and planning for a trip to Chicago. I had no home movies of camp or canoes, no glaring lights invading our regular meetings or excursions to the state fair.

Then came one short film segment of me preparing for summer camp. I was laying out my dull green sleeping bag and neatly packing limited clothes inside it. Girl Scout camp was a yearly trip. We'd bump along in orange school buses to Ruby Lake. Mom couldn't afford to get me the required new flashlight, so I had to use a penlight we had left from Dad's sales samples. It didn't cast much light on anything. Unable to buy a nice new water-resistant sleeping bag, we got a mummy sleeping bag from the army surplus store. Sometimes, tucked inside, I felt claustrophobic. Trapped.

Late in the evening, before bedtime and taps, I'd wander with my friends to the fire pit, which we called a fire scar. We'd sit on logs circling a neatly piled square of firewood and use wood shavings and twigs to light the fire. In my cheap, lightweight, flannel-lined, navy blue jacket, I'd join the others in song. Some loved a raucous round or a complicated ditty. I leaned into mellow lullabies and love songs, crooning, "I know you belong to somebody else, but tonight you belong to me." They touched a very deep chord in me.

The flames mesmerized me, orange, red, and yellow, dancing and receding. The gray coals on the edges spat smoke up into the air. Peace. I looked into the starry sky, gathering courage from the hills and strength to lead from the music. Here I was safe. No scars showing, only a circle of friends in the quiet night, singing, "Peace I Ask of Thee, Oh River."

Having a cadre of good girlfriends was important partially because I felt so uneasy around boys my age. I was active in our church youth group, which had about a hundred members. But I didn't fit in among the more sophisticated kids, who dated and appeared to be much more at ease in social activities.

In high school, two boys showed an interest in me, but I scorned them both.

"Judie," Mother pleaded, "give them a chance. You're lucky to be a sophomore going to the homecoming dance."

Philip, a year older than I, was a quiet person and a good student. He was friendly, but I was critical of his awkward ways. Still, I accepted his invitation to the dance. Few of my friends even had an opportunity. But I was also shy and awkward and transferred my discomfort onto him. Mother helped me choose the traditional plain black wool sheath dress for the dance. It was practical and would last for many years. I wished I could buy something bright and colorful but acceded to Mom's choice. It would save money. I was glad Dad was out of town the night of the dance. It seemed he didn't want boys to date me yet—I was too young, I guessed.

I put the reels from the past away. I decided to make an appointment with Chris and tell him about the films. There were only a few memories of happy high school times remaining on those passing images of my life. Maybe it would give him some insight into my young years.

I described some of the memorable sequences. "You know," I said, "I felt both fascinated and disturbed by those movies."

"Tell me more," he said.

"It was really fun to see some of the old things—the way the house looked, the funny parts that my grandparents filmed in Florida with those parrots, the old Buick before it was painted." I smiled.

"And the other parts?" he said, tipping his chin down.

"I felt queasy with all those men friends around, acting dumb and drinking and wearing Eddie's football shoulder pads. And the pictures under the mistletoe. It was all sort of embarrassing."

He reminded me that I had been at a vulnerable and awkward age, newly matured physically and uneasy around immature adults. "What about your mother's provocative flirting by the mistletoe?"

"Yeah. I hated that. She was my *mother*. No modesty . . . but maybe that's the way adults are."

"Not all adults. With you children in the room, they might have chosen to be more restrained. Was your dad drunk?"

"Oh no. He didn't drink then, but you could never predict about him. Mom was the one who kept things running all through my high school years. We depended on her."

"We haven't talked much about your mother. Maybe before the next time we meet you can concentrate on her. How did she respond to your father? What was she like? Friendly? Quiet?"

I agreed I would think about that and return in two weeks. I knew exactly where I would find mementos that would jog memories of Mom.

When I left home to be married, I took our family's document box—a suit-size metal box that was fire resistant and army green, secured with cloth straps that ran in two directions. In it were remnants of our family's life. I had taken it upon myself to keep track of family matters after Mom died. I also saved other things in the box: pictures, school papers, ticket stubs—memorabilia that traced my story. My pink baby book was there; my brother's and sister's books were gone. There was a tattered gold packet of black-and-white family photos from when I was small. Me as an infant with curly black hair, grinning at the camera, perched among a fortress of pillows. My parents' friends Rachel and Len in heavy coats at a Packer football game in 1942. A manila mailing envelope with four loan-overdue notices from a Milwaukee bank; the cancellation of an insurance policy for nonpayment; a Wedding Day booklet from my parents' private church-office wedding ceremony, along with their county marriage license; Mother's premium book of $2.11 per month for a Prudential insurance policy, never completed. Scattered among the documents were vacation Bible school award folders, the $1,200.00 note for the purchase of our Wisconsin house, and the foreclosure statement on our Plainfield home.

I smiled at childhood birthday cards and a note to the tooth fairy: *Dear Fairy. I lost my tooth. my Daddy pulled my tooth with this kleenex. Love, Judie Marie Thorsen.* My second-, third-, and fourth-grade report cards revealed a good student who was compliant but missed ten to twenty-four days of school each year. Then I came upon my third-grade poem collection, "My Original Poems," singsong rhymes in a yellow construction paper booklet with lavender block letters pasted on. My teacher disapproved of its messy cover.

My mother hauled the box around to all the homes we lived in. We moved every couple of years. Now I had carried the hoard of memories with me for another seventeen years. I couldn't seem to throw them away.

8

THE BIG HOUSE

I suppose that to the people in the world around me, my life appeared settled, like soup in a tureen: its surface smooth and steady as ingredients descended and clustered deep below. My sons were happy in school, and we had good family times together. But the Milwaukee trip had started to stir the ingredients. My past appeared in small glimpses, fragments of memories, distant voices, and glimpses of yesterday disturbing the placid liquid, only to disappear back into the broth. Something was changing.

As I searched the document box and my memories for signs of Mother, I thought more carefully about my first decade in Wisconsin. After the 1944 polio scare in the Milwaukee area, my parents were worried. We had been quarantined all summer. Could we live someplace else? In the spring of 1946, as he washed his big hands under the faucet, Dad proudly announced in the kitchen, "I found us a house." My ears perked up. I was six.

Dad continued. "It's the big house right next to our honeymoon cottage on Clifford Lake." The house was in the vicinity of a small town, with large, pretentious lake homes nearby.

"Can we afford it?" Mother asked.

"Hank has reduced the price to twelve hundred, and we even get the cottage with it. It's a good deal, and we'll live right across the highway from the lake. It'll be good for the kids."

We were three kids by then. We had only girls to start with. Sherri was born in Shorewood and was almost four years younger than I. But Dad had always wanted a boy. At last Edward was born when I was six. For the first two years we called him Eddie-boy.

Mother sat for a moment on the bench of the kitchen nook. She had dark brown hair, a slender nose, and hazel eyes. And she was tall. When she dressed up to go out for a party, she looked pretty. I liked that. Sometimes she painted her toenails, and she kept nice fingernails, which had perfect half moons. I watched her use an orange stick to push back the cuticles. Her hands were smooth, and she had good handwriting, which made me feel proud.

That evening I lingered near enough to hear the details of the sale as I opened a piece of bubblegum. Dad had always insisted we needed to own our own house someday. At last we could stop paying rent. This lake house would resemble his grandparents' spacious summer home on big Lake Minnetonka near Minneapolis.

"Now that the war's over," he said, "I can make more money, back working for the distilleries." He had been selling motors for the Defense Department to avoid being in the services.

Mom agreed with his plan. I think Mom was touched by the romance of returning to their honeymoon cottage. She began to pack up to move us to what I came to call the Big House.

The house was on an oversize double lot with a busy, narrow two-lane highway passing in front between the yard and the lake. It was set far back on the property, and we children were told to stay close to the buildings, away from the lake and the road. There were two hickory trees in the front yard close to the highway. They dropped large, green spongy shells with small, rock-hard nuts inside.

On Mondays, in cold Wisconsin winters or hot summers, Mother carried her big straw laundry basket out to the dark woodshed behind the house. The wind blew through the old building, stirring up the dirt floor. Her basket was awkward to carry, and she grunted as she lifted it and walked carefully down the open, wooden back stairs of the kitchen so she didn't fall.

"Judie Marie, you watch Eddie and Sherri while I get started."

She uses old washtubs and a worn wooden wringer. I stand over near the stairs, watching. Mother is wearing a housedress and a stretched-out sweater. She separates the colored clothes from the whites and puts really dirty ones in another pile. Then she fills the wringer washer with hot water and soap from a box. The machine agitates back and forth, back and forth, so that bubbles rise up to the top of the tub. She puts in white clothes first. I can see them disappearing, a little at a time, until the very last corner of a towel sinks below the waterline and goes under. Good-bye, Mr. Towel!

After the clothes are washed, she dumps them into another wooden tub with hot water to rinse them. Then Mom wrings the shirts and towels through the old wringer next to the washer. They come out smooshed and all wrinkled up. She washes the basket and puts the clothes in. The basket is really heavy now. I can see her bend over as she walks toward the lines. They'll get dry pretty fast today because it's a little windy.

When we go to the house for lunch, Mom pumps the small sink pump for fresh water. It has a funny taste. People say our water is hard. There is a hand-cranked wooden party-line phone hanging on the dining room wall. Our ring is one long, two short. Mom complains, "I think someone is listening in when I'm on the phone." We are isolated. Our nearest neighbors aren't sociable, and Dad travels for weeks at a time. I feel sorry for Mom.

I always felt instinctively close to Mother, a woman of weariness and kindness. She had a hard life. Her name was Jeanne Marie Wicklund. Taller than most of her girlfriends, she was a pretty Norwegian with slightly olive skin, a slender face, and a slim figure. Her mother, Grandma Trina, had emigrated from Norway at sixteen and sewed factory piecework for a living.

Mother's dad was a creative inventor and a poor family provider who was often out of work. Handsome and slim, with dark hair, he met another woman and divorced Trina. Grandma Trina did the best she could to provide for her three children but lacked education. Mother had two younger brothers and had to help with childcare and housework. Her oldest brother, Ronald, used to well up with tears, remembering how often Mom had to sacrifice childhood fun to watch her younger brothers. After a time, to make ends meet, Grandma Trina sadly had to give her sons to their father to raise. He then sent them off to South Dakota to be with his parents. Mom missed them terribly. When he was twelve, Ronnie ran away from his grandparents and took a freight train back to Minneapolis to be with his father. Throughout high school, Mother would walk over to his neighborhood to visit him, and he would do the same.

Mom often went without good food or clothes during the times when Trina had trouble finding work. Despite excellent care, Mom had very bad teeth, perhaps from being poorly fed as a child. She wore cheap shoes, which ruined her feet, and she didn't have money for fine clothes. She had very narrow eyebrows, like her mother, which she kept neatly trimmed. But she had lost all her eyelashes, so she was reluctant to let me use a lash curler on my own, fearing the same would happen to me. Her face sometimes looked barren with no lashes.

When Mom was fifteen, Grandma Trina remarried a warm, bright, and handsome immigrant Swede. Trina and Anders had an open, teasing relationship, and he adored his stepdaughter. It was practical Anders whom Mom came to love as she grew up. When I was in junior high, I watched Anders dictating a letter of apology. Since Mother had good handwriting, he wanted her to write it so he could send it to his neighbor after they had an angry row. I was proud of his humility. He lived a frugal but honest life. I was also attracted to Trina's candid, uncomplicated personality. She loved her daughter and grandchildren, and she was physically warm and embracing. She couldn't take us shopping or to movies, but she cooked delicious food and sewed clothes for the family.

In high school, Mom wanted to have money, to get a job and enjoy life. Early in her senior year, without telling Anders and Trina, she quit high school. Anders was angry and disappointed because he had worked hard to teach himself to read English and could never have a high school degree himself. It was 1934. Job hunting was miserable, but she applied at Sears and eventually worked on the switchboard, which she loved.

Mother stayed close to her father's Norwegian family, especially her Aunt Ida, who was only ten years older. She had a playful side, and they loved to dress up for Halloween. It was fun to see Mom acting silly.

Mother was like the Heaven Sent perfume she wore—very sweet and gentle. I could smell it from the backseat of the car. When I was small, I buried my head in the long fur of her fox-collar coat and breathed in good feelings. I loved her.

But Mother was only tentatively alive. She hesitated to say hard things; she would stutter when she tried to explain her feelings. She avoided disagreements and complained afterward. She pleaded or whined more than directed, and from the time I was three years old, I took care of her—her feelings, her body, her troubles. I noticed it first when we moved to the Big House. By that age, I had begun to take my mother's life into myself. We looked alike, and our personalities had a gentle side. Sometimes she talked with me as if I were a sister or a friend.

I could tell the Big House was old-fashioned compared to our other houses. An enclosed porch wrapped around the front and east side of the house, shading green wicker chairs and a green fiber rug on the green plank floors. Inside, the large main room was divided into dining and living rooms by a sofa. At night the room was warmed by the light of a treasured old brass lamp, Tiffany style, with a rose-colored glass shade, that stood on the side table. Mom said it was a genuine antique. It disappeared in one of our many moves.

Prominent on the dining room table was a cut-glass, tall-stemmed fruit bowl that Grandma Libby had given us. One evening, as Mother prepared dinner, we children were pulling at the tablecloth and the treasured bowl smashed on the floor. I immediately blamed Sherri, who was not at fault. Mother did not scold us as she carefully picked up the fragments of her beautiful bowl, but her voice was sad.

Mother sighed a lot as she raised three kids. Eddie-boy was an infant in a Taylor Tot stroller; Sherri, a three-year-old, loved animals; and I was a typically responsible and self-absorbed oldest child at six. I was a morning dawdler and got the nickname "Slowpoke" because I so often had to run as fast as I could from the house while the school bus driver waited and honked the horn.

The house had one bedroom off the main room where Sherri and Eddie-boy slept. My bed was up the steep dining room stairs, in the attic with my parents. The big unfinished room was sectioned by white canvas curtains, pulled across on wires so that the hangers whined as the curtains were drawn. I tied my dolls onto a long ribbon attached to my wrist so my friends wouldn't fall out of my double bed at night. The large trapdoor at the top of the stairs alongside my bed was always open to allow sound and heat to come upstairs.

Alongside the house was the honeymoon cottage, where assorted furniture and housewares had been left behind, along with a few of our own possessions. One day I went in, curious about the place where my parents first stayed on their wedding trip, to look at the old furniture and assorted household goods. It had one big room with uncovered windows and an empty side bedroom. The kitchen corner had a makeshift counter with a dishpan for a sink. Below the counter were faded red curtains, strung on a wire. The whole inside of the cottage was trimmed with dusty narrow-board wainscoting, dark brown. On the wood floor were scattered a few packing boxes, a rolled-up red carpet, two old wooden chairs, an old, chipped enamel pitcher, and carpenter tools. I gasped. There was a deer head lying on the floor of the main room. Startled, I closed my eyes and turned to leave as quickly as possible. I stumbled on the bumpy ground between the cottage and house and hurried up the back stairs.

I protested to Mother. "Mom! There's a deer head in the cottage. Why didn't you tell me? I was so scared."

"I didn't think you'd see it," Mom responded half-apologetically.

"Where did it come from?"

"Daddy bought it. I told him we might have to wait before we could hang it up."

I scowled. Nobody had warned me. I went up to my bed to be alone.

We bought a second car, a 1934 brown Dodge, so Mother could get out. She found an older woman, Greta, a mile away, whom she could visit for coffee and talk. I think she missed Grandma Trina. Both Greta and Trina spoke with an accent. My guess is that Greta was German, while Grandma Trina had a happy-sounding Norwegian accent.

The car was temperamental, sometimes not starting without the choke being pulled out. One bitter cold winter day, it sputtered and wouldn't start. Sherri called from the backseat, "C'mon, Lizzie, get going!" And with that, it chugged and began to run. From that day on, the car was called Lizzie. We kids laughed with Mother and often repeated the command, "Get going, Lizzie!"

During one of Dad's trips home, he wanted to hang the cottage deer head in the house. I raced into the kitchen when I heard his idea.

"Please, Mom," I begged. "Don't let him do that."

I worried all night, and in the morning I was afraid to go downstairs. Would it be hanging in the living room?

No. They decided to sell it. Mother put it in the backseat of Lizzie so I didn't have to look at it as we drove to an antique store. How could my brother and sister in the backseat be so close to it and not be alarmed? They paid no attention at all. I kept looking straight ahead, and I didn't go into the store with them.

When Dad was home, he frequented the bars that were clustered down the highway a half mile away. We girls would go with him when we could, and he would treat us to Fritos corn chips and a bottle of pop. Sherri liked creme soda, and I had orange. There was a nice, mellow smell to those bars, especially Bauer's on the channel between the lakes. It was the comfort of familiarity: beer, bourbon, a warm room, neon signs, and friendly people. The men would play a dice game with heavy leather cups, pounding them with a thud on the bar and tossing the white cubes out, then shouting if certain numbers came up. We girls didn't understand the game. When we got home from the taverns, Mother would talk to Dad in curt sentences. I had a friend whose family called the Bauers' neighborhood "skid row."

In late spring, I found wild violets on a hillside nearby where I spent long quiet times, picking them and thinking. I made a shelter for myself under the pine trees' branches in the front yard, where I had my own world and solitude. I didn't want my younger siblings to bother me. Mother took a picture of me on the first day of school, and I spread out my flared skirt to look as glamorous as possible. In November I avoided looking at the big deer Dad had shot, hanging in the garage, thinking it might fall on me.

It was a lonely life for Mother and me. In fall, dark brown hickory nuts fell onto the front lawn, breaking open their once-green husks to reveal small, hard, white nuts. We kids and Mother gathered them up and took them inside. But when we pounded the shells open with a hammer, the nuts inside were bitter.

9

PLAINFIELD

I sat one rainy Sunday afternoon, thinking about those early Wisconsin days—how a notice had come: a highway was planned through the middle of the Big House.

The former owner had swindled Dad by selling it when he did. Within only two years we had to move again. Mom and Dad came up with a new plan. The cottage would be moved two miles southwest to a lot near another lake, in a development called Plainfield.

With huge brown timbers supporting the small cottage, a truck transported it up the little hill on Highway 20, the peak of its roof pulling down branches along the road. Wide-eyed, we followed behind in the car. The house was replanted on a concrete block foundation sunk three feet in the ground. There would be no basement and few neighbors.

Sometimes we kids could go over to watch the construction. I liked the smell of fresh cement and wood blended into a new structure. There were large picture windows in the kitchen and living room, which made us all proud. It was very fancy to have big windows to look out at the surrounding land.

If the Big House was where I observed Mother, it was in the barren space of the subdivision that I began to question Dad's behavior.

"How did you decide to go to Plainfield?" I asked Dad one day just before I went to therapy.

"Well," he said, "I did a favor for a friend, and he gave me the acre lot." *What kind of favor?* I wondered. His words sparked images of that eerie place, the days of mystery and threat.

At that time he was selling Meier's wines. I remembered how Dad liked drinking wine better than selling it. Once, after he came home from a bar, Mom said to him resentfully, "You're rocking on your heels again." He looked at her with blurry eyes and said nothing.

Dad decided we should grow potatoes on our acre. Mother did the hard labor of digging and planting the halved old potatoes in the dusty brown soil, with us kids helping in the hot sun. The buzzing sound of insects surrounded us, and we rapidly lost interest, wanting to go off and play. It turned out to be a meager crop. Another of Dad's lost dreams.

There were no children my age living in that new development of modest houses. I liked it best when we had school and I could see friends. Without playmates, summer was painfully slow. Mom finally found herself a friend, Eva, who had sons the age of Eddie and Sherri. Except for Eva, very few companionable adults lived nearby.

Plainfield days were a different life, haphazard somehow. The uncultivated land, once a farm field, was flat. The earth smelled sweet in summer, and grasshoppers were easy to catch. But we had to cut through a neighbor's property to get to the lake. There was no beach, just an old, short dock. We hated swimming in the lake, with its thick, squishy sand and mud and big weeds. It wasn't nice like the Big House beach.

One Saturday Dad told us kids that we were going to eat a "delicacy." He caught a large pail of medium-size lake frogs. What was he going to do with all those little frogs? One by one, using a hatchet, he chopped off their legs, which kept jumping. Eddie and Sherri were amazed, but I grimaced and turned away from watching the executions. I didn't have much appetite that night.

In autumn Dad invited some local bar friends over to shoot blackbirds. Every day at twilight the flocks flew over. He raised his gun, and the men began to shoot. Buckshot and dead birds fell, rattling on the roof. The men cheered. I swallowed hard and went indoors. Mom made a crust, and she and Dad cooked the birds. "Four and twenty blackbirds, baked in a pie!" Dad proclaimed. It tasted like chicken. I decided Dad liked killing things.

We children slept in the back bedroom. On summer nights we could hear crickets and smell the rough grass of the side yard. In any season, I lay in bed and sang Eddie and Sherri to sleep. I had a regular litany of songs: "Cruising Down the River," "Linda," and "My Adobe Hacienda." Sometimes I fell asleep before I finished. Often the music was a way of comforting myself in those lonely times.

Every day at about four thirty, Mom pointed out the "shypoke" that flew over our property in the direction of the lake. The black waterbird, a heron sometimes called a preacher bird, had a huge wingspan that left a shadow on the earth below, flying slowly with its heavy head and slim body. Every day it flew over. It gave rhythm to an unsettled, lonely life.

One Sunday, in church with Eric and my sons, I had a brief image of that pieced-together home. I was being led gruffly by Dad toward the bedroom we kids shared. I pulled back in resistance. "Please, Daddy. I don't want to do that!" In my mind I heard my fearful, pleading voice as my cheeks crinkled up in distaste. I stiffened up in the pew and hoped no one had seen me frowning. As quickly as it had come, the memory faded away when the choir's singing broke into my thoughts. It never returned.

Not everything was strange or scary at Plainfield. One sunny afternoon Dad asked, "Judie Marie, would you like to learn to paint with real oil paints?"

"Sure!" I was nine, and I liked new things.

We went out to an open space alongside the driveway. There was no lawn, just a semblance of even ground with weeds and thick grasses. He brought a black metal box with the name of his uncle, John Albert, gracefully inscribed on the inner cover. I looked with delight at the tubes of color, soon to be identified with names like cadmium blue and burnt sienna. I had seen the paintings Dad had done when he was young—they moved with the family from house to house. Canada geese in flight. A polar bear against a brilliant sunset. Woods and waterfalls.

He brought out a piece of wood and an eight-by-ten scrap of heavy cardboard. Patiently he taught me about background perspective and color mixing. I even used the palette. Eagerly I began, painting a colorful rooster against a blue background on the cardboard.

"Very good," he said. I liked to please him.

After I tried a picture of a tree on the piece of wood, we finished up. The oil had begun to soak into the cardboard. We cleaned our hands with turpentine. Dad was good at giving useful, calm instructions throughout. We returned to the house.

"She's really good, Jeanne," he said, and Mother smiled. I beamed when he said, "We'll have to do that again." But we never did.

Rain fell that Sunday, Wisconsin memories dripping off the eaves. My shoulders fell forward, and I felt very weary. Was it the rain? No. It was the misty recollection of Plainfield. I brought it up to Chris two days later. I told him about the move, about frogs and birds and painting a picture. Then I paused, staring into space.

"You look very sad, Judie."

"I guess I am. There's something that's bothering me. It's like I have a picture on the edge of my mind, but I'm not sure what it is."

"Why don't you sit straight in the chair with your feel solid on the ground."

I did as he requested. Almost immediately I closed my eyes.

"That's a good idea, Judie. Close your eyes so you can concentrate. Can you imagine yourself back at Plainfield?"

I nodded. "Yes, I can see that house—sort of oddly put together on an open lot. I'm looking at the living room with its big picture window. I'm in third grade."

"How are you feeling, Judie?"

"I'm . . . I'm pretty scared. Sort of sick to my stomach." And from there a buried memory unwound into the air of the office.

> It's about a year before that picture-painting day. I'm in third grade. I walk into the tiny living room with its rust and black tiles, where Dad sits in the big overstuffed rocker, smoking a cigarette. He looks at me funny, but he doesn't move.

"Take off your clothes, Judie Marie."

"I don't want to."

"Do as I say. And lie down on the davenport."

My cheeks are crimson as I take off my light sweater, revealing my bare chest. I look away from Dad, trying to concentrate on the piano off to my right. I have nowhere to run. I take off my shoes and socks very slowly. The davenport is directly across from the big picture window. Who might see me?

"Your pants. Take 'em off," he says.

My hands and the fabric tangle as I pull down my pedal pushers.

"The rest. Take it all off."

I take a deep breath. I am naked. Girls aren't supposed to be naked.

He points to the davenport, and I lie down. He sits across the room, smoking and looking at me for what feels like an hour. Why does he do this?

Silence. No one speaks. I don't move. I hope I will disappear into the furniture. Then he leaves. I forget about it. I have to. I can't stand to remember.

I sat perfectly still for a moment, as if still on that living room couch. Gently, Chris asked, "Are you all right, Judie?"

"Yes." My voice dropped, and I stared at the floor. "I was so ashamed. I was so ashamed."

"How are you feeling now?"

"I don't want to think about it for a while," I said. "Can we talk next week?"

"Of course. If you think of things, or have strong emotions, just write them down, and we can talk later." The sound of his voice eased the tension from my arms.

I spent three counseling sessions reviewing and trying to understand how I felt about the memory. I remembered that I didn't have a very good school year in third grade. I didn't like my teacher, and I didn't do as well as I had done earlier. Of all things, there was a deer head hanging high on the wall inside our school room, alongside the door, looking at me. I looked the other way for the whole year.

In those days, adults were unpredictable and sometimes dangerous. The people to the south of us slaughtered a pig in their backyard. It squealed and squealed. I ran to find a place where I couldn't hear. I never forgot the sound, and even at nine I considered it barbarism. More killings. Frogs, blackbirds, and pigs. Deer. And a third grader's modesty.

But after two and a half years at Plainfield, our family took several trips to the bank in the nearby town. We kids fooled around in the car, wrestling and whining, while we waited for our parents. We didn't understand that, for several months, Mom and Dad hadn't made the mortgage payments. In late fall 1949, they moved us back to Minneapolis, their hometown. The dream was done. They had lost the house.

10

NORTHSIDE

After uncovering my country memories, I avoided thinking about the days our family lived on the north side of Minneapolis. The fleeting memories hung heavy in my mind, gray and labeled "Danger." My entire childhood had an edge of insecurity, but when I was ten, our life of isolation in the countryside became an unfamiliar city life. It was nice to be able to walk to activities, but the mystery of strangers and poverty stalked me. Although Mother was happy to be back with her friends and Trina and Anders, and Libby had the family over for meals and us kids for overnights, Dad's shadow loomed over all our activities and left us feeling afraid.

We had come from Wisconsin with few provisions made. Dad's sister Ramona was visiting Grandma Libby for a month, and she took charge. I was glad to see her again when we arrived, as she fussed in her politely aristocratic, condescending way. She had found an old rental home, a lower duplex with two bedrooms, for sixty-five dollars a month. She didn't approve of the neighborhood, but it fit the price. Grandma Libby paid the first month's rent.

Dad got another job selling Jim Beam. When he was in town, he found a favorite tavern called the Cozy Bar. He went there after supper sometimes, and he liked to take Eddie with him some afternoons. On one occasion I wrote a note to Mom: "Today when I asked where Dad is, Sherri said he's probably at the Cozy." I felt I needed to report this to Mother—Sherri had been improper to say that out loud. I wouldn't dare speak about Dad's drinking to Mom.

To my surprise, Mother said, "Well, Sherri's right, isn't she?" It mystified me. Wasn't the family rule to keep embarrassing things secret? To keep the peace? I was too ashamed to speak about being naked in front of my father. Aunt Ramona dropped her voice low when she talked about our not having enough money, and Grandma Libby surreptitiously slipped cash to my parents. Nobody talked out loud about how Dad drank too much, how he came home tipsy or used up the grocery money at the Cozy. What would people say?

I didn't like babysitting my sister and brother in our house. The nights felt darker in a strange place, and I wondered if the doors were locked tight. I wasn't used to all the furniture that came with the rental house. I missed our familiar furniture, stored every which way in the garage. One night, thunder crashed, and the house of brick and dirty stucco shook. Mom was with Aunt Ida at a baby shower, and I didn't know where Dad was. Maybe caught in the storm or probably drinking.

Now the storm raged, and I was on the daybed in the dining room, where Eddie usually slept, waiting for a grown-up to come home. When I babysat, Eddie slept in my bed with Sherri so I could hear if anyone was at the outside doors. The venetian blinds were shut, but I could see lightning when it flashed through the big kitchen window. If someone stood inside the back porch, they could see inside through the big square window on the door and maybe see me. Even though the people who lived in the apartment upstairs were home, I felt alone. It was already ten o'clock on a school night.

I heard a car, then silence and the sound of the back porch door opening. I lay still, watching. Dad came into the kitchen, shaking off his wet gold-colored wool jacket. He threw it over a kitchen chair. Good. Now I could go to sleep.

He turned on the hall light near the day bed. "Oh. Are you still up?" he said.

I knew right away: he was drunk. He wasn't speaking clearly. He looked at me, threw back his head in an unsteady move, turned off the hall light, and came over beside the day bed. I pulled the cover up around my hunched shoulders. I was chilly in my blue seersucker cotton nightgown.

"Sit up," he said. I sat up, my feet still under the covers.

"Where's your mother?"

I turned so my toes touched the floor. "She's still with Great Aunt Ida."

"I want you to do something," he said. I wondered whether he wanted me to wake up Eddie. But I was wrong. He unzipped his pants. I sat very still. The rain slapped the windows, and darkness enveloped the room.

Out from between the zipper, he took his—I didn't want to see that. Fleshy, big. I didn't even know what to call it.

"Come closer," he said, grabbing the back of my head and pulling my face toward it. I pulled back and looked away. Where could I go? His hand covered the whole back of my head. I closed my eyes as tight as I could.

Suddenly there was a noise at the back stairs. It was Mother and Ida. Quickly he tucked himself back together and walked into the hallway toward the bathroom. Just as he disappeared, Ida and Mother put their wet umbrellas on the back porch and came in the door. I breathed a big sigh and sat, shaking.

"I think the rain is letting up," Ida said as Mother walked toward the dining room.

"Goodness," Mother said to me as she turned on the hall light, "are you still awake?"

Ida had driven to the party, and her car was out front. Still standing by the back door, she said, "I'd better get myself home to my hubby. He has to leave for work by six thirty tomorrow morning."

"Thanks for driving, Ida," Mom said, walking over to give her favorite aunt a hug. "I'll talk to you next week." Then she locked the bolt on the back door behind Ida and walked into the dining room.

"It's awfully late for you to be up. I'd better get Eddie so you can be in your own bed."

I spoke quietly, emotionless. "Dad's home."

"He is? Well, we'd better get you settled for the night."

I never told her what happened. I didn't want to say it out loud, and besides, I wasn't sure what Dad was trying to do. The rain had subsided as I crawled between the bed covers, trying not to wake Sherri, and I fell asleep. His actions had been so threatening that I forgot them right away.

I needed a band of security and sense of protection in those Northside city days. Mother joined the Lutheran church seven blocks from home. I walked there for Sunday school regularly, usually alone. One Sunday I asked my fifth-grade Sunday school teacher, "What if parents aren't nice to their children? Do the children still have to obey them?" The fourth commandment was bothering me: Honor your father and your mother.

Diplomatically she said, "Sometimes a child has to obey and pray for justice." I wasn't sure what justice was, but the answer satisfied me. Still, I compared my dad to the father who lived upstairs in our duplex. I wished I had a dad like that. Mr. Dunne didn't drink and did all the shoveling and mowing for our building. His wife had multiple sclerosis. She couldn't walk without leg braces, and he faithfully carried her upstairs and helped with chores. They were Catholics, and their kids went to a parochial school. I thought they had a happy family even in hard times.

It must have been then that I began to separate life's realities from theology. They were parallel entities: faith and reality. In order to hold onto hope, I had to believe that God was good, Jesus understood and shared my suffering, and I would be cared for. In reality my life was at risk or being threatened, and I lived in hidden shame. Had I not been able to separate out those traumatic experiences, I might not have survived. My mind blocked out the dangers and abuses and listened to the stories of the faith. I believed in a compassionate God Father and lived with the opposite. I made a picture with words spelled in glitter: *Prayer Changes Things*. But it was an assertion rather than a commitment. A good idea, but not reality.

A year after we moved to the Northside, I saw a letter open on the buffet. It was to Dad. My eyes fixed immediately on the words "didn't make your quota." It said he was "terminated." I was pretty sure that meant fired.

He'd been drinking too much. My stomach churned with worry. I cautiously mentioned it to Mom. She said little except yes, it was true.

Sometimes Dad was very angry. I figured it was probably because he didn't have a job. I was pretty sure he tried to borrow money from Grandma Libby. Once, he even stalked out of Grandma Libby's house, slammed the door, and left me behind. Grandma tried to make me feel better by giving me some chocolates. Grandpa took me home.

After dark, when we came in from playing kick the can, I hoped not to see Dad. The smell of beer and liquor emanated from his clothing when he'd been to the Cozy. He had bleary eyes, unfocused. Sometimes he was too friendly and happy. He'd give Mother an extra hug in the kitchen. I stayed clear. Other times, he was abrupt and wanted to be left alone.

Dad favored Eddie and yelled a lot at Sherri, who cowered under his power.

"Get in this house and get yourself cleaned up. You're filthy!" he shouted at her one night.

Sherri had been playing in the dusty alley. She was only seven and couldn't help being dirty. I frowned, but I stayed out of the way. She was crying and scurried into the bathroom, where Mom gave her a bath.

Dad was unpredictable—some days friendly, some days scowling with his dark eyebrows. He gained weight: his 240 pounds were imposing on his six-foot-two frame. Those days on the Northside, I never knew when Dad would get upset. I thought about it a lot. Even at school.

My new school was scary, too. Some kids liked to fight, and one boy punched me in the arm all the time. I tattled on him, and the teacher said maybe he liked me. That didn't make any sense to me. Things were not calm, as they had been in the country school, and I complained to Grandpa Anders. Kids were sometimes sassy to teachers, and some students were tardy a lot. Once I even cheated in order to win a race—I pushed the girl who was winning, and she fell, so I won. I wasn't caught, but I felt more guilty than scared of punishment. (We knew that our principal had a rubber hose in her office to handle naughty kids.)

One boy even saw his dad shoot and kill his mother. For half a year the boy didn't speak to anyone, and our teacher had him sit beside me. His tennis shoes were smelly, but he didn't have a mother anymore. I tried to be friendly to him.

I was grateful for my sixth-grade teacher, Mr. Kaplan. He was nice and very tall—bigger even than my dad. I felt safe around him. Mr. Kaplan and my two best friends were Jewish. I noticed that sometimes people from church didn't speak well of Jews. I decided they were mistaken: God cared about all of us and wanted us to do the same. As the years progressed, Mr. Kaplan became a mentor and cheerleader for me, up until he died when I was in my fifties.

Grandma Libby arranged for me to have piano lessons, even though our piano had been left behind in Wisconsin. One day, coming home from my lesson on the streetcar, I sat beside a middle-aged black woman. The woman looked wistfully out the window. I wondered what she was thinking, what made her sad. *Her life must be hard,* I thought. When I got home, I told Dad about the woman.

"Don't even *think* like that!" he snapped.

I got quiet, but I knew I had *already* thought like that, and I was probably right. Dad had something against Negroes, I could tell. He had a bad name for them.

Dad didn't work for months. Grandma Libby always slipped a ten-dollar bill to Dad or Mom when we went to her house. Once I heard Mom call and ask for grocery money. I probably wasn't supposed to hear that. "Little pitchers have big ears." I knew I had better not bring up the subject.

Then, one day, Mom told us she had found a job. A job! Our mother was going to work at a job! I had the feeling that Mother made up her own mind, and Dad had to just go along with her, even if he didn't like it. I was in seventh grade at the junior high. Sherri was in third at Grant School. Eddie had to stay at school after his half day of kindergarten, and he and Sherri had to go to a special room to eat their bag lunch. Most children walked home for lunch.

After school every day I opened the house for us. It felt cool and quiet. I would call Mother right away because she worked at a telephone switchboard. Eddie and Sherri didn't like being different, set aside from the others because their mother wasn't home. She was working to support the family, but they didn't understand. My father didn't say anything about Mother working except that she was a good phone operator.

At last Dad found a job selling notions and novelties as a manufacturer's representative. He drove a showroom truck from place to place, selling goods. The showroom was six feet wide and ten feet long, with shelves on which samples were anchored. There were lamps and dolls, boxes of jewelry, plush animals, and all manner of gifts. He had long stretches away from home, four and five weeks at a time. It was a demanding job, selling, keeping the showroom in good condition, driving constantly. Sherri, Eddie, and I could earn a quarter by helping him dust the showroom interior.

Two months after finding her job, Mom found a double bungalow to rent in Parkland, a safe suburban neighborhood close to where she worked. It had a fresh, clean basement and polished wood floors. It cost one hundred dollars a month. We moved before Christmas into the postwar house, using our familiar furniture once again. I was tired of moving from school to school, but I liked this new house. As before, we children shared one large bedroom. Sherri dressed in the closet, and we each claimed a small space of our own. We found friends in our nice new schools. I spent long days with a friend, Belle, who lived a block away. And, to everyone's relief, Dad stopped drinking.

11

MOTHER

Dad told me my senior year of high school, "You'll have to go to the university and live at home. We can't afford another college." I sighed my disappointment as dreams of living on campus at a school like Mills College for women or even St. Cloud State drifted away. What would my life have been like then? Still, my folks took me to a couple of University of Minnesota football games during high school. Fifty-five thousand people, cheering, music: I was thrilled. It was obvious they were trying to build my interest in college—which I had anyway. I enrolled at the U.

Dad had quit his sales job and rented a building for a store to sell notions and novelties for discounted prices. It would be his breakthrough, he was sure. And he'd be off the road at last. Mother quit her job with great relief, and Dad would be in town for the whole Christmas break that year.

Our long, narrow living room had dark green walls, with lamps casting small puddles of light on the floor. We got the newest lamp, one that looked like an old-fashioned coffee grinder, with Green Stamps. Old carpets, one burgundy and one tan, segmented the room in two. The tan one covered the black metal grate in the floor where the heat used to come up from the basement. In the corner was a Zenith television set on its chrome stand, and beside it stood the Christmas tree.

When I was small, the tree had appeared on Christmas morning, all decorated and sparkling with slim blue glass lights. Magic! "Santa brought it last night." Now the tree was always a spruce. It stood tall enough to scrape the nine-foot ceiling and was perfectly formed. Dad had brought home boxes of ornament samples, and my sister and brother and I tried to make popcorn strings, which mostly became broken pieces cluttering the floor.

The lights were multicolored now, and this was our first year of bubble lights: three-inch glass tubes rising from bulbs filled with colored liquids with a low boiling point. The heat of the light of the bulb sent bubbles up to the tip of the small tubes. Their moving colors were reflected in the mandatory silver icicles that hung on every branch. Dad insisted we use all the glass ornaments possible—large, small, glittery, gaudy. The biggest was a fat red ball with a glittery white Santa face, which I still have. The branches fairly bent to the floor with excess, obscured by tinsel and the reflected light of an otherwise dark room.

Some months before, Mother had had a lump of some sort on her arm, but when she and Dad went to the doctor, there was no clear diagnosis—at least not any that I knew about. So I didn't think much about it. Then, at a Christmas party with her brothers and their families, I overheard her telling her brother that she had new lumps in her groin area. "I have an appointment with the doctor next week," she confided.

College resumed. I was also working at the neighborhood movie theater, happy about my recent promotion from selling candy to cashier. I could sometimes study while sitting there. Boys called often for dates. Surprised by their interest, I was eager to meet as many of them as possible. Early in winter quarter I went through sorority rush, hoping to find a group with whom to identify. It would cost $42.50 a month, including three meals a week, but I would *belong*. No more high school cliques. It would be a home on campus. I'd find some way to pay for it. Before long I got a job directing a children's church choir. The pay was, of all things, $42.50 a month.

After her doctor's appointment, Mom was hospitalized in early January for tests. I took a detour on my bus route from the university to stop by the hospital one late afternoon.

"Hi, Mom."

Her eyes were closed as she rested. Surprised by my voice, she opened her eyes and smiled slowly. She was alone in a double room overlooking the snow-filled park. I remember a high ceiling, terrazzo floor, and spare furniture. I stood back several feet from her bed.

"Oh, hi," she said. "I didn't expect you. Did you have a good day?" Her eyes dodged away from me.

"It was just normal. At least I like my classes. No more French." I had been devastated to receive a D in my freshman French class. I'd never had even a C before. It was a dark day when I took the exam and darker when my grade report arrived. I was glad French was only a one-quarter requirement. I could put it behind me. We smiled knowingly. We looked alike: tall, fine bones, dark hair, blue eyes flecked with hazel.

"Are you all right?" I asked.

Mom paused. "They got the tests back. It isn't good news."

I caught my breath.

"I have cancer."

I was stunned. I looked at her with new eyes. Shock took over, and I felt the room closing in on me. The street sounds outside became muffled, my arms were weak, and my throat was closing down. Mother began to cry.

"I don't know why I'm crying," she said. "The doctor says I could live ten or twenty more years. It's called Hodgkin's disease." I could tell she was reaching for hope, trying to reassure me. But her voice was weak, and her tears betrayed her fears.

I couldn't hold back the terror that filled my chest and brought tears to my eyes. I knew next to nothing about cancer or this particular disease. I straightened my shoulders. "What will you do?"

She adjusted her pillows to sit straighter. "They have something called cobalt treatment. We think we'll try that." She coughed lightly. "The cancer is in my system, in the lymph nodes. That's how it spreads." Again tears flowed through her words.

It was just too much to comprehend. My mother might be dying. I loved her deeply but couldn't reach out to hug her. All I could do was say, "It'll be all right, Mom. It'll be all right."

She smoothed her blanket, looking down. "I shouldn't be telling you all this." Regret waves undulated through her words. "We were going to keep it a secret. But"—her tears began to drip down her cheeks—"I couldn't help myself."

I knew why she had said something. I was the oldest. I was the one she counted on. She had to tell someone.

She cleared her throat. "But we aren't going to tell Sherri and Eddie."

"Okay," I agreed. They were fourteen and twelve. *It would scare them,* I thought.

"And we aren't going to say anything to Grandma Libby. It would be hard on her. Or Grandma Trina and Grandpa Anders either. It would just worry them when they're so far away." They had gone down to Florida just before Christmas with their tiny trailer hitched to their Nash automobile.

"Okay." My spirits lifted slightly. "Mom, maybe everything will work out fine, and they won't have to worry." I couldn't process any more information or emotions or possibilities.

To help ease our tension, we talked a little while about school and the housework that might need to be done. I wanted to get to a bus stop before it was dark. I hugged Mom and walked away, crossing the downtown park, numb with disbelief.

The day was warm for January, and the sun hadn't set, so I decided to walk for a few blocks. *Maybe I could walk home,* I thought, even knowing it was miles away. I could just follow the bus route along Hennepin Avenue. I walked, unable to focus, stopping to look at the display in the window of the Christian Science Reading Room. As the day grew dark, I began to feel cold. There were worn Christmas window displays and noisy traffic. Buses passed by, and I let them go on without me. I trudged on, and my mind was strangely blank. After just over two miles I finally boarded a bus, glad for its warmth and light, and rode to the stop near home. I was glad for the familiarity of the house when I walked in the door. Dad had hamburgers on the stove. I said nothing to anyone.

After dinner, I sought out Dad in the kitchen. Since I had always played a parental role with my siblings, I often referred to them as the kids. That evening the kids were out of earshot in the living room. "Mom told me about how sick she is."

His face fell, and his eyes looked into the distance. There was an ominous silence. Then his whole body heaved with a sigh of desperation.

"We'll just have to hope," he replied. "Medicine is better and better these days."

I didn't respond, and the moment was left hanging on the light of the kitchen and the winter air. I turned to do the dishes.

He continued, "We'll just have to hold things together while she's getting well."

I held my hands in the warm dishwater for comfort, and tears returned, dropping into the sink.

Days were long that winter. February was dismal and cold. I hated February. I had trouble both studying and concentrating. I could never study at home with all its distractions. The television was always on, and we had no desks in our rooms. Everything was unsettled without Mother there. I was in charge of the house and my sister and brother. Dad did his best to handle food duties. He was a pretty good cook and liked to make venison roast or spaghetti and meatballs. Sherri and Eddie pitched in by being invisible and not creating problems. They weren't old enough to be allowed to visit Mom in the hospital. Dad hadn't been drinking for six years. Some of his usual dry-drunk petulance melted into concern and fear for Mom. I had never seen him so worried. He used a three-by-five card to write a Valentine's Day gift message, but I sensed the futility of his hopes in every word.

He tried to cheer Mom up by purchasing new carpet to replace our worn-out living room rugs. He thought it would warm up our old house. Workers laid the carpet while she sat on the couch, wrapped in a maroon blanket made of soft wool, with images of Indian artifacts. I could see she wasn't getting better.

Mother was sick in February, confined to her twin bed most days. I was in her room one evening when she said, "Look in the bottom drawer of my dresser." She was proud of that low, wide maple-wood dresser with its nine drawers and big mirror, which she had purchased with her own money from her job. I stooped down, and there, underneath her rolled-up socks, was a wad of money. A hundred twenty-five dollars!

"That's for your initiation fee for the sorority. I want you to be able to join."

My mouth opened, and then I smiled. "Really? That's wonderful!" I had been scheming about how to earn that large a sum at my part-time job.

"Thanks, Mom. Thanks so much!"

"You don't have to say anything to your father about it," she cautioned. "It will be our secret. I want you to have this chance." Once again, I realized how she regretted quitting high school her senior year. She missed out on many things and wanted more for me.

If Sherri and Eddie were suspicious about Mother, I didn't know it. Dad lived in denial. We were all enveloped in secrets as we always had been. The demands of our home, laden with sickness and fear, were oppressive as each of us tried to maintain school or work with added responsibility and apprehension. At some point Sherri and Eddie began to wash their own clothes.

One late winter day, as I sat struggling with a chemistry equation at the dining room table, Mother came home after one of her many hospital stays. Surprised, I looked up to say, "Oh, hi!" and walked to meet her in the kitchen. Mom looked around, sighed deeply, and said, "I was hoping things would be cleaned up."

I looked at the floor, my smile melting into guilt. Should I apologize or explain my difficult chemistry assignment? She turned away from me and slowly ascended the stairs. I moved to gaze out the window as I made myself stand straight again. My guilt morphed to quiet anger. I understood her disappointment, but it was a big job to manage the house without her, on top of my college coursework. More than that, her own hope seemed to have dissolved, leaving only discouragement.

Mom's aunt and good friend, Ida, knew about her illness, but Dad insisted that she not tell Grandma Trina and Grandpa Anders. Mom wrote mildly cheerful letters to them in Florida. Ida would drop by the house occasionally with a hotdish or a treat for Mother. We never locked our inside back door, probably because one had to enter the covered back porch before reaching it. But as Mom's condition worsened, our common psyche was locked tight. We were a household of solitary individuals. We didn't talk about how we felt. Questions went unasked. Like Grandma Libby, we thought in clichés: Miracles do happen. No news is good news. Time heals all. Perhaps we thought that by not speaking of our fear and suffering, it might go away. As children, we had no idea that other, healthier families would talk about their pain and support one another. We stayed silent, shut in.

Then in early March, Mom had a setback. She looked weary through and through, her face gray and eyes hollow, like a phantom presence. Ida began to visit regularly. Finally, Ida took matters into her own hands and wrote to Grandma Trina and Grandpa Anders. She didn't tell them exactly how sick Mom was, but they read between the lines and within a day they were on the road home. Mom was greatly relieved to see them, and they decided to stay at the house as long as she needed them.

Grandpa Anders was deeply tied to Mom and was annoyed with Dad, as usual. He tried to find ways to help around the house. Grandma Trina took over the cooking and caregiving. We were all worried because Mom kept losing weight. Sherri and I moved to a rickety foldout couch in the finished basement, giving our grandparents our room and moving Mother back to her own twin bed. Still, no one told Grandma Libby, and Mona knew but was not fully aware of how serious the cancer was.

One evening I called Eddie and Sherri together in the living room. The lights were dim, and night seemed to surround us, even indoors. "You know Mom isn't doing so well." I couldn't bring myself to say *dying*. "We'll just have to pray and do the best we can to help. But she might not get better." I thought someone had to warn them. They didn't ask questions, and none of us discussed the illness any further.

Mom had always done the family budget, usually robbing Peter to pay Paul. She had the more steady income, and Dad couldn't discipline his spending.

One evening Dad said to me, "I'd like you to take over the budget and pay the bills. We have a good envelope system. We set aside cash each month for bills when they come due. Then you can take the cash and buy money orders to pay them."

After he explained it to me, Mom called me to come upstairs. Somehow she had overheard the conversation. "I don't want you to do that. You shouldn't have to."

I knew Mom wasn't well, and I hardly dared oppose Dad. Besides, I knew he didn't manage well. "It's okay," I replied. "I can do it for a while."

One evening, just before her April hospitalization, I came upstairs to my parents' bedroom. The only light was by her bed, and I sat on the edge of Dad's twin bed as we talked about my day at school. The distant noise of the television covered our conversation. Mom reached over and turned off the lamp, saying, "I don't think I'm going to make it."

"Mom!"

"No. I don't think so. I'm not getting better. I'm too tired now. I remember I used to drive past the cemetery on the way to work and I thought it looked so peaceful. That isn't right. It's not normal. That isn't how a person's supposed to feel."

I began to cry.

"I shouldn't tell you, I suppose."

In the darkness I couldn't find words. Quietly I said, "I would miss you . . ."

"I wish I could just make it until Eddie finishes high school. That wouldn't be so bad. Just six years more."

"Maybe you will." I struggled to be hopeful and encouraging.

"No, I don't think so. I'm so tired." We sat silently in the dark for an interminable time, light shining in from the hallway. It was more than I could stand. I gave her a hug and left the room. I went to the basement to my shared bed, lay down, and cried softly until I heard Sherri coming. I blocked my tears and slept, exhausted.

On the first of May, I came home from school at one thirty to find Great Aunt Ida at the kitchen sink, washing dishes. Mother had been back in the hospital for a week. I walked into the dining room to put my books on the round table. "Judie Marie," Ida said without looking up. "Your mother died this morning." I've never forgotten the power of those quiet words.

I stood still for a moment, put down my books, and said, "Thank God." I had given up hope; the tension and waiting had depleted me. Her pain was finally over. Grief and relief dropped over me. Ida explained that Grandma Trina and Dad were making arrangements at the funeral home. It fell to me to tell Sherri and Ed as each one came home from school.

Eddie was the first. "Hi," he said as he came in the back door.

"I need to talk to you in the living room," I said. We walked in and stood by the piano.

"Mom died this morning." He looked at me blankly, then his face fell, and he twisted his fingers in silence.

A twelve-year-old can scarcely grasp death and hangs on to whatever is familiar or concrete. "Is there going to be a funeral?"

"Yes, but I don't know when yet. Grandma Trina and Dad are working on it. I'll let you know. Are you okay?"

He nodded and walked quietly away, up to his room, where he could be alone. I ached for him.

I dreaded telling Sherri. She was especially close to Mom. I stopped her on the back porch before she came into the house.

"Mom died today," I said softly.

"No!" she said and began to cry. I took a deep breath, searching for words.

"We'll be all right. We'll all take care of each other." She shook her head in resistance. Soon after, she went to the big wood desk and called her friend Jenny. It was too much for all of us. There were no embraces. And none of us had gotten to say good-bye to her.

All around me the sounds of life were muffled, deadened. I had done my duty by telling the kids the news. I wasn't crying; I was numb. I went to the car, where I had hidden a few cigarettes, since no one knew I occasionally smoked. Maybe it would help me cope. But it offered no comfort.

At five o'clock I rode with Dad to the airport to meet Aunt Mona and her six-year-old son. She was crushed. "Oh," she said, weeping, "I'm too late to see her."

I went to school on Friday rather than breathing the heavy air of loss at home. Riding with some other students, I saw a friend and thought, *Oh look! There's Carol. I've got to tell her that Mom died!* I was consumed by the urgency of letting people know and had no sense of appropriateness. I would have shouted my pain to the world, but I couldn't roll down the window fast enough. And the sound would have been absorbed by a silent world.

Aunt Mona asked my advice for what she should wear to the funeral, since she had no black clothes. "That's all right," I said. "You can just wear something else." Odd, I thought, to be advising my elder. I was eighteen. Mona was forty-two, the same age as Mom had been.

There was a dull murmur in the mortuary: crowds of people gathering to support the family, sharing memories in suffocating sounds. Through the fog I heard my music teacher say, "You'll have to be the mother now." I fled to the hallway, where I sobbed until I saw myself in the mirror and drew up my shoulders, wondering, *What will it mean to be the mother of this family?*

Some days, I told myself, *I will go to her graveside. I'll sit and be near Mother and study and read.* But I never did. Our family isolated ourselves in our sorrow, grieving quietly. Eddie's grade school class made sympathy cards. As the years passed, he eventually forgot how Mom had looked, how her voice sounded. Sherri walked through life blindly, missing Mom desperately but not talking about her feelings, forever searching for a replacement mother figure. She had been dependent on Mom, close to her, and now as a young teenager she felt lost, craving guidance and boundaries.

I took on responsibility for the house and children. I sent special Christmas cards that year, telling distant friends that our mother was gone. Sometimes Dad consulted me regarding the children, but I tried to distance myself from that role. I had two jobs on top of home responsibilities and school. I didn't want to be a substitute for Mother as well. At times Dad even called me Jeanne by mistake. I hated that.

Providing food was one thing Dad knew how to do well. He would make large quantities of Hungarian goulash and put it in the refrigerator for us to eat when we came home. We didn't talk much at meals; sometimes we each ate alone at the kitchen bar. Dad watched television every night and ate a large bowl of vanilla ice cream with chocolate sauce and caramel, topped with marshmallow creme and peanuts. He used music to console himself. Late into the summer nights he would play our small electric organ. The sound of the blues carried through the entire house. I wanted to scream, "Stop playing! Stop that music!" and I covered my head with a pillow. The night was black, and the music was heavy with grief. "Through the dark of night, I gotta go where you are."

12

GRIEF AND SECRETS

M om was awfully young when she died, you know," I told Chris. "And so were you. How did you grieve?"

"I'm not really sure how I coped. I don't remember grieving."

As I drove home from therapy, I intentionally passed by the stately entrance to the cemetery where Mother lay. It occurred to me that my past year had been full of mystery and memories. It was more than the deer and Dad's drinking. There was something that didn't fit together. I was on a new track somehow. I needed to find a way to say good-bye to Mother.

All week long I found myself sighing, images of Mother's thoughtfulness revolving through my mind as I dusted or watered my indoor plants. She loved having plants. I dug out an assortment of pictures of her and framed one each for Sherri and Ed. I put one on the piano and another in my bedroom. I needed to remind myself of her. It had been nearly twenty years since she died, and I had avoided the sadness. I had been left without her protection but with her responsibilities.

It had been our tradition to go to Grandma Libby's for dinner on Sunday afternoon. It was usually pork roast, mashed potatoes, a canned vegetable, and apple pie. For some four years after Grandpa died, when I was in high school, our family invited Grandma Libby to Sunday dinner at our home at our round oak table. Mom loved that table, which had belonged to her grandmother. But a round table represented all that we were not: a circle of companions, equal and approachable, sharing a meal and conversation. Rather, we were children eager to get away to other interests.

We were taught to always thank Mother for the meal before leaving. And though sometimes we laughed around the table, we were usually at attention in order to please Dad. Sherri was especially fearful because she was a frequent target of his criticism.

It was a meager sense of family. After Mom died, the rituals dissolved, a ragged loss of purpose and direction. It became increasingly difficult to throw away broken toys and tools—anything that gave us a feeling of history or familiarity—as we attempted to reassure ourselves that we had possessions and life was stable. We hoarded our past in hope of a future. The space around and atop the cellar doors outside the dining room became a reflection of our cast-off, dysfunctional lives: an old bike, empty wooden boxes, a broken tennis racket, a fragment of snow fence, a discarded white wood kitchen table. It was a collection of worn experiences, insulated with blown-in dried leaves and covered each winter with silent snow.

Occasionally we invited Grandma for dinner with us. She was almost seventy-five, and her vision was diminished by cataracts. Libby was too old to understand my social life concerns. Now I wonder how it might have been had Mother lived longer. I never got to talk with her about her youth. What would she have advised about my boyfriends in college? I had friends, but I needed a mother during those years.

Grief went unspoken and unexpressed for the entire family. Only Aunt Mona clucked, "Since Jeanne died, no one ever sends letters." I stewed: *Does she have any idea what it is like to live without your mother when you are still in high school and college? How much we have to manage with her gone?* Then I'd sit down and write a nice letter to her.

I searched for moments of connection with older women. Sometimes I called Grandma Libby from the university and asked if I could come to lunch at her house. It felt good to be there, and I welcomed the two dollars she usually gave me as I left. From time to time I brought friends, and she charmed them all, humming while she brought us cookies from the pantry. She seldom gave any indication of worry about the family, but she mentioned Mother occasionally.

One day when we were alone, I asked, "How did you feel when you found out the secret that Mom was dying because she had cancer?"

"I figured cancer was probably what it was," she said. She had never asked anyone exactly what was wrong with Mom. *No news is good news. Don't borrow trouble.*

Her big duplex felt like a sanctuary. In that tall white house I was away from the pressure of putting myself through school, tending the family, and paying the bills while always short of money. At forty-five, Dad was a dry drunk, irritable and unreliable. He had lost his business and was back to selling; this time it was electric organs. I had the feeling he was asking Libby for money, but no one said anything.

Nearly fifty-five years apart in age, Grandma and I talked. I would tell her about my classes and what was happening in my social group. When I lamented about Dad, Libby mused, "Last summer I told him, 'You'll be a man yet, Walt.'" It sent shivers through me. *He isn't a boy. How can she insult him like that?*

I was curious about her life. "When did you meet Grandpa Paul?"

"Oh, I was older than you are. We got married when I was twenty-five— that was pretty late back then. We met at a church social." I had seen a smiling picture of a dapper Paul on a postcard he had sent while on vacation. "Don't forget me," he'd written.

I thought the postcard from Grandpa Paul was romantic, a little risqué. One day in the kitchen, over iced tea, Grandma confided that the early days of their marriage had been trying for her. "Paul used to have great rages in the night. I was scairt," she reported.

"Really? What did you do?"

"Nothing," she said. "I just stayed quiet. After we slept in the same bed for a few weeks, it seemed to pass."

I translated the euphemisms: He calmed down once he had had sex for a while. *Odd,* I thought.

It was only later that Aunt Mona told me that Grandpa Paul had run away from home in Denmark as an adolescent and come to America. He had escaped an abusive father. Perhaps he was accustomed to rages.

Lips trembling, I shared those lonely years of seeking a confidant and mother figure during a therapy session.

"Did you ever go to the cemetery the way you planned?" Chris asked.

My head dropped. "No, I never did. It was too hard just to live . . ." I began to cry. "Just to keep things going at home."

"Did you ever really say good-bye to your mother?"

"I did tell her I would miss her . . ."

"And after she died? Did your family talk about your mother?"

"Sometimes. Not really talking *about* her—just mentioning her."

"Did anyone grieve?"

"Cry, you mean? I don't think I ever saw anyone cry. I cried sometimes, when I was alone or with a good friend. But not much." Tears spilled over my lashes. "I tried to keep up with things—making dental appointments for the kids, encouraging them in school. I missed her so much. I was so alone. School, the house, the kids, my dad—so much to do." My tears flowed freely.

On the way home from therapy that day, I bought a single rose, wishing I'd bought roses for her when she was alive. One was all I could afford. I went to the cemetery and found the Hallstrom granite monument. The ground was dry and hard. A crow cawed from a nearby tree. Why had I never come before?

On the other side of the monument was chiseled the name Thorsen. Beside the marker for Grandpa Paul was the ground marker: Jeanne Marie Thorsen, 1915–1958. I felt chilled and worlds away from her. I put the pink rose on the marker. "I missed you, Mom. Why did you have to leave me like that?" I pulled away some of the grass that had grown over the marker. The crow called again and again. Tears ran gently down my cheeks. Years of withheld grief flowed from my eyes and heart. The darkening sky was heavy as I headed home.

A couple of weeks later I sat down at our console piano to play a few old songs. Like Dad and Grandma Libby, I played by ear with simple chords. I had an almost-two-foot stack of old sheet music, some taken from my parents' home long ago and some a collection of my own favorites from the 1950s. I didn't sing along as I played, the way Grandma and Dad did, but I usually found playing relaxing. I often played as I waited for Eric and the boys to get ready to go out. That morning I played Swedish melodies I'd learned from Grandma.

I began to make mistakes. "Darn it," I said. I'd forgotten the next chords. My fingers missed notes until in exasperation I pounded the keys and then slammed down the wooden key cover. "Damn!"

My upper chest felt heavy. Loneliness again. I bounded upstairs, changed out of my jeans, and headed for the car. I drove six miles to the collectibles store I had always liked. The little white cottage contained memories for everyone who browsed there. People like me, who touched and exclaimed over items they had once had in their lives. "Look! A set of Noritake china!" "I've always wanted to have one of these old sleds like we did when we were young." I went straight to the messy stack of old sheet music in the back corner, and only then did I calm down. I went through the worn pages, pulling out the "Black Hawk Waltz" and "Three O'Clock in the Morning," favorites of Grandma Libby. Then I brightened to see a copy of "It Had to Be You." Mother had always hummed that song around the house. It was her favorite.

Once, when I was in high school, Mother had joined Dad and me as we were playing "Mood Indigo" in a duet. Softly she sang along with us.

"You're singing flat," Dad said to her. Mom's face fell, and she walked away. My heart broke for her.

Looking around at the store's disarray, I held the sheet music tenderly, thinking about Mom and trying to make sense of her life and mine. It was more than grief. It was mystery.

When I got home, I played through "It Had to Be You." I imagined that my mother had danced romantically to it with my father. Then I remembered: in the basement storeroom—a diary that had belonged to Mom! I hurried downstairs to see if I could retrieve it from among all the things I'd saved. I had once browsed through it, but now I wanted to read it thoroughly to discover more about her early life.

Mother got the Five Year Diary for her eighteenth birthday in 1933. With gold-edged pages, it was bound in brown leather with a marble-patterned cover. An inscription on the inside cover page read, "Dear Diary. You are a gift from Ruth Benson. For the coming five years you and you only will hear all my secrets!"

Throughout the diary were anecdotes about Mom's best high school friend, Margie Lankowski, who was Polish and lived across the street. She was a jolly, sweet person who finished high school. She had a pleasant whine to her voice and dark eyes eager to tend to others' needs. These two best friends poured out their hearts to each other. Margie brought Mom with her each month to a club called the Zetas, which was made up of about twenty girls from three high schools.

The Zetas would be part of my life as well as Mother's, for they met for over sixty years. The night of Mother's funeral visitation, the Zetas gathered, crying and laughing, unsettled that one of them had died so young. As I read the familiar names in Mother's diary, I tried to imagine them as the girls described in the pages.

Dad's sister, Aunt Mona, was the Zetas' organizer. She made sure they got publicity in the Minneapolis paper's social pages. Grandma Libby hosted the Zetas' gatherings at her house from time to time. That's where Dad first saw Mom. The girls were attracted to him because he was affable and good-looking and flirtatious. He was already off on his own, traveling. He had dropped out of college to go into sales.

When Mother was seventeen, he spotted her at a gathering at Libby's and asked her out for coffee. She was impressed. His family lived in comfort, and with all his travel to Chicago and Milwaukee and even New York, he seemed worldly to Mom.

Over the next six years, when he came to town, he sometimes called her and sometimes didn't, but he always promised he'd call again. When he did call, they'd go out for coffee or to dinner, but several crestfallen entries noted that he had left town without contacting her. Her diary was filled with years of delight at his attention contrasted with frequent disappointment at his disregard.

Reading her reactions reminded me of how sad she looked when we had family plans to go out and Dad let us down. The more I read about his irresponsibility, the more disappointed I felt. But she made excuses for him and covered her sadness with a feeble smile. She dated other young men but always returned to pining for Walt.

In those early days, Mom's friends loved to go dancing at the Marigold Ballroom. They walked the three miles in a group, dressed in ankle-length skirts and medium high heels. Mother always pulled her hair back in a chignon, which highlighted her eyes and slim figure. Dad had a car, and he would drive her home alone. She was taken by his debonair sophistication.

1934—age 19
SATURDAY, MARCH 31

Met Glenn P. He took us home from the Marigold. Nice kid. Seems ages instead of a week since I last saw Walt. Who do I like anyway?

Dad was slender and tall—six foot two—with a full grin and straight carriage. He resembled Jimmy Stewart with dark hair. His smile was full and seductive, and Mom sometimes looked away when he smiled at her. He saw her reserve; it attracted him. He usually treated her to a drink, and she easily slipped into being tipsy. It was fun.

1935
SUNDAY, MARCH 10

Marigold. Met Walt there. We went out. Guess I was drunk. How he's changed.

Mom wrote with such detail that I could even imagine her conversations with Margie. After a walk in the neighborhood and a long talk, Mom sat on Margie's bed, crying about Walt's unpredictable behavior.

"But I love to go drinking with him," she admitted.

Margie pleaded with her, "Please, Jeanne. You've got to stop drinking. It gets you into trouble."

"But I like drinks. And Walt always wants to mix drinks or go to bars when we go out."

"But Jeanne, it's risky! You get too drunk sometimes. Promise me you'll try to quit. You can do it."

"I will. I promise."

Mom stopped drinking, but within two weeks she had broken her promise and ended up weeping with her beloved friend once again.

Reading her words, I was disappointed in Mom's poor judgment. *C'mon, Mom, get a hold of yourself. He's not worth it. Use your head. Don't drink so much.* Then I read on.

1935
SATURDAY, MARCH 16

Walt and I went out to Swing Village, etc. Oh what a night. Love happened!

SUNDAY, MARCH 17

Slept until 1 p.m. Damn when I think of last night. Went down to the Marigold. Lousy time. Home early.

The relationship was up and down, tied together by letters, hopes, and disappointments.

1935
TUESDAY, JULY 13

Al and Walt and I went on a picnic. Fun. Games, ball game, etc. all day. Drinking—and then—the inevitable. Home about 12:30. God knows I love him.

WEDNESDAY, AUGUST 21

Went to work. Got laid off again at noon. Walked home. Loafed all day. Walt called. Movie with him and Bill. Darn him—why should I? Oh, I'm so foolish.

MONDAY, SEPTEMBER 16

Bike races again. Fun. Had plenty to drink. Hagen's Cafe etc. I suppose if he loves me nothing matters. But it's not right.

THURSDAY, SEPTEMBER 26

Out to Sears for my money. Lousy check—no hours. Home all afternoon. Out to Ida's. Out with Walt at 11 p.m. He was drunk. I smashed his car. Fun sort of tho. Home 2 a.m.

They dated for months, then years. The pattern repeated again and again. He would travel. She would miss him. Sometimes he would slight her when he was home. When he left again, she would write to him, and he would go for weeks without writing back. Then he would return, and they would go out together, and everyone was happy.

When Jeanne was twenty-one, Walt's friend Jon said, "That Jeanne is a good looker."

"Jeanne is too good for me," Dad replied. It pleased Mom, and she was also flattered when her cousin told her she would probably eventually reform Walt. She knew he needed to grow up and manage his money better. But then there were times when she cried herself to sleep or said in anger, "Oh that man! I love him."

1937

FRIDAY, JUNE 18

The reason he acts so funny is that the kids razz him about being a rounder. I know he has been. I'm trying to forget.

I looked up *rounder* in the dictionary. It meant "a dissolute person: lacking moral restraint, indulging in sensual pleasures or vices." Did people think he was womanizing? or a drunk? Why in the world did Mom overlook his weaknesses? I could smell bourbon wrapped in her diary accounts—I winced.

I scarcely noticed that the tune "It Had to Be You" trailed through my mind as I read Mother's diary. I had become more aware lately that music wove itself in and around events, often unnoticed. Songs from my nursery rhyme record when I pictured Wauwatosa. The school rouser when my memories returned to high school. Now it was mother's favorite popular song about being hopelessly in love.

I clenched the diary and my teeth. What kind of love is it when you long for someone who is cross or bossy or mean? Someone worth thinking about even though it makes you sad?

The late afternoon sun slanted into the room, leaving me sitting in faint darkness. I lost my desire to know more.

I sighed and took the diary upstairs, where I tucked it into a small bookcase. I hadn't counted on the fact that Mother also drank too much when she was young. My stomach tightened. And all the innuendos about having sex. She sounded reluctant. As a teenager, I had seen those looks when she pulled away from Dad's advances, her lips tight. When I was younger, her face stiffened when he came home with liquor on his breath.

That night Eric and I were sitting in the family room. The boys were in bed, and the house was pleasantly quiet. In the calm light of the room I was more relaxed than I had been when I first read the diary. I brought it downstairs.

"I read my mother's diary today. Listen to this."

He listened, seemingly unmoved. "Don't you feel like you're invading her privacy?" he said.

"Maybe a little. Mostly I feel disappointed. Mom was so . . . so . . . weak. He took advantage of her."

"She loved him, it sounds like."

"Eric! That's not love. She was living an illusion."

"So whose fault is that?"

"Nobody's, I guess. But her story is sad."

"Sure. But she has to be responsible for going along with him."

I flashed a sharp look at Eric. "She was being seduced."

"Maybe," he said. "But women have to admit their part in seduction. And it sounds like she drank an awful lot."

My disillusionment about Mother morphed into shame about her drinking and anger at Eric's dispassionate judgments. I slammed the diary shut. Blame the victim! She didn't have the power to resist. Throughout their life she was the one who worked hard and maintained the family. She stopped drinking too much long before then. He was a philanderer and drank. Neither she nor I could trust him. It was Dad's fault. And Eric didn't understand.

I took a deep breath and glared at him. "Let's drop the subject," I said, and I left the room.

13

APARTMENT MOVE

Two years after my wedding to Eric, Dad married Stella, a neighbor. By then, Sherri was already living on her own, and Ed shared a house with friends while he was attending college. Stella had twin sons, Sherri's age, who had also moved out. Dad and Stella married privately in a chapel. None of their children knew it was planned. Another surprise: he had always been anti-Catholic, and Stella was Catholic. Ten years later he converted to Catholicism.

"You won't have to worry about me anymore," Dad sarcastically told me on the night he called to announce their marriage. It mystified me. Why was he so resentful?

Stella was as petite as Dad was large. She was friendly and usually smiling, with sparkling eyes and reddish-brown hair. She had a good sense of humor. As a young woman she had once led a dance band. She was a good-natured person, forced to be self-sufficient after her first husband had a stroke and died, but she longed for someone to lean on. She and her first husband had owned a small family grocery store in the neighborhood, and she and her sons worked long days and weeks keeping the business going until the boys left home.

One Sunday afternoon, Eric and I stopped by the house to see Dad. I was six months pregnant. It was a wholesome time for me. I was proud to be carrying a child and eager to be a mother.

One of Stella's sons was home, and we all chatted pleasantly in the living room. The twins were nice, handsome young men; I didn't know them well, but I respected them.

Then, from the throne of his overstuffed rocking chair, Dad said to me, "When did you get knocked up?"

My cheeks sagged, and I caught my breath. How could he say that? I looked hastily at Stella's son, embarrassed and shocked. What must he be thinking? He also looked shocked—and disgusted with Dad.

I murmured something to Dad that he knew I was due in a few months, but my heart was crying, sick inside.

Driving away that day, I said, "How could he do that? He knows I'm pregnant!"

"He was drunk, Judie," Eric replied.

As if that excuses him, I thought. Tears flooded my eyes, and a shadow fell over my full abdomen and body.

"Cruel," said Karen when I told her about the remark. "And maybe jealous. Or just angry at your happiness. He's a sick man, Judie."

Soon after, Dad sold his house and moved into Stella's cozy stucco one. They seemed close and caring. It was a symbiotic relationship, each one dependent in different ways. She built him up, and he took care of her. She didn't have to try to manage alone anymore. And I felt relieved of supervising his drinking and financial management. He had Stella now. Maybe she would help him be more responsible.

After working for someone else, Dad had again started his own business, this time selling garages. The cost of the new business drained their budget. Within a year of moving to Stella's place, they were five house payments behind, so the twins, my siblings, and I contributed monthly to their mortgage. But Dad and Stella ultimately lost her house and had to rent an apartment in a fading part of town.

Stella made a good show of the loss of the home where she had raised her sons: "This will be good. We won't have all that house to keep up." Denial and little jokes about life were already familiar patterns of hers. But to my surprise, in the days immediately before and during the move, Stella checked herself into the hospital. The trauma of moving and loss took her down. I felt sad for her loss. She had loved that home.

Preparation for the move was daunting, with two homes' worth of goods to organize and, in many cases, dispose of. Ed loaded their things onto a trailer while his new wife, Marty, did a large share of sorting and packing. I helped when I could. Sherri lived in St. Paul and had little opportunity to assist.

"Dad told me I can have the round table," I told Ed late one afternoon. He took it off the trailer so Eric and I could haul it back to the home we had rented.

I went over to Dad's house the evening before the movers were due to take a few smaller items to their apartment. I found Dad sitting at a cluttered dining room table in the midst of the half-packed house. I could smell that he'd been drinking.

I asked Dad if I could have some of their nice water glasses and Uncle John Albert's paint box. "Take what you want," he said with sarcastic disregard. "We can't use it anymore." I went downstairs for the paints, which were in a pile of assorted housewares in the middle of the room. Despite a small set of antlers only inches away, I retrieved the old black metal box.

I was in their kitchen, washing a few dishes, when a friend of Dad's knocked at the front door. "Hey, Shorty!" Dad called. "Glad you're here." The man stood by the front door, waiting.

Dad turned to me. "Judie Marie, have you got a little money I can have?"

I searched my purse and came up with two dollars.

"Thanks," he said. "Me and Shorty are going to Jennings. Maybe I'll see you at the apartment. Here's the key." They were headed for his favorite bar.

I watched through the living room window of Stella's once-pleasant home, now nearly empty. Shorty drove, with Dad behind him in the back. As the car sped away in the twilight, Dad fell over onto the backseat. My stomach turned. I projected despair into his actions—another home gone. He was on his way to anesthetize his feelings.

I loaded up my car with some household goods and headed for the new apartment. Later, when I was in the midst of organizing things, Dad arrived—drunk. I was making their bed in the single bedroom. Dad watched me, unsteady, filling the bedroom doorway. I tensed.

I looked around the room, trying to appear at ease. I reflexively feared being trapped with him, not knowing why.

"Nice of you to do that, Judie Marie. What can I give you?"

I quickly looked around the bedroom. "I'd like some of those giant old phonograph records from Grandma Libby's house."

"Sure. You just take whatever you want," he said expansively.

I went through the albums on the dresser and chose two records, surreptitiously watching him in the mirror that was above the dresser niche. He was still blocking the door. I took a deep breath and moved toward him.

"I have to get going, Dad. I've got to be up early tomorrow."

As I approached the door, my shoulders back and feigning confidence, he stepped aside and let me pass.

"You just come any time now," he said, and when he moved in my direction, I quickly headed for the door and left. I had no idea if he would stay there that night or find some way back to their near-empty house. I got into our car on the dark street and drove home, clenching the steering wheel and eager to feel safe with Eric in our own home.

14

TREATMENT

I wrote in my journal, "I don't think I have the ability to survive life." Seeing the words on the page scared me. But I had noticed lately that I didn't breathe deeply: I held my breath, or I sighed loudly as I went about my day. I couldn't sort out all the factors of my dull, heavy pain, and I had no sense of how I could change my life. I was walking through heavy mud.

Had I created my own cell from which I could not escape? Was I too focused on my past? I had written and published a book, *I'm Worried About Your Drinking: Feelings of Family and Friends Who Care*. It was at least some catharsis, putting into words the effects of being with a parent who was unpredictable and even thoughtless or abusive because of an inability to manage alcohol. After it came out, Stella phoned Sherri.

"I don't like that book about Walt," she said.

Sherri replied, "That book is about me too, you know."

Good for Sherri, I thought. But I didn't have her straightforward manner. Sherri could more easily speak her mind. She was the strong one, I thought. And, of course, despite my efforts, Dad was still drinking. Early memories of Dad's insults taunted me, and now I had the shameful memories of being naked on the couch. Those were the worst.

"Can't you put that behind you?" Eric asked, and my heart sank.

We had moved to an outer suburb. It was the second time Eric had made a work location decision without including me. I became involved in community activities, but I felt isolated, quite out of place. It was like being in rural Wisconsin once again. My having published a book and being a pastor's wife had a negative effect on some people; they set me aside as unapproachable. Eric wanted me to wait to go to work outside the home until both of our sons had finished kindergarten. I acquiesced for a couple of years, but I missed being employed.

Those days, people had signs in their homes saying, "I'm okay, You're okay." Vietnam pounded at our doors daily, and Watergate shook our confidence as a nation. Our preschool boys and I would dance together in the living room to "Aquarius/Let the Sunshine In," arms and legs flying as we smiled. On morning television we watched *That Girl*, the story of a young, independent woman. Things were changing. But I felt trapped.

We had marital skirmishes. Eric had forgotten to buy a birthday gift for me again. We went to Target and looked at radios for the kitchen, something I wanted. We perused the shelf samples. He chose one. I, another.

"I like the sound of this one better," I said.

"Sound doesn't matter. This one is cheaper," he snapped.

With the boys nearby, I gritted my teeth and added, "Sound is what a radio is for."

We bought the radio I had chosen, but it was tainted with Eric's reluctant obligation.

In many ways I felt successful. I loved my children, and our family was usually a happy unit. Still, I was reluctant to be honest and intimate with my husband. I was critical of his angry outbursts, his carefree approach to his work, and his tendency toward miserliness. Would we be able to work that out over time. *What's wrong with me?*

I looked out at the field across the road, permanently empty of crops. The swaying willow in the yard was a playground for the boys, but sweetly sad. I didn't fit into the culture of the area, where few women were like me, and I thought I was a failure as a wife. I put on a Neil Diamond record, *Moods*, and turned up the portable phonograph as high as possible. The strings of lonely despair crescendoed in the song "I Am . . . I Said." As in the song, nobody noticed. Nobody heard.

I took a part-time job with Minneapolis Public Schools, writing radio programs for elementary school children. My concern over my father's drinking was woven beneath our busy family life and my activities. Dad and Stella lived in their small apartment on a meager income. He kept drinking in excess. I avoided bringing my children to visit them.

The two-day national church committee meeting on the East Coast was a welcome break. The semiannual meetings gave me a chance to expand my limited home horizons. Eric was happy to watch the boys and willing to let me take two extra days to visit Aunt Ramona and her husband, Hugh, in Washington, DC. Mona had always been supportive and eager to see me succeed. My house was full of antiques and small treasures they had sent from around the world. They were great fans of history, and Mona had once taken me on a White House tour. On this visit we toured Monticello and stayed in a motel near the University of Virginia. I was intrigued by the creativity of Jefferson and the apparent contradiction of his writing the Declaration of Independence while holding slaves. We all have our blind spots.

The spring day was warm and mild. We took short naps, and before dinner I joined Mona and Hugh in their room. It was modest with dark brown furniture and a view of a local park. Hugh didn't touch alcohol. It was too risky because of his high-security State Department job. However, after her time working in Portugal, Mona liked a little port.

"Would you like some wine?"

I nodded, not sure I'd like the taste. She put out small, gold-trimmed glasses from Portugal that she had brought with her and set them on the small bedside table. She poured the wine and walked toward me with a glass. It gave me a perfect opening to update her about Dad.

It was hard to keep my thoughts straight. Mona always spoke of the family as better people—proper and respectable. I was sweaty, anticipating what I had to say to her. I mustered courage to tell the truth.

I took a deep breath and tentatively said, "We've had some trouble with Dad. He's drinking again."

She paused and returned to her chair. "He's all right, isn't he?"

Mona always did that—just like Grandma Libby. Her question told you what answer she wanted.

"He's had a DWI. We didn't tell Grandma."

"That's good. Maybe no one will see it in the paper." She sipped her wine.

"And we're thinking of talking with him about getting help."

"It's not *that* bad, is it?"

"It's dangerous, Mona."

She flashed me a look of concern that startled me. "He never hurt you, did he?"

Reflexively I lied, "No."

"Well, that's good." She frowned beneath her exactingly coiffed beehive hairdo. "I don't know why he can't control himself. We'll just hope he'll stop."

My shoulders drooped. Another trait of Grandma Libby. Denial. It was automatic to avoid disagreeable things.

"It's a complicated situation," I said. "He's become dependent on alcohol." I knew better than to say *addicted*. "But in Minnesota we have treatment programs to help people break the dependency." I needed to assure her that this was a good thing so she'd stand with us. We had to be unified.

"Not one of those *asylums* . . ."

"No, not at all. But a chance for a person to learn a new way to live," I said.

"Well, I always say that you Minnesotans know how to do things best. The Mayo Clinic, even Dayton's. There's not a store like Dayton's anywhere in the country."

I nodded as she turned to look out the window at the park, glass in hand, lost in thought. Then, to my surprise, she said, "I'll do what I can if you need some financial help or something."

"Thanks, Mona. I hope we can get help for him."

Hugh was quiet, sitting on the edge of one of the beds. Mona turned back to me, put on a smile, and said, "Did you enjoy Monticello?"

I returned home with mixed feelings. At least I had told Mona part of the truth. But I was desperate to know. What made Dad the way he was? I read everything I could about alcoholism. I concluded that alcohol had taken over his life. I realized that it is a chronic disease with predictable symptoms and outcomes. I decided I had to help him. In the weeks ahead I talked it over with our family doctor, Dr. Beasley. "If you ever need my help, call me," he said. "I've dealt with this before."

Despite the pain, at times I felt compassion for Dad. I went to a local grocery store and ordered a few bags of groceries to be delivered to Dad and Stella, with the grocer's promise not to say who had sent them. I remembered the Halloween when he eagerly bought candy for the local children—a chance to be generous and important. They had left the light on at the apartment's front door, only to have no children knock. It felt immensely sad to me that he didn't get to enjoy giving. And yet his drinking impaired his judgment and his life. He had been cruel and thoughtless toward me at times. I desperately sought some way to help and change him.

Then an opportunity arrived. Stella was worried that Dad was drinking so much that he was developing diabetes. I rallied the family, hoping to have Dad admitted to an effective alcohol treatment program. Everything relied on timing. He had to be willing to acknowledge his need and seek help, and simultaneously there had to be beds at the treatment center.

Ed and Sherri were hesitant. "Maybe he can straighten around if we talk with him," Ed said, quiet and stoic. Once before, he had tried to talk with Dad about cutting back on drinking, with no success.

"He's never responded to suggestions to quit before," I reminded him.

Sherri was open to the idea of getting Dad into treatment, although she wasn't sure she would be able to contribute to the expense.

Before turning to Mona, I wanted to get everything organized. From a work phone, I called hospitals, the treatment center, our doctor, and my family, trying to coordinate everyone. After I had been working on a plan for four days, Stella changed her mind and wouldn't agree to the idea. I wanted to scream at her. She couldn't face being in conflict with Dad. I was exhausted, and Dad wouldn't budge. Tears in my eyes, I turned to a secretary at work and said, "Why does he do this? What's wrong with him?"

"Sometimes people are just mean," she replied. I was speechless. Mean had never occurred to me.

Overall, I was the one who tried the hardest to deal with the problem. Sherri and Ed scarcely backed me up. It was the familiar pattern: one member of the alcoholic family takes charge and is labeled the hero, while others respond in less-direct ways. I assumed I had to "fix" the family, particularly Dad, since he was the primary problem even while Mother was alive. I was, and expected myself to be, the hero. I concluded that I had failed.

Then one evening Stella called. "I'm sending Walt to the hospital in an ambulance. He's been drinking a quart a day, and I can't handle him. Ed will bring me to the hospital."

"We'll be right down," I said. I called Dr. Beasley and arranged to meet him there. I threw on my yellow cotton sleeveless turtleneck, and Eric and I headed to the hospital.

We were all in the lobby of the hospital, Dad in a wheelchair, Stella shaking and silent, and the doctor close at hand to admit him. It was a cold, early spring night.

"Walt," said Dr. Beasley, "I'm going to admit you to the hospital. You're very sick, and your wife can't care for you the way you are."

Dad looked at him blankly, since he was inebriated and had never met Beasley before. Then he turned to look my way.

Dad smiled at me and said, "I didn't know you could fill a sweater so well."

I had no words. I blushed and nearly cried. My own father making a lewd remark about me. In front of other people. Humiliating me. I wanted to disappear—surely everyone was looking at me. Who had heard him?

No one said a word. It was as if it never happened. I never again felt at ease in those cotton sweaters. I seldom wore them, afraid to draw attention to myself.

After Dr. Beasley registered Dad, Ed and Stella pushed him in the wheelchair to the elevator, where all of us rode up to a single room. An assistant joined us and suggested that some of us should leave so he could help Dad get ready for bed. Ed offered to stay with Stella, so Eric, Sherri, and I left, just as Dr. Beasley came down the hall.

"I'll get something arranged at a treatment center by morning. Why don't we all meet here in his room at ten in the morning? You can leave it to me to handle things at that point."

We were all relieved. Sherri left us in the lobby, and Eric and I drove home.

"Thank goodness for Dr. Beasley," I said. "He really knows what he's doing. We're finally going to get someplace."

"We can hope so," Eric replied. "But don't get your hopes too high. You never know how Stella or your dad will react."

The next morning, after Dad had begun to dry out, we met in his room. Stella stood off to the side, near the dividing curtain, slightly out of Dad's view. Ed, Eric, Sherri, and I were there. The window curtains were half closed to keep the light less severe.

I was surprised when Beasley wasted no time at all. "Walt. You're a drunk. You need to get treatment. I can get you admitted by tomorrow."

"I don't need any treatment. I'm just fine."

"You do, Dad," I said. "You're sick from the alcohol. You need to get help."

Ed said, "You've been dealing with this for a long time, Dad. Now it got you into the hospital. You need treatment."

"Do what you want to do then," he said. "Obviously I don't have anything to say about it."

I took a startled breath. Could it be that easy?

Dr. Beasley knew the ropes for admitting him to Forestwood, a treatment center for alcoholism just south of Minneapolis. Ed took him there within twenty-four hours, with Eric and I following behind. Stella stayed home.

After a patient dried out from drinking, the in-house treatment program typically required small-group and individual counseling to encourage drinkers to look at their behaviors and tendencies toward excuses or denial of the problem. It commonly lasted four weeks, which was all we could afford. Afterward, many patients entered an Alcoholics Anonymous program to maintain their sobriety.

Forestwood was a 1940s-style brick institutional building with minimal furniture in the front lobby. The floors were terrazzo and the walls beige; the utilitarian rooms had doors with frosted-glass windows. Patients' rooms were not open to visitors. This particular program did not have family group work, which might have been helpful but was a scary idea for all of us. We dreaded telling the truth about Dad's drinking in front of him.

After two weeks at the center, Dad was allowed to have visitors. I drove down with a pastor friend, Jim, who was skilled in working with alcoholics. That morning, in a recreation room in the basement, I told Dad of the memories I had of his excessive drinking. Sherri and Ed had fewer memories because Dad had been sober for eight years during their childhoods. As the oldest one, I recalled more years of alcohol use than they did.

"I remember the phonograph record you made at that bar in Milwaukee when you were drinking so much. And the time you and Earl spent a whole afternoon in the basement drinking those little cordial sample bottles from work. And the night you passed out in the dining room when I was in college."

"I didn't think you'd remember those things," he said. "I don't remember passing out."

"I do, Dad. And your health is getting ruined by drinking. Once you start, you can't stop. That's why you're here, getting help with stopping."

Pastor Jim reinforced what I said in positive tones, and after about forty minutes, we drove home.

"I'm glad we did that," I said. "I've wanted to speak up for years."

"You did well, Judie. There are no guarantees, but you made a good effort."

Five days later, Eric and I drove down. Visitors usually met with patients in the lobby, which echoed. There were three men in the room, all of them silent and, like Dad, smoking. Two were watching a basketball game on a small television set.

"Well, it's not much of a place," Dad said to Eric. "But I'm better than the rest of these guys. One of 'em tried to sneak out so he could walk to the town."

"How do you think you're doing, Dad?" I asked.

"Hell, I'm fine. I'm gonna beat this thing. I didn't drink that much anyway."

I knew that kind of talk: bravado. I could only hope the remaining time would bring him more self-awareness. I was quiet for most of the drive home.

After his four weeks, Dad went home. He had never bought into the concept of disease and addiction. He was "better than that." Stella was relieved to have him back. He treated her with consideration. But within weeks he began drinking beer again, and after a few months he was as sick as he'd been before he went to the hospital.

15

AIRPLANE RIDE

The jet engines roared as our plane began its taxi down the runway. Dan and Andy were leaning to see out the window, and I smiled. It was their first plane trip. We were going to see friends in Colorado and then continue on to Santa Fe. Since the boys had never flown and we wanted to drive between most destinations, Eric drove to Omaha while the three of us took the plane. The boys, eight and ten, chattered to each other through the whole flight, pointing out landmarks and proud to be served their own sodas and peanuts. I told them I had gone on a plane for the first time when I was six.

I had loved to travel, but something had come over me shortly after I got married. I was afraid of flying. I did everything I could to distract myself from the air pocket jostling and chewed gum madly on takeoffs and landings. I hesitated to take even a short trip. Where had it come from?

"It's odd," I told Dr. Hayes. "You know, I was fine for a long time. Then I got this fear."

"Would it help to talk about it?"

"I guess. I'll tell you about my first plane ride. That was amazing!" As if by habit, I untied and removed my shoes, closed my eyes, and began to remember.

I'm in first grade and home for lunch. We live in Wauwatosa, near Milwaukee. Mother gives me a peanut butter sandwich cut into triangle shapes, which is special. "Eat your lunch right away, Judie Marie. I have a surprise for you."

Usually I'm very poky about eating, but a surprise sounds wonderful. Then Daddy comes home, which is another surprise. I finish my sandwich and declare, "I'm done." I smile.

"How would you like to take a plane ride to Minneapolis?" Daddy says.

"A real plane?" I get up from my chair. "When?"

"This afternoon. Mother has your suitcase all packed, and you and I are going to see Grandma Libby. I have some business to do there."

Now we're at the airport with a lot of people. We walk out to the movable stairs, and we sit in the second row of seats on the plane. I'm wearing my good powder-blue coat. Now the plane makes a lot of big noise, and we're taking off. The windows aren't very big, but I can see the houses get small. I am very polite to the stewardess. She's nice, and she gives me chocolate-covered mints. I print my name in big letters on the folder the stewardess gives me. I talk a lot to Daddy about what we can see below.

Now the stewardess says I can come up to the cockpit and help fly the plane. I get up on the pilot's lap. There are a lot of dials with numbers, and I can see all the sky in front of me.

"You can hold on to the wheel and drive," he tells me. I trust him, so I take the wheel and push it and turn it. I notice that the other pilot is moving his wheel the opposite direction at the same time I am. They give me a pin with wings on it. I'm a pilot now.

I go back to my seat, and Daddy asks, "Shall we write a letter to Mother?" I tell Daddy what to write to Mother on the paper inside the folder.

Dear Mother:

I hope all of you are fine. How is Eddie? How is Sherri? Is Sherri being nice?

I saw the wings on the airplane. It bumps up and down. There are lots of people in it.

There are lakes around. I saw trees and fields that are small. We are almost up to the sky. I saw the propellers. It is fun to ride in the airplane. The windows are made of plastics—I have lots of ideas. I worked the jigsaw puzzle. Mother will like this letter!

The lady gave me some milk and cookies. I went to see the pilots. The lady took me up to see the pilots. I saw the front of the airplane.

I think that should be the end of the letter, don't you, Daddy?

Love,

Judie Marie

We fold up the letter and put it in an envelope. We'll mail it at Grandma's house. It costs 21 cents for special delivery.

Just before we land, I get a little sick. It must be from those mints. The stewardess helps me clean off the front of my blue coat.

When we get to Grandma's house, nobody is home. Daddy knows where the back door key is, so we go inside. The house is quiet. It has big rooms.

"Do you want to take a little nap on Grandpa's brass bed?" Daddy asks me. I feel a little tired, so he helps me climb up onto it. Then Daddy—

Then Daddy—

Then Daddy puts his hand inside my panties and moves his fingers. Why does he do that? I lay very still. I feel strange when he does that. Then he goes away.

Pretty soon I wake up, and Grandma is home. It's time to fix dinner.

I sat perfectly still in the office chair for a moment, except to rub my shoe-less feet back and forth on the carpet. Back and forth. Back and forth. *Is that what happened to me? When I was six?*

My insides filled with a heavy sick feeling. Then something burst.

"How could he? No wonder I dread airplanes. He was so—so awful!"

I cried bitterly into my hands, crying at the image of me as a six-year-old. The little girl who always smiled. "Why me?"

I quickly grabbed a tissue for my hands and face. "I still have that letter and folder from the plane in my document box. How could he? Why?"

Chris leaned forward. "How do you feel about it right now, Judie?"

"Why would he do such a thing?" I gasped.

"Try to stay with your emotions. What are you feeling?"

I looked away from Chris and wiped away my tears. I didn't feel much of anything. I was closed off, except for my questions.

"It was bad enough to remember being stared at with no clothes on. But now it's worse. Now he's touching me. Why would he do that to his girl, right after our nice trip? It spoiled it all."

Tears gathered again, but they did not fall. I sat suddenly straight.

"I think I have to go soon. My time is almost over, isn't it?"

He did not resist my poorly disguised need to flee. I gathered my purse and put my shoes on. I said good-bye and walked, dazed, to my car.

Driving home, I felt more paralyzed than alive. I was sad for that little girl who went from joy and trust to fear and disappointment. She was so young. I could scarcely believe she was me.

The memories of the plane trip lingered in my mind, much as the garage memory had clung close. Days passed, and I would think of it in the midst of driving or while playing piano. There was no one I dared tell, not even close friends. I walked around the enclosed mall every day for a week. One day I drove out to sit by Lake Harriet, on the western edge of Minneapolis. The quiet cold of winter calmed me as I sat on a bench and looked out at the lake.

My memories had been cut, boiled, and stirred like apples into apple-sauce. I couldn't tolerate being around Dad. I avoided family conversations.

I became distant at family gatherings, suspicious when Dad was there. My anger was deep down and cold, but unexpressed. I worked hard not to feel my pain, afraid of losing control.

Sherri had called and asked me, "Why are you getting rid of our family?"

"It's not about you," I said. I talked about Dad's drinking and how busy I was with Eric and the boys.

"This is your family," she scolded. "You belong with us."

Sherri was fully involved in a new marriage. I emphasized Dad's drinking problem to her because she knew it well. I couldn't muster enough courage to tell her more.

Even before the plane memory surfaced, I had told Eddie, over coffee, that I was struggling with dreams about deer heads and Dad. He affirmed that I should be seeing a counselor, which felt like support, even though I knew he didn't want to talk about it. I had fantasies, though.

Pushing open the door at a family party with a bang. Striding in, with everyone aghast, and shouting, "Quiet! I have something to say." Pacing the room. "This family is a sham. We pretend we're happy and we get along. It's a lie. Dad is an abuser. We cover up for his drinking and his abuse. Our mother was never happy. She didn't know what to do. We cover up so the world won't know we're a broken family. But I won't stand for it any more. I will speak the truth!"

I smiled at the dream of liberation and confrontation. People walking their dogs went by, unaware and uncaring. Just a fantasy.

Sherri's question plagued me. Guilt crept up my shoulders until it choked me. How would I tell her? I could never do it alone.

Finally, I realized I had to act. At my request, Chris agreed to have a family meeting at his office. I invited both siblings and their spouses. I wanted them to know and to support me when I confronted Dad. I had figured out how to take back being an adult, not a helpless child, in Dad's presence. Eric came for support, as did Karen. I practiced what I would say for days.

I called Sherri, then Ed. "Dr. Hayes is the therapist I've been seeing. I have some stories to tell you," I said.

"Is it important?" Sherri asked.

"Are you sure this is the right thing to do?" asked Ed.

I told them both plainly but not emotionally, "It's important to me, and I hope you'll come." I wanted to defuse some of the fear I heard in their voices. They said they were willing to come to "help you with your counseling."

It was a sunny afternoon in early March. The whole city was weary of winter, but the sun held promise. Eric and I arrived a half hour early, just to be sure we could welcome the others when they arrived. Even he didn't know what I was going to tell them. He had never asked about my counseling; he didn't resist it but also didn't inquire or seem to observe how I was affected after a therapy session.

The outer office had Danish furniture with neutral gray upholstery. Eric paced the floor as we waited. I sat off to the side, fixated on the Berber carpet. I checked the clock every five minutes; neither Eric nor I had much to say.

Karen joined us and stoked some conversation with talk of the weather and questions about our kids. Just then Chris came in and greeted Karen as a longtime colleague. It set my shoulders at ease, and I smiled.

Chris offered us coffee. I asked for water, and he brought a clear plastic pitcher with water and ice. It was then that Ed and Marty came in, with Sherri and her husband, Phil, walking behind them. The atmosphere was stiff. I introduced each person. Everyone was polite but not chatty, as if we hardly knew each other—which was true. Chris invited us all into his office, where we took seats in the half-circle of armchairs facing his small desk. Karen sat alongside Chris, close to Ed and Marty. Sherri and Phil were on my right. I took my place near Eric, and Chris put the water and glass beside me on a small table.

I suddenly had a dry throat and felt shaky. I looked at everyone and felt like a stranger. I knew that Chris and Karen supported me. Eric was quiet. Did I dare speak the truth? Would the others believe me? I had to begin the conversation. I reintroduced Dr. Hayes, reminding Ed and Sherri that I'd been working with him for a long time.

"He's given me great support and help," I added. "Now it's time for me to share with all of you some of what I've discovered." I stopped to take a drink of water.

"As you know, Dad has been a hard person to live with." No one moved.

"I was always scared of him," Sherri said softly and began to cry.

Rubbing my feet across the carpet, I unfolded the stories of the Shorewood garage. "I was so afraid and so small," I stammered. The room suddenly felt cold, like the November garage. Sherri cried, and Ed sat, unmoving.

Then I told the story of the plane ride. All of them were following along with me, partners in the surprise lunch and trip. I paused to gain strength and had a drink of water. "But there's more. After we arrived at Grandma's, Dad took me to Grandpa Paul's bed and . . ."

Ed frowned. Marty was focused on every word I said.

"And he . . ." My voice speeded up. "He fondled me inside my underpants."

The air was heavy and ponderous. Ed's hands were wringing, and Sherri held her breath between tears.

"Things with Dad were always mixed up," I said. "I never knew when he would be nice, or angry or punishing. I couldn't trust him."

Ed ran his fingers through his thick brown hair, mumbling, "I didn't realize."

My voice began to shake. "There's more," I said. "When I was in third grade, I came into the little living room at Plainfield. Dad was sitting in the big overstuffed rocker." My mind gathered back that scene in the room with its picture window directly across from the couch.

I couldn't look up as I continued. It was as if I sat before them, stark naked all over again. My words stumbled. My cheeks burned.

"He made me lie in front of him on the davenport with no clothes. He didn't say anything or touch me. He just stared at me. I was so embarrassed—probably eight years old."

Sherri cried throughout the stories, reaching for tissues again and again. Phil sat beside her, putting his hand on her shoulder. Ed, speechless, sat unmoving. Marty seemed to be absorbing all that I said with compassionate eyes.

I hastened to comfort them. "None of this is your fault," I said. "I don't blame you for anything. You could not have helped." I poured another glass of water.

The room was quiet except for Sherri crying. Ed folded his hands under his chin, his elbows on his bent knees, looking at the ground.

Suddenly, Eric hit his hand on the wooden arm of his chair. "I'm furious at Walt!" He had cut the palm of his hand and took out a handkerchief to cover it.

Everyone pulled back from his violence. Karen stared at Eric. Startled, I cringed with fear and disgust. Even though he had expressed the unacknowledged anger of decades, his fury drew me directly back to the source of his passion: my helplessness. Karen had been right that day at the lake: He was bound to be angry. The less he knew the better.

After a moment, as I took yet another sip of water, Ed tried to lighten up the atmosphere. "That water must have something special in it." People smiled, and Sherri choke-giggled through her tears.

I was intent on finishing.

"What I need to do now is confront Dad. I have to hold him accountable to regain my own strength. I have to tell the truth out loud in front of him. I'd like you to go with me for support. You don't have to say anything or do anything. Just be there if you can." I was trembling inside, and I looked to Dr. Hayes and Karen for visual support. They both nodded.

Sherri stopped weeping, and Ed looked off into the distance. Neither of them spoke. Phil kept his hand on Sherri's back, silent.

Hastily I tried to calm the tension. "If you can't do it, I'll understand. But it would be a big help to me to have your support."

Ed rubbed his chin. "I have to think about it. I'm sure all you said is probably true, but I have to think about whether I can be part of that. I'm not sure this is the best way to handle it."

"What means the most to me is that you believe me and you care," I said.

Sherri drew up her shoulders but couldn't meet my eyes. "Me too. I have to think about it. I don't know if I can be there."

"Why don't you both think it over and let me know? I plan to do this in about ten days—on Friday. I hope you can come."

"If we don't go, are you going to do it alone?" Ed asked, shifting in his chair.

"No, Chris will come, and Eric will be there. And Karen. We've planned it carefully. We want to support Dad as well, not just attack."

We parted with tense hugs and their promise to call. Unbeknownst to me, Karen called Eric the next day. With a clear, steady voice she said, "If you cannot control your anger, it would be advisable that you don't come to confront Walt. It sets Judie back, and she needs to use her own power." He assured her that he would behave appropriately. She called three days later to tell me about their conversation and give me confidence.

Even in a small family, one cannot know all that is happening to every person or how they feel. And nobody likes to discover that the idealized family one imagined or reconstructed is not a true reflection of reality. Perhaps my siblings had memories they didn't want to recall. Perhaps they felt afraid or guilty. Confrontation always terrified our family. They needed time to think.

Two nights later both of them called. Sorry, they would not be coming, but they wished me well.

I had tears in my eyes, but I was determined that the meeting would proceed.

16

CONFRONTATION

The dismal March Friday morning came, and I lay in bed, planning. *After I confront Dad, if he comes after me, where can I hide? The basement is too obvious. Closets invite searching. We don't have an attic. He has guns.*

I remembered the tiny storage spaces behind the dormers. They would be clean and dark. I would have to squeeze carefully to get through the ten-inch door, but he might not notice the openings.

I got up and took a hot bath to calm myself. Eric had sent the kids to school and would return from work by twelve thirty. We were due to meet Chris and Karen at Dad's apartment at one o'clock. I couldn't eat, and I paced the living room, gazing out at our neighbor's quiet house. *Will I be able to tell the truth and be safe?*

We hadn't given advance warning to Stella and Dad, very sure that they would be home. It would have been hard to explain why we were coming without sounding uncomfortable. I hadn't seen them in months. Better to "drop in."

Eric came through the back door. "Are you ready?" he called.

I went to the front closet to get my coat, pausing to wonder if we were headed for a big conflict. "Just about ready," I said. I walked into the kitchen, nervous, which as usual made me quiet.

In the car, we avoided digging into heavy emotions, trying to stay relaxed. I asked about his workday. Fortunately, Dad's place wasn't too far away, so the time passed fairly quickly. Eric parked near the apartment house on a side street where we would not be seen from upstairs.

In the week since his explosion at the session with Sherri and Ed, Eric had tried to support me. I knew he didn't like the idea of an intentional confrontation, but he understood it was important to me. He would stand with me. I just hoped he'd keep his temper.

"Are you okay?" Eric asked me.

"I think so. It will help to have Chris here if anything goes wrong."

Chris drove up, Karen behind him, and we stood on the slushy sidewalk.

"Do you think I can do this?" I asked them all, my voice cracking.

"It's up to you," said Chris. A damp breeze blew over us.

I drew my shoulders back. "I can. I *have to*." We headed for the back entrance of the white stucco building. It was a worn facade in a tired neighborhood, with no garages for residents, only a small parking area. There were no security devices, so we could go directly upstairs to the second floor. As afraid as I was, I had to believe that telling the truth wouldn't harm me.

I knocked at the door, trying to hear if anyone was inside. Stella came to let us in. "Look who's here," she announced cheerily. "It's Judie and Eric. C'mon in." Her smile sat uneasy alongside her curiosity about the two strangers with us.

"Hello, Stella," I said. "These are two friends of mine." My goal was to get in and get out. Speak my mind and leave.

"Here. Let me take all those coats," she said.

"We can just keep them," I said. She pulled back slightly, her pose wary.

"Well," said Dad, "this is a surprise." Eric and I led the others through the kitchen toward the living room. Our first view, above the couch, was of a large watercolor painting of a dilapidated barn, gray and red, its door off its hinges, standing in the weeds of an untended field. It reminded me of Plainfield.

"Dad, this is Dr. Hayes. I've been working with him. And you remember Karen." I had taken charge of the encounter, and as I expected, Dad was surprised and didn't question why two strangers were there. I thought he'd probably think "doctor" was a reference to my health, and he knew Karen was a longtime friend.

He took the role of host. He sat in his gold, padded kitchen chair and reached out his hand to shake with each guest. "Nice to meet you. Do you want coffee, anybody?" He nodded to Stella.

We all declined, and we each took a chair in the space between the kitchen dining area and living room. Stella took her place at a beige card table in the living room, where she had been eating a bowl of cold cereal. She was shaking.

"I haven't seen you for a long time," Dad said to me, his back to the kitchen window. "Nice of you to drop by."

"I've been pretty busy, Dad. But I wanted to come over and talk to you about something."

He nodded and lit a Viceroy cigarette. "Sure," he said congenially. "About what?" He shook out the match.

I sat facing him. I had a burst of confidence as I continued.

"Do you remember the time that you got mad at me and put my head into the gut of a dead deer hanging in the garage?" He didn't move except to draw on the cigarette.

"I was three, Dad, and you knew I was afraid of deer heads. That was a scary thing to do to a little girl." I glanced at Stella who paused, her spoon in midair.

Dad was stoic, smoking, looking right at me with a blank stare. "I don't remember that," he said.

I lifted my voice to be more cheerful. "I was remembering the other day about the time we killed all those frogs at Plainfield. Do you remember how you chopped off their legs so we could have frogs legs?"

"I sure do," he said with a cigarette laugh.

"Me, too. That was scary to me." I squirmed in my chair, the one that matched his.

"Aw, it was just frogs. You didn't have to worry." He had a drink of coffee.

Eric shifted in his seat. Chris and Karen were in my line of sight, sitting very still and concentrating on our conversation.

"But something else happened at Plainfield. It was in the living room. You made me lie on the couch naked while you just stared at me. I felt ashamed, Dad. I didn't understand." I held back cresting tears. "That was wrong."

His change of countenance was obvious to us all. He stared at the picture of the barn, as if he heard nothing. He adjusted his position. "I don't remember that," he said blankly.

I could see Stella, sitting rigidly in the easy chair, put her spoon into her cereal and not move. Eric was breathing deeply and wringing his hands. Chris and Karen remained silent and unobtrusive. The air was stifling, suffocating. "One more thing, Dad."

"What's that?" he said in a testy voice.

"There was that time when you took me on a plane trip when I was six." For a split second he lightened up.

"Wasn't that something? You were only six. We wrote a letter to your mother."

I returned to my voice of remembrance. "But when we got to Grandma Libby's house, you put me on Grandpa Paul's bed and reached into my panties and you were touching me."

Dad sat stone still, looking straight ahead. His eyes glazed over, clearly covering his emotions. He met no one's eyes. Then he leaned forward and crushed out his cigarette. A smelly trail of filter smoke cut through the silence, all emotion suspended. No one moved.

He spoke. "I didn't do anything to your brother or your sister. And as far as I know I never did anything to you." His voice trailed away to silence.

The air went out of the room. He knew, all right. He remembered.

"Mr. Thorsen," Chris offered, "these kinds of memories are hard to acknowledge. It's possible to restore relationships if you work with someone on them."

Dad sat straight in his chair. He was calm and spoke evenly. "I don't know anything about what she's talking about. There's some mistake. You're her doctor. You'll have to help her." Then he stood up, unsteady with age and shock.

I rose immediately. "I think it's time for us to go," I said hastily. "Time to get home to the boys."

Dad smiled. He returned to the safety of etiquette. "You say hello to the kids. Tell 'em I'll get 'em something special from the store one of these days."

He accompanied us to the door. Karen, Eric, and Chris preceded me through the door. Stella stood at a distance in the living room, watching with suspicion. As I walked out, I turned back in the doorway to look at Dad.

"You take care of yourself, Judie," Dad said, leaning on the doorjamb for balance.

I looked at him. Suddenly he was a shrunken old man. The giant of my childhood was gone. I stood taller, and a sense of empowerment coursed through my body. I had dared to confront his mistreatment of me. I had challenged my fears and won. I had spoken the truth, even though he denied it. He was small, and I had the power.

I didn't smile. "Thanks for having us, Dad. I'll see you sometime." And I joined the others at the stairway where they waited, grinning. Eric put an arm around my shoulder.

"I did it!" I said in a loud whisper, beaming.

Karen spoke first as we left the building. "It might be a good idea to debrief what happened."

"I'm dying to talk about it," I said. "Could we go someplace like a restaurant or something? I'm starved."

And that's what we did. The ribs place was bright with red and yellow lights and full of happy people. We found a round table away from the crowd. Liberated, I laughed openly as we talked through the whole encounter, and I soaked in their affirmations, full of personal pride and power. Then Eric and I headed home to meet the boys, talking excitedly. He didn't mention Karen's phone call reminding him to maintain his composure. I was relieved: he had been there for me when I was scared.

That night Dad called Sherri and Ed. "Your sister is on drugs," he exclaimed. He and Stella took turns shouting indignant and angry accusations about me.

"She told all kinds of lies," he told them.

"Can you imagine such a terrible thing to say to your father?" Stella demanded.

I don't know how Ed and Sherri responded, but they called to report the accusations back to me, knowing how empty they were. It was their way of supporting me. The truth was out. For now.

17

DAMAGED GOODS

I couldn't stop thinking. I had spoken the truth to my father, and even though he denied it, courage had risen up in my psyche—my whole body—and strengthened me. Why, then, did I continue to feel depressed? Was it the fact that he continued to drink—a sign that he continued to block out the reality of his past acts with me? Or was it in hidden memories that I carried on my shoulders, perhaps still unknown to me, the bundle of pain and self-hate that I could share with no one. I am, after all, an extrovert. Who could I tell?

It was clear that Eric wanted to stay on the edge of my pain, avoiding the hard stuff. As he said once, "Life for me is just a big ball game." One of his attractive traits was his lightheartedness. I had often thought of him as a clown in my pocket—a wonderful contrast to me, often serious and responsible. Perhaps it was too much to expect that he would handle it with objective understanding. He was angry, and his anger intensified my fears of unpredictable male behavior. I didn't press him. I needed him as an appropriate father to his sons, not a therapist or even a friend.

I replayed in my thoughts the memory of a morning at the lake when I lay in bed in our loft. I had slept late. Eric had made pancakes, but I could not face going downstairs. The boys were out building a tree fort. Eric energetically climbed the spiral staircase and stood beside the bed. "Are you coming for breakfast?" he asked. "I made some pancakes."

Unmoving, I looked at him. "I feel dead inside," I said.

My life was miserable—fearful, lonely, and unable to relate to Eric. His forehead furrowed, but he said nothing. My despair seemed to slide over him. I had no words to rescue him in the moment. I had no energy and no desire to live that way anymore.

"That makes me feel sad," he murmured and went back downstairs. We said no more.

I waited a few minutes, sighed, and got up to eat some cold pancakes. I realized that I was depressed. I hoped that Eric would bring up my withdrawal and sadness, but neither of us spoke of it again.

Chris was there to guide me, but I also needed a regular friend. Someone I could tell and not be afraid of responses. I had confided in some women friends but was afraid to be so honest with any men. After several weeks, my inner quarrel eased into a decision. I chose Ken, who was married to my good friend Joan. He was a pastor with a kind and understanding affect. I thought I could take a chance on his knowing. I met him for lunch.

"I asked you to come because I need to tell you some stories about myself."

I didn't add, *Stories that I am ashamed of, stories that may make you think badly of me.* I proceeded, stuttering occasionally, to speak of a little girl and her father's history of intruding on her privacy. I didn't use the word *abuse.* It was too clinical. I described the afternoon on the couch at Plainfield and, more hesitantly, the experience following the plane ride. They were such personal stories, so intimate. I was waiting for him to look at me with disgust. He surely would think of me as tainted and misshapen. "I just needed to tell someone who knows me," I added. "It's been a secret for so long."

He paused, and I caught my breath.

"I'm so sorry that happened to you."

There was no condemnation in Ken's face or his words. He heard me as a friend, not a judge. I sighed my relief. He didn't think of me as a filthy person. He was my friend.

Still, as I drove home afterward, I realized I felt less a person, now that Ken knew. Even though he accepted me, I felt defective.

Without realizing it, I had been building for years an escape from the pain I had stashed inside me, memories I had not yet encountered that were poisoning my self-esteem. Since third grade I had been writing: first sing-song poems, then stories and news articles for my grade schools. Without knowing it, I was also building and saving in my memory a repertoire of true, painful stories that someday I would release to the world. They would be my path to liberation and truth. Someday.

After college I had taught elementary school. Eric and I were married after that first teaching year, but three years later I resigned, hoping to soon be pregnant. Within months I was. As my two sons grew into busy toddlers and then preschoolers, I began to write.

I submitted poems to Augsburg Publishing House, our Lutheran publisher, and to my amazement, they offered to publish my first book. It changed my life. Using free verse and conversational tone, I revealed the delights and frustrations of being a young mother, my feelings about friends, and my fears about failure. It sold well, and as years passed, I wrote more books: about motherhood, about being a young teenager, about being a working mother, and about living more simply in a materialistic culture. My doubts about religion were scattered through it all, and to my surprise, I was not alone. People identified with them. One friend said, "I would never have the courage to tell people those things." I frowned in disbelief. *What courage?* I wondered. *It's just the truth.* I would sit on the floor of our living room, my portable typewriter balanced on my knees and my sons playing around me, and I'd write. Write and write and write.

Soon women's groups asked me to speak to them about being a woman and raising a family. I traveled throughout Minnesota and sometimes to cities far away, talking about life's complexities, about forgiveness and mystery, and about hope. Eric supported my work by staying home with Andy and Dan when I had to go to a banquet. I earned money, which I set aside for our sons' education. I was often asked to be interviewed on the radio—it was a heady affair. I published six books in ten years.

During that time, I seldom saw Dad. We sometimes attended the same family events, but his drinking and my memories of his abuses disturbed me. I didn't feel safe around him, nor did I want my children to be influenced by his behaviors. However, one day Eric and I visited Dad and Stella in their apartment. I had been told that they were selling off some of their valuables, and I asked to have a clock that had been among the treasures Grandma Libby had given them. It was a large, decorative shelf clock with glass sides and French works. I didn't want the family to lose it. Dad easily agreed that I could have it.

Dad had a piano again, and I encouraged him to play for us. I smiled to the sounds I still loved. "It sounds great," I told him.

"I can play better than you can write any book," he said. I swallowed my surprise and disappointment. *Is this a contest? How mean!* I said nothing.

"Why did he do such a thing?" I exclaimed to Eric as we drove home.

"Just let it pass," he replied. I gazed out the car window into deep, isolated sadness.

I appeared to be competent and confident. Thousands of people knew my books and, with them, my honest feelings about life. Except. Except no one knew about Dad and me. Not even I knew for sure. And the books did not say that my marriage might be dissolving.

I took a speed-reading class at the university one summer and walked those familiar walks on the mall where I had once greeted college friends. Reminiscing about college days, I paused outside the building in which, my sophomore year, I'd had to declare my major.

I had gone to an unfamiliar liberal arts counselor, who wore a white blouse and navy suit and met with me in her small basement office.

I told her, "I'd like to teach high school history or political science or social studies."

She replied blandly, "You can't do that."

I frowned and said, "Why not?"

"Because the coaches get those jobs. Social Studies and Math. If you want to teach high school, you can major in English," she suggested with a half smile.

Intimidated by her assurance, I scraped together some courage and said, "I like English, but I don't want to teach it."

"Well," she said, "how about teaching elementary school? You can teach more subjects there. We always need elementary teachers."

I shuffled my feet and adjusted the books on my lap. I had no idea whether I had any power in the situation. I just wanted to have a job someday and move out of my parents' home. I took her word for it: women don't get to teach social studies. I did enjoy children a great deal and thought it might be good "training" for being a mother, which I never doubted I would do some day. So I agreed with her and entered the college of education in the winter quarter.

More and more mornings that sophomore second quarter, I went to the women's athletic building, where there were cubicles with cots. I would sleep before classes or between them. I was tired all the time. I had little interest in my elementary education classes, which concentrated on theory rather than methods. Being active in sorority activities and dating didn't help—I couldn't shake the darkness. Mother had died less than a year before. The idea of grief never occurred to me.

The next year, I met a premed student, Mark, who was good-looking, bright, and fun to be with. We spent several months dating, and our relationship had possibilities. We had some differences, of course. He liked small towns and had nostalgia for his family's farm. I was a city girl, and I harbored jealousy of his high school girlfriend, who was also at the university.

That summer Mark took an intense eight-week science class at a small college an hour and a half from the Twin Cities. We wrote regularly but had no opportunities to see each other. One week, to be humorous, he wrote that he was "horny" and missed me so much his antlers could barely fit through a doorway. A gate dropped down. A crack appeared in my trust, and the relationship began to fade for me.

It was the word *antlers* that brought me down. Why did he have to say that? Didn't he know how terrified I was of those hunting trophies? I began to notice and be annoyed by small comments and actions. I could never marry him, I concluded. Soon I drifted away.

My biggest crush was on a boy named Clark who was glamorous, wealthy, and intelligent. He was already well on his way to being an alcoholic. By then I was a senior, and we dated in the fall. During the summer, I had been selected princess of our Minneapolis Aquatennial Royal Party, a huge surprise and honor. I had no experience with fine clothes or society, so my sorority friends lent me clothes to wear for all the contestant events. I was thrilled with the whirl of appearances, riding in a limousine, attending lovely parties at lake homes, and traveling to small towns to be in parades. To tease, Clark sometimes called me "Princess," which made me feel cared for. Clark also humiliated me occasionally, especially about my lack of taste in clothing, and I did nothing to stop him. In a sense it made him more attractive.

I had other steadies, too, most of them very good men. As soon as we became entangled enough to consider a future together, I gradually lost interest and drew away. I never stopped to ask myself why. What was I afraid of? Why was I fickle? I felt guilty, walking away, but I couldn't maintain a connection.

There were ten Judys in our sorority house, so I took the nickname Jamie to distinguish myself from the others. "Jamie," my sorority friend Jan said to me. "You should get a red dress for that frat party. Something with a low-cut neckline."

"Not red," I replied. "It's too bright." I hated standing out like that— drawing attention to myself, to my body.

"But you look great in red!" she asserted. "With your dark hair and clear skin."

"Can't do it, Jan. I just can't. Besides, I like blue best." I didn't tell her that I also hated to emphasize my breasts. I compared myself to Mother, who had nice breasts, and my grandmothers, who were plump at that time. Ever since high school, Sherri and I had both felt flat and skinny, and shy about both. I tried to distract people, especially boys, from my bustline. I had little to offer, and I hated how some boys virtually drooled over the "stacked" girls. Not for me. *Not safe.* Fortunately, blazers and plaid skirts were popular. I borrowed a dress from another friend for the party: full skirt, jewel neck, and three-quarter sleeves. It was black.

Looking back on those college days, I see that I gleaned pebbles of success: the glitter of being a princess and the pride of winning awards by directing peers in music, along with sorority and campus leadership accolades and a special trip to Indiana for a national convention. But I also carried boulders of shame for decades. I couldn't let my fickle immaturity go—had I been capricious, a coquette? I didn't realize that I had a poignant memory stuffed deep inside that was influencing many of my college choices. It was years later when I relived it with Chris.

I am a sophomore, almost a junior. It is afternoon, and no one else is home. I'm back from university classes, wearing only a plain nylon slip on the hot spring day, standing in the kitchen watering the violets. Our kitchen has a wide shelf above the sink, facing northeast, where violets thrive. I try to keep routines as they were before Mom died. "Once a week is enough water for violets," she taught me, and I follow her instructions. On the other side of the room is the stairway to the basement alongside a closet, with a door made of three-quarter-inch plywood and painted apple pink, where we squeeze in our coats and Dad keeps his rifles.

Dad rumbles in the back door.

"Hi," I greet him, my body stiffening. I try to stand confident, tall.

Dad reminds me, "Hold your shoulders back." I hunch over as if my arms are weighed down by sacks of flour. More than a habit, it is a self-understanding—abased and wrapped in hidden shame.

He doesn't look at me as he passes through the kitchen and slams some folders onto the big desk in the dining room. I avoid looking at him, and all is quiet, but his tension floods the rooms. The sun shines into the dining room, a long patch of light through the narrow eight-foot windows.

Everything stood still. I discreetly turn to work on the violets again.

"Get yourself downstairs," he orders.

My stomach turns. I hesitate.

"I said, get downstairs," he says as he steps toward me. I set down the brass watering can by the sink and try to slip past his tall, strong body to get to the second-floor stairway. He steps into my path. I squeeze by, but as I reach the door of the closet where the rifles stand, he pushes me in the direction of the open basement door. I catch my balance as best I can and scrape my arms on the stairway walls as he shoves me down three stairs to the landing.

The wood stairway down to the basement is bordered by foot-thick stone walls, painted white, with a two-by-four makeshift railing. It's dimly lit by the small window above the landing and a single bulb at the base of the stairs. The basement has been remodeled since I was fifteen. We created a large recreation room and smaller sitting room, all of it in natural light-birch paneling. We do our ironing in the small room because it is cool.

My head swirls as I struggle to keep my balance. Dad's face is intense with determination. His dark eyebrows are frowning.

"Dad!" I plead. *What in the world is wrong with him*? I can't breathe.

He pushes me again, and I grab the railing tight to keep my balance. My foot slips on a stair, and I strain my shoulders to hang on, trying not to fall.

At the base of those stairs is an oversize, heavy white wood door with a long wood bolt. Behind it are the tall, open wooden stairs leading to the outside ground level, covered by the folded-down cellar doors held closed by assorted junk. The faded gray doors close off outdoor light and air. I avoid the gray stone walls of the stairs. They are damp and musty, and spiderwebs link shadows and dust—barriers to getting out. Whenever I climb the cellar stairs, fragments of rock fall from the sides, protesting my intrusion. *No exit*, they seem to proclaim. *No escape.*

"Move!" he orders. I look up. Ahead of me is the bolted cellar door. I have no escape route. Even if I could open the white door, the cellar doors above the stairs are sealed with junk.

"Get over there." He points into the smaller room, where the ironing board is permanently set up. He shoves me, and I bump into the metal furnace and carom through the entrance into the small room, which is cool and dim, and avoid colliding with the ironing board. He catches my shoulders from behind, pushing me down to my knees. I have no strength to push back against his weight on my slim shoulders. My knees crumple until they hit the floor. I put my hands down to steady myself. The room has one small window, and the tile floor feels cold in the darkness.

"Dad!" My plea is lost in the silent room.

Then I feel warm urine cascading on my head. I bend my head low and fold my arms in front of me, eyes closed, as if I am praying. *How can this be happening?* The whole room fills with my aversion, trapped on the floor with no way to escape. I shudder.

Dad says nothing, but I hear his heavy breathing. It sends chills through me. He zips up, turns, and stomps upstairs. I do not watch him leave, but the old Bendix washer with its round door window saw it all, witness to the debasement.

I bow low, weeping. I gag on the smell of urine as I raise myself slowly from the floor. Suddenly shivering in the cool room, I hurry to find a rag to clean up. Tears run down my face as I take the soiled rag to the nice new sink we had put into the half bath. The fresh rooms with their birch paneling have become a sewer. As I squeeze out the soiled rag under the clean running water, I wash the memory away, hoping to make myself clean. My shoulders slump in, humiliated. My body is worthless. I gather my shame into my flat chest.

I didn't remember the event for years. I never understood why he was so angry. The sense of filth that permeated that afternoon clung unidentified to the pretty dresses I wore and, like a flame, burned the edges of even the most wholesome relationships I had. I was a hidden slut. Defective. Damaged goods.

18

SAYING GOOD-BYE

Memories temporarily abated as I was caught up in all the activities of my growing sons. I had turned forty, and it was late March when a phone call came at 8:24 p.m. It was Sherri's twelve-year-old daughter. "Aunt Judie, something's happened to Grandma Libby."

"Where are you? Where's your mom?" My voice was intense.

"Mom got a phone call and went to the nursing home right away. I'm scared!"

"Are you alone?" I checked the clock and thought about where my sons were at the moment, in case I would have to drive to Sherri's house.

"My sister and brother are here. They're watching TV. What's going to happen?"

"I'll try to find out what's happening and let you know. Just be safe in the house—check the doors and stuff."

"We're fine. Is Grandma going to die?" Her candid question confronted my distress.

"I don't know, honey. But I'll try to find out." As we hung up, I looked up the phone number of the nursing home.

After selling her home, Grandma had lived in an apartment for a while, but within two years, Aunt Mona came to town and helped move Grandma into a Swedish nursing home. My hands shook as I paged through the phone book for the number. In the midst of my search, the phone rang. It was Sherri, saying that Grandma had had a stroke and died. She was three weeks short of ninety-four years.

I sat for a moment, stunned, without tears. The path of rationalization appeared first: She had a nice long life. She wasn't afraid to die. Then memories flooded my mind: her clocks chiming in the night, the sound of her short-heeled shoes walking from the kitchen to the dining room, her nail polish. Tears dripped down my cheeks. Grandma Libby was gone. I sat down and played "Three O'Clock in the Morning," as she so often had done. My hands didn't have her touch. It would never be the same.

The service was at a funeral home, the same one where Mother had lain twenty-two years earlier. The casket sat in the center between two half columns with large bouquets of flowers.

I avoided Dad, as I had since the confrontation at his apartment. His face was puffy from alcohol, although he was sober for the day. Stella stood, a loyal little soldier alongside him. Fragments of memories from early childhood froze in my mind like a curtain of ice between us. Ramona was prominent in her hostess-like role, eager to be hospitable and proper. "Mother would be so pleased you came."

Dad hung in the shadows except when his friends came in. His affect was wooden, his dark eyes blank. Several commented on how Libby had welcomed them for coffee or bought magazines they were selling. People praised her hospitality and said how they missed the old house. Gradually a group of around fifty people arrived, and after subdued conversation and viewing her body, they took their places on oak pews. Dad, Stella, and Mona sat in the center directly in front of the casket. The directors closed it and covered it with the pink roses. Since I had a place on the agenda, I sat over to one side, where I could see Dad and Mona on my right.

I was invited to the lectern. My legs were a bit weak, but I took a breath and went forward. Accustomed to speaking before a group, I read a poem about Grandma.

As the service progressed, I looked at the gray metal casket on its stand in front of my father. Suddenly, my arms tightened. A powerful bolt of electricity filled my whole being, and I held my breath. I had the impulse to go over to the casket, pick it up, and with all my strength throw it onto Dad.

Anger! At whom? At Grandma? At Dad? At both of them? I stifled the urge and embedded it in my memory, wondering if anyone noticed me during those moments.

The cemetery trip was familiar after traveling there week after week with Grandma when we were young, visiting Grandpa Paul and her parents. The slight hill to the proud granite monument had been cleared of snow, and artificial grass lay around the opening in the ground. The trees had not budded yet, and a light wind blew across the grave. Sherri and I cried, and Ed wiped his tears as he put his arm around his daughter. Dad stood dignified, and I caught a glimpse of tears rimming his eyes as well. Stella and Ramona stood side by side, holding hands. The sky clouded over as I was distracted from the rites of burial. There was so much I didn't know about all of these family members. And now our matriarch was gone.

19

DISSOLVING

K aren and I went to the new exhibit at the Minneapolis Institute of Arts. Its stately front columns had presided over the nearby park since 1883. The new portions of the building had large, sleek rooms. A portrait called *Frank* by Chuck Close dominated an entrance. Among the many exhibits, we stopped by the silver tea setting made by Paul Revere but decided to skip the Egyptian rooms and instead go for lunch at the indoor balcony restaurant. The restaurant was a modern design, set high above the lobby entrance with expansive windows, white and chrome furniture, and simple lines. It was a cloudy day, and we were glad for some extra light.

I was eager to talk. Shortly after we were seated, I told her, "I'm struggling."

Ever willing to listen, she asked, "More memories?"

"Not really. It's more about Eric and me. I feel so—I don't know how to say it. It seems like I'm always the one to get things organized and finished—except our social calendar. He refuses to let me use his company car. He insists on doing the bills but doesn't know how to keep a budget. He forgets my birthday or complains if what I'd like to receive is too expensive. And he blows up over unimportant things. I suppose that's small stuff. He's great with the boys. And deep down I think he loves me."

"You feel resentful?"

My face contorted in a grimace. I took a deep breath and said, "You won't believe this, but I don't know what *resent* means." I looked away for a moment to avoid blushing. Surely everybody knew what *resentment* meant.

"You weren't given many opportunities to express emotions growing up. It's completely possible that you don't recognize them."

"What do I do about *that*? It seems so foolish."

"I'll tell you what. I have a list of emotions and also a chart showing people's faces when they feel emotions. They're at my office, and I'll get you some copies."

"That would be great!" The sun came from behind the clouds, and the sterile room warmed. Our lunch arrived, and I chewed on my feelings about Eric.

Three days later, the material arrived from Karen's office. The face chart was entertaining: "How Do You Feel Today?" Little round faces had wrinkles of aggression or frustration. Some were quizzical, some mischievous, and others drawn down in disappointment. It was a revelation to me. So many words and descriptions that I had probably read but could not identify in myself or others.

The list of emotions had hundreds of words. I lost track, reading them. They were listed in ten categories of three intensities each: strong, medium, light. *Anger, depression, confusion, fear*: how had I lived over forty years and never known some of those words, let alone used them in conversation?

I tucked the lists near my typewriter in the family room. I would have to start practicing the words, I thought, if for no other reason than my sons needed to be able to use them.

I called Karen from the kitchen phone just before the boys were due home from school. "Thank you so much for those emotions lists. They'll be a big help."

"Did you take a good look at the list under Anger?" she asked.

"Not especially," I admitted. "I'm not a very angry person."

"Every person has anger. You just may not be very well acquainted with it." I could tell she was smiling over the phone.

"Do you think I'd better introduce myself to anger?" I joked.

"Couldn't hurt," she said. "It might teach you something."

I had no idea how I was going to manage getting acquainted with anger that I didn't feel in the first place. Still, I knew it was probably a good idea, especially if I was going to communicate with Eric. He had plenty of anger for both of us. I set the idea aside with the internal promise to work on it.

Karen had told me that we tend to marry people who have the same inclinations toward intimacy. In our case, it was true. We both had limitations: I was stifled by my childhood experiences with physical intimacy, and Eric was unable to be intimate with his range of emotions. He could be openly angry and fun-loving but was not in touch with nuances such as self-examination. I often said to him, "I don't *know you*." It was part of why I didn't share my therapy experiences and emotions. He wasn't interested.

I longed for deep conversation and honesty, although we both avoided confrontations. It got us through to about our mid-thirties. But that's when the memories started to return and all equilibrium was upset. We struggled on, our bond growing ever weaker. My journals filled with days of my crying alone. I had a period of stomach problems that were caused by stress, and soon I realized I was often clenching my teeth. The skin beneath my wedding ring became irritated and raw with no apparent cause.

At my pleading, we finally joined a small group of couples working on marriage issues. Our leader observed that we were the quietest pair. We did not reveal our disagreements. I knew Eric didn't like to attend, but I felt desperate to reassemble our marriage. After eight weeks the group disbanded.

There were pronounced tensions about finances, especially when Eric took money I had saved for the boys' educations to pay taxes—without telling me. My father had done something similar with my siblings' Social Security death benefits after Mother died.

It was by accident at a clergy couples' party that I discovered Eric's job was being eliminated within a few months. He had known for weeks but said nothing. When we went for career counseling, he had no plan for our future. The counselor offered strategies and resources, but Eric did not respond. Finally, the advisor asked, "How do you keep yourself from knowing what it is you need to know?" I was stunned. Can a person intentionally choose not to know or learn how to solve a problem?

But bit by bit, our truncated or passed-over power struggles were tearing at the foundation of our marriage. My body quaked before Eric's anger, especially when it arose over what I deemed to be unimportant issues. His anger felt like danger. Over years, a residue of resentment built up and collected, blocking free-flowing communication. I swallowed my anger until it turned cold, and sex became an issue of control. Romance languished.

Nineteen years guarantees nothing. Our marriage became empty, except for our sons—they were the treasure. As a foursome we were happy, so our boys were unaware that we were crumbling as a couple. We worked with a kind counselor, a colleague of Chris's, talking through our troubles. There were brief moments of hope for a new future, but it was as if we were on a see-saw, one feeling high when the other was low, and then reversing the pattern. I didn't want to hurt Eric, but I knew that I might not personally survive in the marriage.

Ultimately we concluded it would not work to stay together. The synod staff helped him find another church. We agreed that we would share custody of the children, who were twelve and fifteen, and we would not diminish each other in front of the boys—and we did not do so. We found ways to cooperate.

Danny was angry in surprise, his blonde hair blowing in the wind as he stomped outdoors. Andrew, pensive and quiet, suggested to me that the boys could move out for a while so we adults could work out the marriage. I wept to hear them. I still do at the memory. I wondered how much my troubles with my father were poisoning my relationship with Eric. But the marriage was a cardboard container. After years of our trying to fill the box and crying over its weak seams, divorce was inevitable.

Legally separated, we sat together at Danny's confirmation service. Tears filled my eyes, looking at our dear sons. "We let them down," I said to Eric. "We let each other down," he replied.

The ribbon was cut. Tainted by the guilt of causing our children pain, I blew free to be myself. The winds of self-discovery that would follow were unpredictable. I got caught in some of the old branches of self-criticism or fear, but I persevered. I was on a new journey of revelation—of both the future and the past.

20

SEMINARY

"You ought to go to seminary."

I must have heard that a dozen times in the six weeks after Eric and I separated. I supposed people said that because of all the devotional books I had published. I knew I would not return to an elementary school classroom, and my part-time church work would not provide enough salary. I served on the board of the Lutheran seminary in St. Paul, but it was a far cry from imagining myself as a student there. Still, a friend who was an executive of the larger church encouraged me, which built my confidence.

Even as a young girl, I had a persistent curiosity to understand why things happened. Mother carefully recorded events and my comments in my baby book. My first questions about God happened at three years old. In her documents box I found a four-line text, typed on a rectangular slip of tagboard, that I had recited when I was five at the church Christmas pageant.

At the Big House we went to the Presbyterian church in town. I remember my teacher saying, "My, it's been so long since you came to Sunday school," in a syrupy, accusative voice. I felt embarrassed but angry. Then we sang, "Climb, Climb Up Sunshine Mountain." I was six, and I knew life wasn't about sunshine.

The summer after fifth grade, I went to church camp and loved learning the energetic songs. When I got home, I was motivated to be helpful to our family and went outdoors, unbidden, to rake the backyard. Mother came to watch from the back door. "Well," she said, "you learned to be a do-gooder at camp." It felt more like ridicule than praise, and I soon gave up the chore. Still, I was drawn to be part of a church wherever we lived, and Mother made sure I went to confirmation classes in junior high.

When Mother died, my faith was on edge. We got sympathy cards saying things like "She's in a better place now" or "It's God's will" and "Do not cry; she isn't gone, she only sleeps." They disturbed me. Were people saying we shouldn't feel sad? I had already questioned the virgin birth and a seven-day creation of the world. Avoiding or discounting our pain at death was too much. At that time I belonged to a huge Lutheran church. On Sunday evenings it had an all-ages program called Fellowship for All. After activities arranged by age group, we all gathered in the sanctuary for a short service and sermon. One night I decided I had something I wanted to say. I volunteered to speak.

The pulpit rose high above the pews, and the sanctuary could hold hundreds of people; that night there were perhaps 150. As was customary, the lights in the entire room were dimmed, and a spotlight shone on the pulpit. Standing there with all eyes on me, I described the loss of my mom and my search for comfort and hope. It was a transformative experience. I felt that people had heard my sorrow and acknowledged that my loss was natural and painful.

Of course, in 1958, it never occurred to me that a woman might be in ministry. When I was ten, living on the Northside, I mentioned being a missionary to my parents.

"Oh, that's too hard a life," they said. End of discussion. Since there still were no women pastors by the time I was in college, I dismissed the idea of ministry for over twenty years.

As I wrote about my faith journey in my application to Luther Seminary, I felt a call—despite my doubts and questions, or perhaps because of them—to explore the work of ministry. Where better than seminary could I confront the paradoxes and gifts of life, the mysteries of the universe and human existence?

Deep within I knew I had a life struggle ahead. How would a woman of faith integrate a life of shame and rejection into her psyche? This was my core struggle. I was in the midst of discovering that I lived two separate lives. One of them was visible on the surface. The other was buried in memories that allowed only occasional glimpses of its existence. But internally I knew both existed. At some point there would be a battle. Which person was I? Who told the truth? Did anyone care about my spirit? What holds a life of such contradictions together?

The search for understanding would require more than words or platitudes. It would require ritual and practice and human beings who embraced my broken self. I desperately needed the living witness of a universe that, although full of both goodness and terror, would ultimately hold wounded lives in love. I needed to unearth the hope that life overcomes our most destructive moments and renews the spirit. In seminary, I needed to experience what everyone professed: that God is good, that light and life prevail over darkness and the death of our spirits. I had to walk directly into the depth of the battle of memories and hope.

Seminary was no small challenge. It required three years of ambitious classes and a year of intern work in a congregation to earn a master of divinity degree. I was intimidated to be studying again, after twenty years away from the books, surrounded by hundreds of young people, many of them fresh out of college. I was older than some of the professors. I also worked a thirty-hour week at our local congregation and had primary responsibility for our teenage sons. Greek nearly did me in. One morning, amid the confusion and tension of the separation and divorce processes, I spent an entire class weeping in the back row. The teacher graciously overlooked my tears and was supportive of my efforts. I passed the class—but not by much.

Piece by piece I found my place in a culture of people largely younger than I, but friendly and warm. Faculty members became my friends. The one who knew me best was Professor Don Juel. He was my advisor for a while and taught the course on the Gospel of Mark, about which he was considered an expert. Tall and dark, he was outgoing and sometimes explosive, sometimes critical. Some were put off by his brilliance and arrogance. I found him compassionate and real.

The feminists were concerned about language and gender. So was I: How does one talk about God as Father when *father* means invasion and pain? How will I fit into this view of God? At Luther I found other women who knew that struggle, even those with abuse histories. It was difficult to reconcile our experiences with our patriarchal religious history. I concluded that God was more than father, or for that matter, father and mother. Occasionally in chapel I would begin the Lord's Prayer, "Our Mother in heaven . . ."

"You should read more about women in the Bible," one student said. "There's even the book called Judith that didn't make it into the official canon books of the Hebrew Bible. She was really something. She rescued her people from a tyrant."

I found materials on brave women of the Bible: Susanna, Esther, and yes, Judith, who took leadership as a faithful widow and destroyed the enemy of her nation, a general called Holofernes. I had seen a painting of his murder at the Art Institute. In a similar way, I took the risk of seminary in midlife, which empowered me. *Judith had power. So do I.*

Nevertheless, I felt inadequate alongside all the young students. I admitted my feelings to a young woman who was an accomplished artist and who had fine grades in college: "I don't have any idea how to write a paper anymore."

"You've been writing ever since you left school. Just look up the information and tell the story of what you learned," she advised. "Write like you talk." It worked.

At lunch hour, I was frequently invited to sit at a table with faculty. I usually had to listen more than contribute because they knew so much more than I about our curriculum, but we also shared stories about our growing children and our family struggles, which made me feel at home.

Most days I would finish classes and hurry back to our church, where I worked in communications and the ministries of helping others. Dan and Andy had their own after-school activities, so we all arrived home in time for supper together, our small terrier, Mindee, delighted to see us. In the evening we all could study. There was no time for me to meet with small study groups on campus during the day, but I met many students who became supportive friends. Sometimes I felt they included me because I was like a mother among them. They insisted I was welcome. Seminary was an intense undertaking, but a community of stimulation and growth.

One autumn evening took me totally by surprise. A physician and his wife, leaders in our congregation, invited seminary students to a football party at their charming home in a nearby suburb. They were interested in theology and supportive of students. Dr. Esterly was known by many at church as a remarkably kind man, affirming of his son, gentle with his two daughters, and attentive to his wife. His patients also respected and loved him. I rode to the party with a couple from school.

The last thing I expected was to walk into the Esterlys' den and meet, ten feet ahead, two deer heads. They hung at eye level, and a jolt of surprise and fear tore through my body like lightning. I felt nearly faint, but with a student directly behind me, I had to move ahead. I turned my head to the side as I passed by the trophies and, shaken, stood tall, pretending I hadn't noticed them. I pondered. *Dr. Esterly is a hunter. Could he be a person like my father? Someone who is cruel? That doesn't make sense—there are good people who go hunting.* I pushed my confusion deep inside and moved carefully toward the adjacent country-style kitchen, where there was laughter and conversation among the women. I walked toward the fireplace wall, where I could engage in conversation, but the surprise had spoiled my whole evening.

I was glad when my friends wanted to leave early. "That's fine with me," I told them. "I'm not feeling great." Then, in the car I asked, "Did you see those deer heads?"

"Nope. Where?" my seminary friend Bob said.

"They hung right out front, in the den. I never would have thought Dr. Esterly would shoot animals."

"Millions of men do that." Bob dismissed me, and I bristled. *He doesn't realize how intense my fears are*, I thought.

Even so, my voice was meek when I said, "I've always been afraid of them for some reason," and my voice trailed away.

"I'm sorry that they surprised you," Bob's wife said. I was grateful for her kindness.

I couldn't face explaining more about my fears to them. Tears filled my eyes in the dark of the backseat. *Friends don't understand. They tolerate my reactions, but they don't understand. I hate this phobia. There's something wrong with me if I can't manage this. Now, I suppose, I'll have a dream about them. Nobody understands.*

With all the changes of marriage and school, I had been feeling vulnerable. I resumed therapy. "I think I need to pursue that phobia," I told Chris. "Something must have happened, even besides the garage incident, to make me terrified of deer heads. I want to find out." Although I had pressing family and work responsibilities, I felt compelled to pursue my demons.

21

THUNDERBIRD

There was a well-known deluxe motel in a southern suburb of Minneapolis named the Thunderbird. People from all over the state and country stayed there when there were major sports events, and many held dinners or special parties there. The lobby displayed American Indian clothing and artifacts in wall cases, and the decor used colors and patterns inspired by Plains Indian cultures. I had been there once, for Eric's high school reunion, when I was startled to discover several deer heads and elk trophies in an upstairs hall near the ballroom. I stayed as far away from them as possible that night, and I had avoided the Thunderbird ever since.

My deer head experiences during seminary had made me intolerably wary and fearful. I found new resolve to try to overcome the phobia and decided I would try again to erase my fears by confronting them. Determined, I chose to go to the Thunderbird.

I asked a longtime friend, Todd, to meet me at the motel. He was a pastor who had seen me react to trophies before, so he seemed to understand my terror better than most friends. Short and stocky, Todd was the sort of person who maintained physical distance but had an intimate and nonjudgmental gaze. Our friendship was strong because his wife had died three years before and he had talked with me about the disruption and intense loss he felt. We trusted each other.

We met in the motel lobby. It was afternoon, and the bar and cafe were relatively empty. Here and there businessmen passed through the corridors, and people checked in and out at the dark wood desk.

"Hi, there," I said, trying to calm my voice.

"Are you doing okay?" he asked with a slow smile.

We sat on brown leather chairs for a few minutes as I tried to talk away my anxiety. "Why do I do this to myself? Why don't I just set this fear aside and try to forget? Get on with my life?" I smelled coffee and a frying hamburger. It would be so much easier to go for a bite of food and talk.

"Maybe you just need to know," he said. It was true. I could not ignore my past. Those fears came from somewhere. I yearned to know in order to understand.

I explained what I had in mind. We would go upstairs to the wide hall where several hunting trophies were displayed. By awakening my terrors, I hoped to gain insight into where they came from. I would take charge and conquer the fears. He nodded as if to say, "I'm with you."

I stood up. "Okay," I said. "We might as well get it over with." I grimaced and took a deep breath.

With heavy legs I walked toward the sixteen wide, red-carpeted stairs to the second-floor lobby. They were roped off with a thick velvet cord attached with brass hooks to the railings. We ducked underneath the cord and checked to see if anyone was watching. No one noticed. We began the climb.

The noise and people now behind us, I was leaving security and comfort. I took Todd's hand. Then, arms tensed and heart thumping, I forced myself to look up from the carpet and down the spacious gold-and-brown hallway, where I could see all manner of heads hanging on the wall. There was a bull elk, posed in the midst of its bugling cry, mouth open as if in pain. I heard the call in my mind, grotesque, as if he cried out for mercy, not rutting. A mule deer. Small as it was in comparison to the others, I still feared it would hurt me. Another elk with a gigantic rack and dark face. I swallowed hard and gasped.

"How're you doing?" Todd asked.

"Pretty scared," I said. I wanted to look aside, but with my hands trembling I kept my gaze. One moose, huge and dark. It was as if I stared into a long, dark hall full of monsters poised to attack me. I was afraid I would faint with the shock.

I stayed close to the stairs, about twenty-five feet from the trophies. One after another, I forced myself to look at them. Each was a shock to my system. I squeezed Todd's hand. I became small again. Three years old. Terrified. I smelled the ugly salt-leather cavity of the deer in the garage decades ago. I talked to ease myself.

"That one looks in pain," I said in a little voice.

I protested with adult vigor. "How can people kill like that? Cut off an animal's head and hang it on the wall! It's repulsive. Grotesque. Morbid." It was as if there were pools of smelly blood on the carpet beneath each creature. "It's mutilation," I told Todd.

I talked faster, and my words became young.

"Ish. I don't like those things. They're too big. They hurt people."

Wisely, Todd said little, holding my hand and listening intently.

"I feel like I need to hide. To get away."

I could not bring myself to get closer. I had always been afraid the animals would fall on me—crush me and trap me so I could not get away.

"I think that's all I can stand for now," I said.

"I saw an elevator down there," he said. We turned right and walked to the end of an adjacent hall so I didn't have to retrace my path. I took a deep breath.

"I'm glad that's over."

"How about a little tea?" he wondered.

"That would be so good." The tea in the motel coffee shop was warm and soothing, fragrant with jasmine. For half an hour I just talked, describing what had happened in disconnected statements. "They're so big. I think if I were normal I could think of them as handsome animals. But I can't—they're too dangerous. I felt sorry for them. They were mutilated. I was—I was angry. Why was I angry?"

I talked myself back to a modicum of calm, thanked Todd profusely, and drove home. The image of that long hallway full of animal heads overlaid my vision as I drove, my hands sweaty on the steering wheel. I was glad to get home and have Mindee greet me, happy and so alive! I took her out for a short walk to clear my head and fill my sight with flowers and green grass. When we returned, I lay down on the couch and slept soundly until my sons came home from their afternoon activities. I was numb but proud. I had faced the frightening moments and survived. Maybe now I would overcome this unexplainable terror.

"Well, I decided to do something about my phobia," I told Chris, smiling. "I went to the Thunderbird."

I described to him my anxiety and then the process of forcing myself to look at the heads.

"I was a child around them. Terrified."

"You *felt* like a child," he reminded me.

I slipped out of my shoes. As I spoke, I began to curl inward. A memory was coming. My eyes closed. "I'm very small."

I'm playing on the rug of Grandma Libby's living room with my wood blocks. I am two. Now from the dining room I hear Daddy's teasing voice. I don't see him yet.

"Judie. Ju-die Ma-rie!" I look up. It's Daddy's playtime voice. We're going to have fun!

Now all of a sudden there's a tall, scary figure. It has horns on its head and brown eyes, and it roars at me. I'm scared. I don't know that the big figure with horns is Daddy holding deer antlers on his forehead, growling. I've got to get up! Terror! I scramble to get up from the floor, my feet get tangled with each other, and my blocks go all over. Run, Judie! Run! Run! I'm screaming. The monster roars again and laughs. I run into the parlor, and it chases me. Where can I hide? I'm so small . . . so small . . . so small. Roar!

My legs are weak, and I stumble. I crawl across the floor on the blue rug. I hide behind Grandpa's big chair on the shiny wood floor, screaming. I'm shaking. I have to close my eyes and squeeze them tight. I have nowhere to run, so I "go away." I leave the room. I'm floating away from the terrible monster. I hide in my mind.

The monster gets tired of chasing me. He stops roaring and walks away into the living and dining rooms, out into the kitchen. Everything is quiet again. I'm safe. I can come back now. I crawl out from behind the big gold chair and walk unsteadily into Grandma's bedroom. I go into the corner by the window where the sun shines in. I lie down on the rug by the great big dresser. I curl up into a ball and fall asleep.

Later, Grandma Libby comes into the room. "Judie. Wake up. Grandma's home." I take Grandma's hand and walk into the kitchen.

I came back to awareness of the office. I slowly opened my eyes. I sat still, nearly void of affect, stunned. "The Thunderbird awakened all that. No wonder I've been afraid of deer heads." I frowned. "But how could I remember what happened when I was two years old?"

Chris folded his hands. "Emotional memories of trauma do not go away. They linger in a brain's limbic system until we're able to reclaim them and even change their effect."

"I carried that terror in me all these years."

"Your brain couldn't compute that the noises that frightened you were coming from your father and created your fear. A child that age cannot identify that fear is caused from anything outside itself."

My eyes flashed. "All these years. Dad must have known! He must have known he scared me that day. What a mean thing to do and then not admit it!"

"It's possible he forgot too. We'll never know."

"Mother said I got afraid when I was two and a half. I saw steer horns hanging on the wall with a display of Indian blankets in a downtown Milwaukee store. I ran to her, hysterical. She picked me up and held me until I could stop crying. I couldn't explain why I was afraid. I thought that's when I first became afraid of deer and antlers."

Chris's eyebrows rose. "Or maybe you were reliving your trauma with your father."

I paused and looked out the window for a long time. I heard birds singing and smelled apple blossoms sweetening the backyard.

Then I snapped back into the room. "What about that part when Dad was chasing me and I 'left.' What does that mean?"

"Some people who are creative can go into another state of consciousness and leave their bodies, almost as if they become observers of what's going on, rather than experiencing it. Children who are traumatized learn to leave for self-protection."

"A two-year-old can do that?"

"Think about how children daydream. They can easily leave the present and be in another world."

"That's true. I see kids do that."

"And adults are able to do it too, especially if the trauma they're experiencing is profound. It's called dissociation."

My eyes narrowed. "Are they sort of crazy?"

"No. It's a way of creatively enduring something that might be dangerous to one's psyche. You did that to save yourself when you were only two years old."

I straightened up and grinned. "Kinda smart, wasn't it?"

Chris smiled at my sudden confidence and insight. I didn't often grin.

I nodded. "Well! That's really something! Do you think my fear of the heads will disappear now?" I took a deep breath of hope.

Chris pulled his shoulders back and paused. "I'm not sure. It may take some additional time and work. But it's a very important memory to work on."

I knew it wasn't over yet, but I didn't care. I was exhausted but hopeful.

In my adult years, even before I started therapy, I had a recurring experience. Sometimes it happened at a basketball game in the midst of a crowd. Sometimes I would feel it while standing on a street corner or sitting at a concert. I lost touch. It was as if I watched the world through heavy glass. I was observing myself doing whatever it was. I wasn't caught in a daydream, but I was not present. I was separate from the world around me. Then some stimulus would shake me back into the moment, and I'd wonder where I had been. There was an element of dizziness to it—not a physical imbalance, but rather a mental stirring. I didn't pay much attention to it. I mentioned the strange feeling to one or two people. Had it ever happened to them? They said no, so I dismissed it as indescribable and probably normal. Looking back, I think I may have been dissociating. Faced with a reminder of traumatic reality, I "left" for a while in order to save my sanity.

22

LET'S PRETEND

It was a weary time. I continued in therapy. Second-year seminary work was demanding on top of maintaining a household. I noticed cloudy weather and rehearsed in my mind the mistakes I made from day to day, whether they were in schoolwork, my relationships with my sons, or forgetting to attend an event. Thinking about the Shorewood garage and the plane ride, the unrelenting struggle with Dad's alcoholism, and missing Mother had brought me to the threshold of a door into darkness. Now I was carrying around a terrified two-year-old girl who felt broken and scared. The victory of confronting Dad with the truth at his apartment had faded. He hadn't acknowledged it. I maintained my pleasant exterior, but my arms wrapped tight around me most of the time.

Despite efforts to remember good times, of which there were many, I felt limp from sad memories. Why hadn't anyone taken care of me? Why was my dad so mean? I caught myself sighing, with no apparent reason, as I drove from place to place.

"Nobody took care of me," I wept one day to Chris. "I was so alone. I can't seem to rise above my sadness. It's like I'm still in my unhappy child self."

"You need to find a way to take care of yourself," he replied. "You've survived for a long time. You nurture others well. You can also learn to nurture yourself."

It sounded like an impossible task. How could I treat myself with care when others had not? I walked away from therapy pondering where to begin to change.

Soon after, I was wandering through Sears one afternoon. The lingerie area where I was shopping was adjacent to the children's department. I walked over to the children's shelves and perused the stock. Maybe I could find something to comfort my child self there. I touched a soft yellow crib blanket. I looked at teddy bears, blue and tan.

Then I saw it. A doll. She was dressed in a navy blue dress, just like the one I wore when I was four or five. There was white lace trim on her sleeves and skirt. Her dark hair was set in my five-year-old braids with bangs. She had my blue eyes and fair pink skin. I bought her immediately. I named her Judie Marie. I was going to care for myself.

At home, I found an inexpensive pearl bracelet that I seldom wore and put it around her neck. "Don't you look nice in your very own necklace?" I said to her.

I wrapped her in a pastel-striped flannel receiving blanket. "There you are, Judie Marie, warm and safe." She slept beside me that night and for several more. Every day she sat in the middle of my bed, leaning against my pillows on the straightened spread.

My doll, in her white anklets and Mary Jane shoes, was me. I talked to her from time to time. I held her gently. I consciously nurtured her in ways I once needed, and still need. I learned to nurture myself. She lives with me still.

Not long after I purchased the doll, I watched a television documentary about the struggles of aging people, their isolation and the difficulties of managing physical tasks. I bent my head, reflecting that in her last years, Grandma Libby used to eat lunch meat rather than cook for herself. I could have brought a meal now and then. The next day, as I drove through a modest neighborhood near Danny's high school, guilt weighed on me. *Did I give Grandma enough attention? Should I have visited her more?* My thoughts were dreary on that early February day, with ice along the curbs and no sign of grass on the boulevards.

I was stopped at a stop sign when across the street I saw a tall, old man awkwardly climbing out of his car into the busy road. Leaning on the car, he walked cautiously on the wet pavement. He carefully placed his foot on the snow-covered curb, heading slowly for a small convenience store. It was a documentary right before my eyes. An old man at risk. Would he fall? My shoulders tensed up around my face as I started to drive by. Then I looked more closely.

Dad! It's Dad. The old man is my father! I gasped and grabbed the steering wheel tightly, turning my face away from him. I didn't want him to see me. *Am I afraid of him or worried about him? Do I hate him or love him? Why does he show up in my life now, when I've avoided him for nearly a year?*

I drove straight home. My hand was weak as I turned the key and opened the door. Nobody home. I avoided Mindee as she tried to greet me happily. I pulled off my jacket and tossed it on a kitchen chair as I walked into the living room, dropped onto the couch, crushed a pillow beneath my chin, and sobbed.

Karen was waiting for me at a back table in an English Tudor restaurant. She smiled, and we hugged.

"Let's order popovers," I said. "My favorite comfort food."

"How are things going?" she wondered as I settled into my armchair.

Stopping only to unfold my napkin and put it on my lap, I said, "I'm having a hard time. I doubt myself. Maybe these memories are fake." Just saying the words sent a chill through me, and the room darkened. The dark wood beams seemed to close in on me.

"Do they feel like a fake?" she asked.

I paused. My mind flooded with images of Plainfield and Dad passed out in the dining room and the Shorewood garage. I gripped my napkin.

"No." I looked up at her. "Not at all. I feel so shaken up by them." I thought of the times when I wept in Chris's office or felt a jolt of fear sear through me as I remembered Grandpa Paul's brass bed. I rubbed my forehead.

With conviction I said, "They're real. I know they're real. I wouldn't even be able to make them up. But sometimes I doubt myself. I don't get it."

Karen looked me in the eye with compassion and certainty. "It's common for a person to have doubts when you've repressed experiences for so long," she said. "You've held those memories away from your consciousness for decades. It's natural to feel doubtful."

I gathered my courage to say what I feared. "Maybe I'm just trying to get people's attention and sympathy."

Karen laughed, which startled me. "It's a pretty unusual way to get attention. Do you tell a lot of people what's happened?"

"No. Hardly anyone." A tall, slender male server in black and white interrupted us, pouring water and handing us menus. I kept quiet until he left and then said, "I don't like telling people."

"That doesn't sound like trying to get attention to me," she assured me.

I pushed air out my lips loudly and looked up to the ceiling. "I get mixed up. I totally believe what happened. My memories are so strong. And then, sometimes I sort of feel like I'm crazy or something."

Karen nodded calmly. "What do your memories tell you about your family?" she asked.

I looked down at my place setting. "Mostly bad news. We were just five isolated people. Four of us were bullied into submission and silence . . ." I paused.

"Do your memories threaten your dream or your idea of what it means to be a family?" she said.

"Absolutely." I placed my palms on the dark table. "We just floated along as if everybody knew what was going on and loved everybody else. We didn't talk about what was happening to each person. We didn't face it at all. And for sure, we couldn't let the outside world see the truth."

Karen shifted in her chair and looked at me with understanding. "Many families in deep trouble create an illusion of what their family is like. Pretending helps them survive."

"*Let's Pretend*," I mumbled, remembering the kids' radio show. The melodies of the commercials for Cream of Wheat sang in my head as I thought about the pleasure of hearing fairy tales dramatized on Saturday mornings over the airways. But then my eyes teared up. Images of Dad drinking too much or yelling at Sherri seeped into my mind. There were no happy endings in our family.

"I just wanted to believe it could be different someday . . . and it never was," I said. Tears rolled down my cheeks just as the tall server, quiet as a ghost, came for our orders. Karen distracted him by ordering first so I could blot my cheeks with my napkin.

"I think I'll have two popovers, if that's okay," I said with a friendly smile. "And extra butter." Hide the pain. Cover the truth. After the server walked away, I could think of nothing to say.

Karen said, "Do you think you have a lot invested in *wanting* your memories to be not true?"

I sighed. "I do. I really do. I don't want to know that I was treated so horribly. I don't want to know I'm damaged goods." I began to cry.

Karen leaned toward me and extended her hand. "You're not damaged goods. You're a good person who was mistreated." She gazed firmly at me. "And you're very strong."

"Strong? Me? Look at how I never stopped Dad. I kept quiet. I'm just a pile of nothing." I twisted my napkin on my lap.

"You were just a child," Karen said.

For a long, painful moment, I waited to speak, rubbing my hands on my thighs. Then I took a deep breath and, without looking at Karen, spoke the truth.

"I'm scared. What if it didn't stop when I was a child? I don't think I could stand to know that."

"You've been able to handle knowing everything else," she said. "If there's more to face, you'll be able. You're one of the strongest women I've known. You're confronting the hardest experiences of your life with honor and courage."

All I could do was shake my head slowly back and forth. My throat was clogged from tears. My family was not a happy, normal family. We were a wreck. No wonder I wanted to doubt it.

And it was all true. It was all just terribly true.

23

MASSAGE

August, as usual, was hot and humid. The boys were working part-time jobs and going to sports practices. No new memories had surfaced since the Thunderbird, but I worked with Chris every other week. I missed Grandma Libby, and from time to time I'd drive by the big old duplex where I had made such good memories. Life was normal except that I had been craving chocolate, eating Hershey's kisses in the evening and even a candy bar after seminary classes. In four weeks' time I gained several pounds. It annoyed me. I felt out of control.

Karen had given me a gift certificate for a massage, saying, "You might need this. It may help restore you." Self-care: I decided to use the certificate before a therapy appointment.

Only once before had I had a massage, when I was a young mother. I had been embarrassed to strip to my pants and lie on a bench. My stomach had swirled with old feelings. I hurried to cover myself with a sheet and blanket—even with a woman masseuse, a nun. A friend had recommended her after I had some back trouble, and she was nice, but it seemed to double my embarrassment to let a stranger touch me and see me half naked. Now, again, I felt tense, vulnerable. I was tempted to skip the appointment, but I climbed the stairs to her office above a clothing store, reluctant.

The woman was gentle: a tall brunette in a turquoise Southwestern skirt and top, named Mary. Soothing music played, and sandalwood incense was light in the air. "How are you feeling today, Judie?" she asked.

"Oh, I don't know," I said softly. "Kind of tired, I guess."

"This might be just what you need," she said. "You can relax. Who knows, you may even fall asleep."

She began carefully, and we talked a while. I gave her a very abbreviated version of my life story, with references to Dad's alcoholism and abuses. Mary's hands moved lightly and carefully. The music lulled me as I worked at relaxing.

"I guess I shouldn't work so hard at relaxing," I said with a smile.

"That's pretty common," she replied. "Just let go a little."

Without much time I began to drift in and out of sleep. My muscles relaxed, and the music calmed me. Then, unbidden, I started weeping. Tears dropped onto the mat slowly, more and more. My tears made me choke.

"I'm sorry," I whispered.

"Not at all! That's common," Mary said. "You had to let go of a lot of tension—to allow it to wash out of yourself."

"But I don't know why I'm crying. I'm sorry."

"Please. You don't have to apologize. You needed to let go."

My tears gradually subsided, and after another twenty minutes, the massage ended. Slowly I came back to feeling alert. I lay still for a few minutes and redressed. I went out into the center office and thanked Mary.

"I feel very tired, but it's a good tired. I guess I needed that."

"I'm glad I could help, Judie," Mary said and smiled. "Come back any time. I'd like to see you again."

I drove pensively but with no focus to the therapy office. The tears had taken a lot out of me.

"I didn't have anything special to talk about today," I told Chris. "But something happened just before I came here. I went to have a massage. I didn't expect to like it, but I did, and in the middle of it all I started to cry. I *never* do that."

"Why do you think it happened?"

"I can't say. I know I've been missing Grandma Libby. I've been thinking of my other name for her: Soft Grandma. She was kind of like that, you know. Soft skin, and sort of fat when I was young, and . . . well, not firm somehow. A soft person. Nice and all, but she didn't have a clear shape in some way."

"You've been talking about her lately," Chris said, and I nodded.

"And for some reason I've been eating a lot of chocolate, and it makes me mad. I've gained weight, and I can't stop. What does all that mean?"

"I don't know," he said, "but you usually find a way to figure it out."

I paused for a moment as a wave of nostalgia swept over me, remembering how the back stairs at Grandma's house wound upward between panels of dark, waist-high wainscoting. They smelled of sweet wood, and rubber treads muffled the sound of our steps. It was a comforting climb.

At the top of the stairs, on the second floor where she lived, Grandma had an old, heavy metal icebox, no longer used, and atop it was an eight-inch-high metal funnel. When she lifted the funnel, there was a skeleton key beneath it, and she used it to open the door to the kitchen.

To the left of the icebox were the stairs that continued up to the attic. In the attic, on the south side, was a larger room with old toys from Dad and Mona's childhood and a second room, which was locked. There were three small rooms on the north side. The first north room was locked; I knew Dad had kept antlers and one deer head there. I felt uneasy around it, even with Grandma near me. The open middle alcove had a window that let in light from above the house next door. The room farthest from the stairs had huge, framed oil paintings leaning against the walls. It was really dark in there. The most visible painting was six feet long, in a huge decorative gold frame: a picture of a lion mother, a piece of torn meat in her claws, dripping blood. The first time I discovered it, I gasped and jumped back. At the far end was an open space and a window with three arches that overlooked the street where streetcars ran, their rails singing. In cold weather Grandma hung her clothes in the aisle near the stairs. I would climb upstairs with her and peek around at the rooms, not eager to go into the darker ones, and always avoiding the deer head room.

The nostalgia passed, and I was completely quiet for what must have been a minute. Chris said nothing as I closed my eyes for a while, then opened them. "I keep picturing Grandma Libby's house." I took a deep breath.

"Grandma's house had back stairs, going up. They weren't tall, so I could climb them even when my legs were short."

Then it happened again. "Oh, I'm starting to . . ."

Chris leaned in a little.

" . . . remember. I'm remembering the back hall stairs." I stiffened. "I don't want to know this," I begged.

Chris was intent but silent. He always let me lead.

I squeezed my eyes closed. My stomach quaked, and I felt my whole body resisting the memory. Then I took a deep breath. "I have to do this. I have to know."

The story unwound, closing in around us in the still office air.

It's late summer, and it's been a mild day. We live on the Northside. No one is playing Kick the Can tonight, and I'm indoors. Dad says, "I'm going to Ma's. I'll take Judie Marie with me." Mother nods. She is working in the kitchen, and the kids are outdoors someplace. I might as well go along. I'm following Dad to our beige-and-brown Fraser car. I wonder why Dad calls his parent "Ma" when I'm supposed to call my parent "Mother" or "Mom." We drive for about twenty minutes, passing through downtown. I look out the window. I like to watch people. Our poor neighborhood fades away, and we're coming toward Grandma's, where only white people live. Dad always has a key to Grandma's, so we let ourselves in and close the heavy front door, which shakes the whole hallway. Now we're climbing the stairs with the purple carpet and brass fixtures and dark wood all round, oiled and shiny. I'm ten. I weigh about sixty pounds, and I have long legs, but I have to hurry to keep up. Dad isn't talking.

We're coming into the large kitchen. Petey, Grandma's blue parakeet, screeches. Grandma walks sprightly across the linoleum floor, her short heels clicking. "Well, look who's

here!" she says. I'm smiling at her. She doesn't give me a
hug, but she's glad to see me. Her voice is happy, and she's
looking right at me.

Dad is impatient, and he says, "I need to talk to you, Ma." I
don't like his demanding sound.

Grandma's voice is uneven, shaky. "Let's go out on the
porch."

"You stay here, Judie Marie," he barks at me. They're going
out past the icebox to the door of the small balcony. It's gray,
with falling-apart wood railings and a black asphalt floor.
When you stand there, you're on the roof of the porch below.
You can see the small backyard with its pansies and sweet
peas.

I'm talking to Petey so I don't have to hear Grandma and
Dad, and I look around the familiar kitchen. It smells warm
and sweet.

The ironing board is always up, covered by a white
tablecloth with red flowers. Behind it on the radiator is
Grandma's sewing basket, a dark brown woven circle
decorated with small colorful beads on top. I can hear Dad's
voice, but I don't know what he's saying. I listen for the
robins instead.

Now Dad's angry. I stiffen up and try to ignore the two
of them. It's twilight, and I'm looking at the south skyline
over Great-Grandma's house next door. Grandma Libby grew
up there. Strangers live there now. The sky is pink-gray
peaceful. It helps me feel better. Calm.

Now there's a rustle as Grandma steps from the porch into
the back foyer, with Dad behind her. I'll just go out to meet
them. Grandma meets me first.

"Here," Grandma says as she reaches into her apron
pocket. "Take this and get yourself an ice cream cone at the
store."

Her voice and hand are shaking as she pushes the dime into my hand. I don't understand. I'm not allowed to go to the corner store alone. It's almost dark.

"Take it," Grandma insists, pressing harder into my hand. Dad strides in. Standing in the light of the open door, he's bossy. "You come with me." He reaches for my wrist. I shrink away. Grandma stands between us, but she fades away as his hand reaches around and grabs me.

"Please, Walt," she's pleading. "Don't!"

Who will help me? My wrist is small and hurts because Dad squeezes it tight. Now he's pulling me, and I stumble up the curved stairs toward the attic. My mind is swimming with fear. What's going to happen to me? He's pulling me behind him, past the deer head room and the alcove and beyond the scary room with the lion. He's shoving me to the floor. Ouch. I hit the floor hard. The wood is dirty.

I can't fight. I'm too small. Too scared. He rips off my panties and falls over me. Oh! he's so heavy! I have to squeeze my eyes real tight. Pain! What has he done? He moves and rocks, and my head hits against the rafters where they meet the floor. Rock, rock. Ow! Hold on tight! Then he makes a loud noise, and his whole weight falls on me. I feel something wet. It makes me gag. Now he's back up, hitching his trousers, making grunting sounds. He stalks off, down the stairs. I don't move. I'm lying there, and I feel the dust on the floor. It's getting dark. I'm not supposed to take off my underpants. Shame. I'm dirty, filthy. I squeeze away my tears. I wait. In a few moments I hear and feel the heavy front door slam. He's gone.

Where is Grandma? Did she hear the noise? I mustn't let her see I have no panties on. I'm getting up. My hands are shaky, but I put on my clothes. I'm walking slowly toward the attic stairs. I'm uncomfortable. It hurts to walk. I'm walking carefully downstairs, away from the deer and the lion holding the bloody meat. One step down and then another. Alone.

The light is fading from gray to indigo, and night is setting in. Grandma comes to the kitchen door. Petey is quiet, cheeping occasionally.

"So there you are. Come over to the table," she beckons me. I'm walking carefully and slowly, trying to look normal. I go over to the white metal table and sit down.

"See what I have," Grandma sings. "I have some candy for you." Her hand is shaking, and she's holding out a box of Fanny Farmer Old Time chocolates, the most favorite in town. From the box's white cover, the picture of the proper candy lady in her old-fashioned upswept hair and metal-rimmed glasses smiles at me. On one side of the box is a picture of an old farmstead, and on the other is the Statue of Liberty. Grandma lifts the lid, and I take one. It's a dark chocolate creme, which I like, but it doesn't taste sweet.

"You can have another one. Here, help yourself." Grandma is talking very sweetly, and I like chocolate. Maybe it will help me feel better. I take a second piece. It's chewy inside. But that's all I want. I'm too tired to eat. It doesn't make me feel better. She puts the top back on the box, and I can see the Statue of Liberty on the end of the box.

"Grandpa will be back soon. He can take you home."

Grandpa doesn't talk much to children, but he's nice. I'll be safe with him.

It's later now, and Grandpa comes. I ride with him in his light green Plymouth. It's a pretty car, with fuzzy gray seats. We don't talk much. It's already nine thirty when I get home. Grandpa walks me into the Northside house.

"Where's Walt?" Mother asks. I shrug my shoulders. Grandpa says that Dad left earlier. No one asks why.

"Thank you," I say to Grandpa. He smiles at me, which he hardly ever does. Then he leaves. Now I'm going into the small bedroom where Sherri and I sleep together. Eddie is sleeping there, and he moves to his dining room daybed to make room for me. Sherri is friendly and talkative, but I'm too tired to talk.

"Don't forget to brush your teeth," Mother says. She washes my face with a cloth. Then I go to sleep. I already forgot everything that happened.

Chris said nothing. I did not move. Without tears, in shock, all I could say was, "Nobody took care of me. Not even Grandma." I don't remember leaving therapy or driving home.

When I got home, I went to my bedroom to change clothes. There on the dresser was the old silver hand mirror with Grandma's initials engraved on it: *O.T.* Olivia Thorsen, scrolled in graceful script. I could smell her perfume in my mind as I picked up the picture of her as a girl.

"How could you do that, Grandma?" I sighed. "How could you not help me?" Tears ran hot on my cheeks, slow to start and then breaking into sobs. "How could you let him . . . ?" I caught a breath, and the tears stopped. Numb, I put the picture down and walked over to my bed. I crept onto the bedspread like a ten-year-old, curled up, and fell asleep.

24

BLAME AND RECOVERY

I purposely drove past Grandma Libby's house two days after therapy. It was in growing disrepair, like my image of her. She had been Soft Grandma, all right. No spine. A cheery ball of flesh and fear. I couldn't lean on her. She would sink into folds of nothing.

Chris scheduled me for less than the usual week between appointments. Two more days seemed endless as I carried the weight of the attic memories, which tortured me when they poked into my thoughts. I was grateful for school because it distracted me from that late summer night's pain. I cried as soon as I got into Dr. Hayes's office.

"I'm devastated. I was betrayed. I loved her—but she didn't love me." My tears were like barbed wire on my face, scraping away any semblance of beauty or idealism. The truth was pain. My own grandmother had betrayed me.

Suddenly I rose from my chair. "She knew! She knew! She didn't do anything to help me. She could've called the police! She could have called for help! She pretended nothing happened." I sunk back into my chair, fists clenched, beating on my own legs, weeping. "Betrayed. I was betrayed."

At last I calmed my breathing and sat with my head tipped to the side, dejected. "I was only ten. Ten years old."

"What your father did was wrong. He also betrayed you."

"He was a monster. But what she did was wrong, too. I *know* she could hear my head banging on that rafter. I *know* she must have known something awful was happening. She was a coward! My own grandmother who—I loved—" I sobbed, rocking back and forth, back and forth. "I loved her. She was good to me."

A cloud passed over the sun. I was silent, then asked, "How could this be? How could she not do something?"

"Do you have any ideas?"

I sighed heavily. "I suppose nobody would have helped. The police hardly paid any attention to that sort of thing in those days, did they?"

"No," he replied. "And what might have kept her from telling?"

I paused a long moment. "Well, fear, for sure. He was a big man." My eyes squinted closed. "And shame. It was shame, wasn't it? She would die if anyone knew what a terrible son she had. She was ashamed of him."

"What do you think she did when you were in the attic?"

"Oh, I don't know." I shook my head with disgust. "Turned up the radio, I suppose. Or talked to Petey. Or went outside—I guess she could've done that. I don't know. She was such a coward. Afraid of my dad." My voice changed to mockery. "It's a man's world, you know." I was absolutely exhausted.

"We'll probably never know what she did or told herself. Do you think she remembered?"

My voice dropped. "No, I don't really think so. She was always really nice to me, but—but I don't think she was trying to make up for anything. I just think she didn't have the guts to stop my dad."

"She tried, didn't she?"

"She *didn't* try. She didn't help me," I insisted.

I could see in his eyes that he had another point of view. Doubting his words, I suddenly raised my eyebrows. "Yes! You're right. She tried to help me escape. She gave me that dime. And she kept saying, 'No, Walt!' She *did* try."

There was silence. My eyes looked at the floor. My chin stiffened. "But she didn't try hard enough. She was too soft and small to fight. He's a big man, you know."

"I know. Big and angry and strong."

"I need time. I just need time, I guess. I'll figure it out. But it was hard. Hard."

"And I'm here if you need me," he said.

When I got home, I went to my bedroom for sanctuary. I walked to the dresser, and again I saw the silver hand mirror. Tears gushed out as I steadied myself against the sturdy surface. There was her crocheted dresser scarf as well. She was everywhere—except when I needed her. I wept. Then I picked up the mirror and saw myself, red face swollen with tears. I hated the sight. I stopped crying and set the mirror down, went to the bathroom, and rinsed my face with cold water. All I was hungry for was soup, and I went to bed as soon as Andrew and Dan came home.

The next week, in class, we had to present information on aspects of pastoral care. One of the groups talked about the elderly.

"These people need our care, and, in many ways, they're kind people who are overlooked by our society."

I raised my hand. "Some elderly people are not nice. Some of them are plain ornery or abusive." The room went quiet. Classmates stared at me.

I continued. "I know. It can be very hard for older people. They have fewer resources and more problems. But we can be too sentimental about them."

The group waited for the professor to say something. He was silent. Then one of them said, "We're talking about people who are disadvantaged and whom we're trying to help."

I felt my face turning red as the whole class shifted to look at me. But I didn't care what they thought of me. *My* elders had left me hanging in the wind. I wasn't about to be Pollyanna.

The class proceeded. I tuned out and watched the clock until I could get out of there. I had revealed my true self in front of twenty-five people. Gradually my anger melted into shame. *I do care what others think about me*, I realized. *I am a nice person—or I want to be.*

I rambled aimlessly down the hill toward my car. As I approached it, I slipped on wet leaves and fell. My books scattered over the ground as I hit my head on the side of the car. Young students hurried to assist me, helping me stand and gathering my books. I felt like a vulnerable old woman. Damn!

Again I drove past Grandma's house, front and back. The old tall elm was gone, replaced by a misshapen catalpa tree. The alley in the disintegrating neighborhood was littered with trash, and I had to drive cautiously because of broken cement. I peeked over the weathered wood-plank fence at Grandma's house. I could see that the door to the second-floor porch where Dad and Grandma had stood talking was nailed shut and secured with two crisscrossed planks. The neat strings for Grandma's sweet peas were long gone, and there were no pansies, only a dirt yard with no grass.

I began to think that Grandma was probably the reason Dad was mean and drank. I didn't know how it fit together, but certainly something must have caused his behavior. Maybe it was Grandma. Maybe that's why I wanted to tip her casket over onto him.

I took out my photo albums in search of clues—Grandma Libby's life in black and white. Did she punish Dad too much, or not enough? What about Grandpa Paul? Since Paul was abused as a child in Denmark, did he do the same to his son? No, there were no indications of Paul's complicity. He was generally stoic, but around young children he often smiled in pictures. It warmed my feelings about him.

Pictures of Grandma as a young and midlife mother were curious. Mona stood with her arm around her mother, Grandma Libby not reciprocating. Characteristic of her day, Grandma seldom smiled in photographs. Cousin Lois told me that the person who spoiled Dad was Libby's mother, Great-Grandma Marin. Marin would set a standard but overlook when Walt broke it. Lois tipped her head in pride and disgust. "I always had to mind my elders," she scolded. I wondered, *Did Grandma Libby also spoil Dad?* I heard both Mona and Mother say that Mona and Grandma would bring breakfast to Dad when he overslept for work as an adolescent.

For weeks, I pondered Grandma Libby's relationship with Dad. Her disregarding his youthful mistakes. Telling him, "You'll be a man yet, Walt," when he was already in his forties. Overlooking his drinking.

Ultimately, after hearing the prosecution and the defense battling in my head again and again, I acquitted her. She did the best she could. He was responsible for his own actions. She let me down, but he did the deed.

Hundreds of times she prayed for me or welcomed me for lunch. She did love me. That dreadful summer day she was, as she always said, "scairt," trying to tuck a dime into my palm and send me to safety. I surely understood about being scared and silent. I lived with silence and secrets in order to survive. For years I had told no one, not even myself. I was like Soft Grandma.

25

SUPPORT

The oaks were rusty red, and splashes of aspen yellow announced the second phase of autumn. Sandy, my former sister-in-law, flew in from Milwaukee, and I eagerly established a touring itinerary for the two of us. It was my third year of seminary, and I had a weekend break.

Sandy hadn't been in Minneapolis for a few years. Eagerly we drove by the lakes, which were quiet and reflective, like the season. The Minnehaha Falls were barely dripping after a dry summer, and only a few people gathered to look at the shiny bronze statue of Hiawatha, financed with pennies donated by schoolchildren over a century ago. We strolled through the Walker Art Center and stopped at the band shell at Lake Harriet for ice cream.

I trusted her to know my story. We had never lived close to each other, but since the first time we met, I had felt an instant bond. When the memories returned to me, I came to rely on her quiet but emphatic support as we discussed them during long phone calls.

"That garage gave me the chills because when I was small, my dad came home from hunting and punished me by sticking my head into a deer's open stomach cavity there," I told her with minimal emotion.

Sandy, always a tidy person, was put off by the gruesome image. "That's an awful thing to do to a child!" she said. Her indignation encouraged me.

When I told her about the day when he scared me with antlers, I could hear her palm slap a table. "That's terrible! No wonder you were so afraid at that restaurant. I'm really sorry, Judie." Her voice consoled me. She believed me, and that was what I needed most: to know people didn't think I was crazy.

One day during her visit, we drove by hometown favorite haunts—our grade schools, the drive-in—and then through the southwest side of the city.

"Let's go past where I lived in high school," I suggested. "It was an old farmhouse. I visited there once, when the boys were small."

"Was it hard to go back there?" she asked.

"Not too much. The owners had changed it some, and things were less messy. I was mostly curious, and I haven't had too many memories from there—yet."

"Maybe things were all just okay there," Sandy said, as her voice trailed off.

We had an early walleye dinner at a spacious restaurant overlooking Lake Minnetonka. The water was calm and the diners quiet. As we drove back toward the city, I said, "Remember Parkland? I used to live near there in junior high. Shall we go by that house, too?"

Patient as ever, and uninhibited by schedules, Sandy said, "Sure." Then she paused to look out the window. "We're so different," she said. "I lived in one house my whole childhood, and you had so many different ones."

We drove through the alphabetical streets of Parkland, with all its postwar two-bedroom expansion tract homes. Trees that I remembered as saplings were now mature, and families had planted shrubbery and built modest fences. I could still imagine the heavy asphalt smell from the old creosote factory, long before it was censured for land and water pollution. We used to like that pungent smell, probably because it was "ours."

I drove around a corner. There ahead was the double bungalow my family had rented, still in beige stucco with dark brown shutters and roof. It looked small, and the once-short evergreen out front had grown above the roofline.

I slowed the car. The early darkness of autumn closed in on me. I felt weighed down with deep sadness.

"Sandy—I've never gone back to that house," I said with surprise. She looked at me quizzically.

"I've gone to every house I've ever lived in, Wisconsin or Minneapolis, except the Northside one that burned down." I held my breath and frowned. "Why didn't I go to this house? It's so available. So close." My voice was low and ominous. Surely it was somehow important that I had never returned there. I sat riveted in dread, and my mouth went dry.

"Maybe you didn't have a reason to go there," Sandy encouraged me.

"No. It's not like me to avoid one of our homes. They all hold memories." I felt a chill through my entire body. "There must be a reason why I've passed it by . . ."

Sandy looked directly at me. "I don't think we can go visit the house tonight," she said hastily, with a note of insistence. "People wouldn't understand." I couldn't blame her for not wanting to get into another potentially difficult situation.

"No. It will have to wait," I said. I accelerated slightly, turned at the corner, and slowly drove away. "I can't deal with this now."

I was shaky inside. Why had I not gone there?

Sandy distracted us both by bringing up her new job in Milwaukee, and I welcomed the opportunity to set aside my dread. I drove her back to her hotel, and we made plans to get her to the airport the next day. I knew enough not to stir up too many ghosts.

That night I lay in bed, curled tight in a fetal position. Fear pressed down on me. *I can't go there now. I have to finish seminary first. I can't face any more counseling right now.* I scarcely moved all night long, caught in a heavy, foreboding sleep.

Ten months later, the next autumn, a shadow rose as I began my last year of seminary. It lacked definition and crept in gradually, but I knew something was coming. Dread slipped into my posture. For some time I had noticed that when I put my head on the pillow at night and closed my eyes, I instantly returned to whatever dream I had been having when I had awakened earlier that morning—and I dreamed nearly every night.

My unconscious was very accessible, even in the daytime. I sensed that something disturbing was about to happen to me. I planned to go back to therapy, but I was afraid to face it alone. I searched for someone who could anchor me. Someone safe. An answer came.

David Miller was eighteen years younger than I, studying for a master's degree in theology. I don't remember meeting him. He was just there, studying with Don Juel, the professor who had been a mentor and friend to me almost from the start. We talked about Dr. Juel's class on the epistles of Paul in the early fall. David was new to the seminary community and expected to go into the foreign mission field. He and his wife, Amelia, were expecting their first child. From time to time we would have long talks over lunch in the cafeteria. I heard stories of how he and Amelia met, each coming from a family of five children, and his college experiences abroad. He loved sailing on Lake Superior. He walked with a swagger, which wore down the outside edges of his shoes, and he had a deep voice that radiated confidence.

"You sound like an FM radio host," I kidded.

He was superior to me academically. An alpha male, he took on professors about theological ideas and did not easily back down or admit that he might be wrong. It appealed to me, although I felt tense in the midst of conflict, as always.

I felt secure telling David about some of my history: the memories of the plane trip, my fears of deer heads. "I'm sorry you had such a difficult childhood," he said. "I was lucky to have a close family." He didn't pull away from what I considered to be my strange and unpleasant childhood stories. He listened.

I finally realized that I had a sort of schoolgirl crush on this broad-shouldered young man with chiseled German facial features, deep-set eyes, and a good mind. I think he knew—perhaps he was flattered. Certainly I felt shy with him, as if I were still fifteen. I'm never sure when I am blushing, so I hoped my emotions were hidden behind my composed expression.

What would he think if he knew how I felt? I wondered whether I was, in a way, still fifteen. My comfort with men may have been arrested young.

Despite my confusing shyness, I needed people who listened and, perhaps most of all, a strong, trusted male friend other than Chris whom I dared to tell the truth. And David would look straight at me with his dark brown eyes and tell the truth in return. It was an intimate relationship—not sexually but in honest sharing.

Sometimes I would say unusual things, like, "What color do you think my eyes are? It seems like they aren't either blue or green."

"They're hazel," he replied, overlooking my adolescent curiosity and need for personal attention.

I second-guessed myself. *Why did you ask him that question? He'll think you're so dumb. How can you be so attracted to someone eighteen years younger than you?*

I even played a Roger Whittaker tape for him in the car one winter day, saying, "I like this song so much." The words were intimate and spoke of trust and understanding. I had no courage to say them aloud. He just listened and let my uneasiness dissipate. He knew what I meant but did not shame me.

David and Amelia occasionally included me in a family meal or evening outing. Amelia was gracious, and I tried earnestly to behave as a friend, not competition, which I knew I was not.

"You two should sit together," I said when I joined them to see a movie, but she insisted it was fine that I sit between them. Once, Amelia introduced me to someone using David's last name: "This is Judie Miller." Why did she say that? Although I yearned for a man in my life who loved me, I knew he was completely dedicated to her.

In December I spoke to him. "I feel like I may have some difficult times coming soon, maybe some new memories. Do you suppose you could be a support person if that happens? I may need a listener who I trust. Someone I can tell, in confidence."

He hesitated, and I took a deep breath. "I have to think about that for a while," he said.

It was only fair to let him think it over. Still, I drove home that day preoccupied. I feared he would say no.

He said yes. We both knew he couldn't, and wouldn't, try to be a therapist. But he would be a friend. The edge of my dread softened now that I knew I had a reliable confidant, and our friendship grew in the deep days of winter. Squeezed between his part-time job, our schoolwork, and my job at my congregation, we had playful times: walks in falling snow, running errands, tea at the nearby tea house. He taught me about trees and Papua New Guinea and what he was learning about the environment and reverence for the earth by reading Albert Schweitzer. In some ways it was a relationship I had never had before, one that was relaxed and stimulating. Despite uncomfortable moments of adolescent infatuation, I felt secure with David. It was a time of preparation for the storms that lay ahead.

26

SATURDAY VISIT

E arly February. Mist blurred the landscape, gray with patches of white snow and indistinguishable trees in the distance. Closer stood barren trees, black pencil strokes along the faint edges of a lake and path. Nothing was crisp or clear. The air was too warm to break through the fog settling heavy on all the world. Snow would have been welcome, or color, and surely sunlight, which remained hidden. In the few moments of faux spring, the birds sang briefly. The cardinals signaled that change would come, but during most Februaries I faced a bout of depression. This year was the same: dreary and oppressive. My spirit dragged.

I was four months from graduation from seminary. I had returned to therapy with Chris. He had me take notes on all my dreams. Then my nightmares increased, perhaps because Dad, at seventy-two, wasn't well. One Saturday morning, when Andy was away at a friend's cabin and Danny was in Japan on a yearlong Rotary scholarship, I awakened with a clear premonition. It was February 23. I called David.

"Would you be willing to go someplace with me today? It's important."

"Sure. I'm free after one o'clock."

The fog seemed to fill the entire house as well as my spirit. It was almost a year since I had driven through Parkland with Sandy, wondering why I hadn't visited that house yet. I felt shaky inside, so I tried to keep busy with housework as I waited for David to arrive. The front closet was cluttered, and cleaning it distracted me. I pulled out boots and gloves, a baseball, and a misplaced umbrella cover, casting the dusty items into the hallway. I was ready when David arrived on time.

"I want to go back to the double bungalow where we lived when I was in junior high," I said. "I don't really understand it, but it has to be today. It won't take long. This is the one house I've never revisited. It doesn't make sense—it's so close. But I have to go today." I wrapped my arms tightly around myself against the chill.

We passed the two-bedroom house where my best junior high friend, Belle, had lived, she and her five siblings now grown and gone. The house had been repainted. I pictured their kitchen, so tiny that a table hardly fit, leaving the dining table to be squeezed into a corner of the living room.

As we drove slowly toward the end of the next block, I pointed out homes to David, recalling which kids had lived in them. We turned at the site of the old creosote plant. There it was: the side-by-side stucco bungalow. It looked smaller than ever.

We stopped out front. "Let's try to go in," I said.

"Really?" David looked at me with reservation.

"I need to see the inside of that house. There is something in there that I have to know."

He looked off toward the neighborhood park without speaking.

"The worst that can happen is that people will say no," I said. "I'll just tell them I'm a writer who used to live here. People always let me in." David's pace betrayed his reluctance, but we walked up to the front door, knocked, and were greeted by two girls about ten years old. They had curly blonde hair and wore jeans and T-shirts. The television set was on in the small living room. The dark green walls of the 1950s had been repainted in beige.

"I lived here when I was your age," I said. The girls giggled, standing away from the entry, which had no foyer. "Is either of your parents home?"

They looked at each other, still giggly, and shook their heads no.

"Would it be okay if we come in to see the house?" Without pause, the gangly pair let us in. I hesitated to cross a boundary with such young girls. They had no doubt been taught not to let strangers into the house, and I was asking them to ignore the rule. I knew we would cause them no harm, but I was breaking my own ethical boundary related to protecting children. I figured their parents would scold them good when they found out—if they found out. I just hoped they wouldn't come home while we were there.

We moved quickly as I narrated. David followed me, beginning with the big upstairs bedroom, which looked very small, considering that three children had slept there together. I hastily described which corner had belonged to each of us and the plywood door at the top of the stairs, where we had stored a few items under the roof.

We went downstairs and passed through the living room. The girls paid no attention to us, but sat playing with Barbie dolls. We went down the open basement stairs. I still liked the open spaces of the basement, which was light and largely empty. We returned upstairs to look at the compact, pleasant kitchen facing south. We had been proud to have real wallpaper there instead of paint—a cheerful country pattern on a mint-green background. It had our first wall phone.

We walked quickly to the small bedroom where my parents had slept. "It looks pretty small now," I said. "They had a double bed, a dressing table, and a dresser in there." Its window faced the street, where David's car waited. The whole tour took less than ten minutes. Not wanting to linger, we thanked the girls and left the house.

David drove us a mile east, and we came to the white frame church where I was confirmed, just down the street from the big old hippodrome roller rink. I was reminiscing about our small girls' choir when suddenly I reached for the dashboard and gasped. "Stop. Stop right here."

David must have heard fear and distress in my voice and pulled over immediately.

"Something terrible happened in that house where we lived!"

"What happened?"

"It was this day, February 23. I know it was. I can't remember what happened. All I know is . . ." I began to cry. "All I know is, it was terrible. Terrible."

"Are you all right?" David frowned. The gray afternoon and dark trees conspired to bring back my chills. I thrust my hands into my coat pockets.

"I'll be all right in a minute. Just give me time to catch my breath." I breathed deeply and calmed myself. He said nothing but reached over to lightly touch my shoulder. We sat still for a few minutes. David seemed careful not to disrupt my thoughts. Everything was silent. I couldn't focus on identities, but adult faces swirled in my mind. I was fighting to hold back a memory, my whole body tense.

"I'm sorry," I told him, pulling out a Kleenex to blot my tears. "I'm sorry."

"Judie, you're always being nice to people. You don't need to apologize."

I sat, numb. At last, I took a deep breath. "Okay. I can go now." Tentatively I added, "This must be why I went back to counseling. Something's really wrong. I've been depressed all month."

David resumed our journey, and I pointed out familiar scenes from those junior high years. But even those good memories gave me a feeling of unease, so we changed the subject to classwork until he dropped me off at home.

"Take care of yourself," he said.

"I'll try," I said, feeling remarkably tired.

The next day was Sunday, and I stayed home from church, too upset to attend. I had slept fitfully and could barely eat. I fought to close off memories that appeared in my mind like ghastly, unidentified shapes, laughing and taunting me. Finally, I called David at noon and asked, "Can you come over? I'm having an awful day."

He came immediately, and I talked incoherently for an hour, crying but not knowing why. After he left for a family event, I checked all the doors to be sure they were locked. I paced the floor, unable to bring myself to call anyone. Finally, I made an emergency appointment with Chris and tried to find mindless chores to do. I turned on the television set and saw nothing that interested me. I made some toast and waited for night to come so I could go back to bed. After a warm bath, I slept at last.

27

FEBRUARY TRIO

The usually welcoming office felt strangely foreign and still.

"My friend David and I went to the house I lived in, in Parkland," I told Chris. I related the Saturday visit. I folded my arms close around my chest. I closed my legs together, twisted at the ankle.

"Do you think you have a memory from there?"

I nodded. "I'm afraid so. I've had an awful weekend. I know there is something terrible to remember. I need to know, even if it's awful." I paused for a moment and closed my eyes. I took off my shoes, and I began to recover the memory.

It's Saturday afternoon, February 23. I'm in seventh grade. Vern and another hunting buddy of Dad's, Earl, are at our Parkland house. Sherri, Eddie, and Mother are going to a movie. I don't want to go. I'm going to go over to my friend Belle's. So they leave in the car, and I stay behind.

Earl is about ten years older than Dad and Vern. He has curly, sandy red hair and a freckled face. He doesn't often come to visit from Sioux City. Children like him because he can imitate Jack Benny and has a pleasant, cheery disposition. As always, Vern seems to leer at me with his blue Swedish eyes and strange smile. He likes to sing when Dad plays piano, and he laughs loud. With his strange lisp, he tells a lot of story jokes that I don't understand, but I'm pretty sure they're dirty. I try not to listen. He and Earl are having a highball, and Dad has a ginger ale. He's been on the wagon since we left the Northside.

I go down to the basement to find a pennant from the high school that I want to take over to Belle's. I'm coming slowly to the top of the stairs. I click off the light.

"Judie Marie," Dad calls from the living room. The closet with its sliding door is straight ahead, so I hurry to look for my jacket. He's insisting. "Come here, Judie. I want to talk to you." I move slowly and just barely enter the green living room. I have to be polite. My heart is beating hard. I am alone.

"Say hello to Vern and Earl," Dad is saying.

I smile weakly and say, "Hi." I turn to go.

"Just a minute. Come here. We want to show you something." Dad stands and walks toward the small bedroom down the hall. I'm staying very still. Maybe I can go soon. I'm trembling inside.

He's annoyed. "I said, 'Come here.' " He moves toward me with a menacing step, so I walk quickly toward him. He grabs my hand. My hands are sweaty.

We enter the small room, crowded with my parents' double bed and dressing table and dresser. Dad coaxes me. "Here. Sit here on the bed." My face feels worried, eyes wincing. Vern stands in the doorway, Earl just behind him.

Dad begins to take off my blouse very gently. I pull away. "Be nice, now," he persists. His big hands and fingers have black hair on them, and they fumble with the small buttons on my blue blouse. I want to hide. He's removing all my clothing while the others watch. My shoulders collapse, and my whole body quivers as he pulls off my slacks. And my panties. I can scarcely breathe. He pulls back the spread and covers. "Lie back now and scoot toward the head of the bed." The world is starting to spin around me. *Make it go away!*

I don't move. "I said scoot back and lie down." It's Dad's insistent, angry voice.

I move back slowly, looking away from all the men.

Vern takes a turn first, climbing onto me with the aid of my father. I'm desperate. I cannot stop him, and I'm melting with shame. Dad is smiling. Earl ducks away, out of the door a little. *I have to not feel this happening.* I look out the window into the front yard, through the four-inch opening of the pulled shade. There is another world out there. Gray. Dreary February cold. No one to help me. I promise myself, *I will not go insane.*

Now Dad takes a turn while Vern stands on the side of the bed, urging Dad on. I squeeze my eyes closed. I don't want to see. After Dad is finished, he rises from the bed and bounds out the door toward the living room with Vern, leaving Earl in the doorway. "Go ahead, Earl!" They're laughing, Vern and Dad. They're like wolves in winter. Laughing.

Now in a gentle way, Earl rests himself on me and uses me. *I don't want to look.* I feel the sting of blocked tears as I close my eyes. He's pausing. I watch him look at me as he tenderly finds and arranges a sheet to cover my naked body. It seems like he cares about me. Then he leaves.

Out in the living room, Walt and Vern are frolicking, half naked, slapping each other with rolled towels and laughing madly. I squeeze my eyes tight to block out the sounds and the pain. I forget it all. I quietly and very slowly climb the stairs to our large bedroom and go to sleep, and forget everything that has happened.

When Mother and the children come home, they are surprised to find me there. "I didn't feel good," I tell them, "so I didn't go to Belle's." Nobody asks any more questions.

The men left while I was asleep.

I sat looking away from Chris, tears running down my cheeks—small puffs of sobs. The therapy office was still.

"At least Earl was nice," I said. "He treated me gently."

"That wasn't nice," Chris retorted. "That was assault and abuse." He clutched his pen.

Weary, I thought for a moment and then said, "I promised myself I wouldn't go insane." Angry determination swelled through me, and I glared. "I will *not* go insane."

A gray cloud enveloped me nonetheless. "The day was gray. I was gray. Ugly men! So-called friends. Running around afterward and laughing." My voice cracked. "I hate them!"

"You have good reason to hate them for what they did."

"What was wrong with me? Why did they do those things?"

"It was not your fault, Judie. They were the aggressors. What they did was wrong."

"I forgot it all," I said in wonder. "Forgot the whole event—until now."

"You have been strong in your ability to protect yourself from memories that might harm you. You're a strong woman."

"A weak girl," I said, tears welling up in my eyes.

"A *strong* girl who decided she wouldn't go insane." he added. "Very strong."

After I took a few more minutes to calm down, Chris offered to see me later in the week at my usual time, and I agreed. I knew I might keep going back to thoughts of that little bedroom throughout the week. I would need his reassurance.

When I got home, I called the library answer service to ask about the days in February of the year when the attack happened. There were four Saturdays: the second, ninth, sixteenth, and twenty-third. My mind had never forgotten.

The next day on campus I pulled David aside.

"How did things work out?" he asked.

We decided to meet at a local hamburger place, where I discreetly told him the story. The only person I dared tell outside therapy.

His anger fortified mine. "Cowards. Jerks." His eyes sparked as he crushed his napkin. "Cruelty. They shame all men."

Just what I needed to hear. Support from a friend who believed me. Someone who walked the site of the assaults with me. Someone who could assure me that the men were corrupt. But my heart kept wondering what was wrong with me, that those grown-up men would do that to me. My anger wavered and melted into gray shame.

28

HOTEL

When you live in the Northland, seasons are distinctive. Fall leaves turn brilliant colors in sequence—gold, red, brown—and fall beneath our feet to exude the full fragrance of a completed life. Sparkling winter. White snow and sun in the brisk cold. Scolding blue jays and an occasional white-throated sparrow calling out hope. The wonder of spring stretching out toward warmth, renewing us. Robust summer demanding notice.

Less distinct are church seasons. Created to measure the movement of life, the markings are seasons of the heart: days of anticipation and waiting called Advent. Then Christmas. Epiphany is next, when we remember how the work of Jesus was revealed. And then Lent: the forty religious days squeezed between winter and spring, often dreary, calling the world to reflection and penitence, which we prefer to ignore. Lent is neatly segmented into six weeks and resists finality or closure until we uncover Easter and the launching of hope and spring. Each week of Lent commemorates the journey of Jesus to Jerusalem and his crucifixion on a cross at the hands of the Roman Empire. Lent commences with Ash Wednesday.

It was three days after Ash Wednesday in 1985 that I felt compelled to visit Parkland, when I dramatically began to unlock many caverns of my history. After loosing that wild memory, with Chris at my side for support, I knew more was to come. For six weeks, like boiling lava, my pain and memories erupted, spilling over the floor of Chris's office and burning away my confidence, my self-worth. This Lenten journey compelled me. Would it end at a cross? There would be no going back. I had to clear it all out. It was almost as if I were hypnotized because my memories were so close to the surface every day.

I went to therapy twice weekly. Again and again, just before my appointment, a remnant of a specter from the past emerged, foreshadowing the memory my therapy would soon unleash. A week after my memory of the three men, I saw a pack of cigarettes, crushed on the sidewalk. I stopped to look closely. It was a pack of Viceroys, the kind Dad smoked. It was crumpled and dirty alongside the boulevard. I picked it up and saved it. Why would I do that?

"I found this cigarette pack on the street," I told Chris. "I know it means something. I think I need to go back to high school."

Dad is talking. "Judie Marie, why don't you come with me today? I'm going to see Mr. Herbert to talk business."

I don't have anything to do today, and I know Mr. Herbert. He's kind of good-looking. He's nice, and he has a pretty wife. I'm almost fourteen, and I look carefully at women and how they dress and act. Mrs. Herbert wears pierced earrings. Mother says that women who wear pierced earrings are cheap. In the car on the way down to the hotel I'm telling Dad that I'd like to be a singer someday.

"That's a hard life," he says. "Mrs. Herbert did that for years, and she had to travel a lot, and it's a lot of night work."

That's nice of my dad. He's protecting me. I'll think over whether to be a singer.

Now we're at the Curtis Hotel, where my music teacher lives. But we're going up to a regular room, on the fourth floor, walking down the long hall with dark red diamonds on the carpets. This hotel smells tired. It's an easy smell, like an empty room.

Dad knocks, and the dark wood door opens. "Hi Fred. I brought Judie with me." Dad and Mr. Herbert shake hands, and we all go into the small room.

I'm always polite. "Hello, Mr. Herbert." He smiles back at me. He's not as tall as Dad, and a little thinner. He slicks his gray hair back with hair creme. He has a white shirt on, with the sleeves rolled up to the elbow. It looks kind of classy. Mr. Herbert is from a small southern Minnesota town. He's pretty rich because he has a big car business—a lot of sales lots, I think.

"You've been growing up quickly," he says. "How old are you now?"

"Thirteen and a half." The room is plain and boring. It has tan wallpaper and a brown rug with swirls in it, a double bed, a plain wood table and chair, and a small, brown upholstered chair in the corner by the window. The view from the window is mostly buildings. Some are gray, and some are brown. It's a cloudy day. There's a bathroom with white tile and a mirror on the door. This hotel is getting old.

Dad pulls up a straight chair from the table desk and lights a cigarette. The smoke trails rise toward the ceiling, and I wonder what I'm supposed to do. "You can sit right there on the bed," Dad tells me. He and Mr. Herbert talk about business for a while. I sit on the side of the bed facing the door, but I don't listen much. I just look at the design in the carpet and try to find pictures. I try to write the alphabet with my feet to exercise my ankles, like my gym teacher taught us.

I stopped talking to Chris. My throat got stuck, and I felt shaky.

"Are you all right, Judie?"

"I don't know. Something feels very—scary. I maybe don't want to go on."

"That's up to you, Judie. Whatever you think best."

"This time of year—Lent—it can feel very heavy." I sat for a moment, consumed by dread. "I wish I didn't have to go back there. But I do. I have to find out what happened. I'll try again."

I pulled my ankles close together and twisted my hands in my skirt. Eyes closed, I began again.

I'm back in the hotel room. Dad just said he needs to go out for a pack of cigarettes. I start to stand up. Dad looks at me and says, "Just wait for me here, Judie Marie." I squint my eyes. I slowly sit back down, and I look at my feet. My arms feel very weak. Why doesn't he take me with him? I don't say anything. I start to rub my upper arms, crossed over my chest. The door closes.

"Well, Judie Marie. What grade did you say you're in?" Mr. Herbert is sitting down beside me. The bed sinks a little.

"I'm in ninth." I can't think of anything to say. I squeeze my arms tight on my chest. He touches my arms and pulls one of them away. Now what should I do? I try to turn away toward the headboard.

"Why don't we try something new to do?" he tells me quietly, his other hand reaching up my skirt. I'm worried. The room is very quiet. His hand rubs my thigh.

Now my body feels different. Like it did the time at a church dance, when I danced close to a boy I knew from school. I felt tingling all over. It was nice. But he was a boy. This is a man. I hardly know him.

"Don't you worry about anything," he says quietly. "Everything will be just fine." His hand inches upward on my leg.

I don't know what to say or do. He's leaning on me now. I push back a little, but he's moving his hands up and down my thighs. My feelings around my legs are getting stronger. It's like I want to be touched. But Mr. Herbert is a grown-up man.

What should I do? I look at the ceiling. *I'll have to be like Mother. I'll have to do whatever she would do.* My stomach is shaky. He is leaning on one of my arms and holding the other one down with his strong hand. I'd better not fight him.

There is no sound anymore. No sight. I am gone someplace else. I just do what I'm told. And I forget. Forget.

When Dad comes back to the room, things are dim. He and Mr. Herbert are very friendly and a little loud. "Well, we'd better get going, Judie Marie," Dad says.

I don't talk to anyone except to say good-bye to Mr. Herbert. I don't look at him. They talk to each other but not to me, and they shake hands again. Dad lights up a cigarette, and we go home together.

The therapy office was still except for muffled traffic passing somewhere nearby. I sat unmoving in the chair, looking at the floor. I had nothing to say. I squeezed the crumpled cigarette pack tightly between my fingers, sick at heart.

"Judie. Are you all right?"

"Yes."

Silence. I twist my feet around each other.

"Do you remember what happened after that?"

"Not really. I just know by how my body feels. He—he—had me." Tears rolled down my face, hot and stinging. "He wasn't a nice man at all, no matter how he looked or how important he was in his town. He ruined me."

"You are a whole, good person Judie. What happened to you was assault. You are not to blame."

"But I feel dirty. Used. Debased." My words slapped the air and fell to the floor.

Firmly Chris said, "You were assaulted, and it was *wrong*. You are a good person. You're not ruined."

I spent another half hour talking through my experience, slipping between my adult self and the young girl who felt betrayed and used.

"What about that part with Mother?" I asked.

"What do you think she was doing in the memory?"

"I think she was telling me—she was telling me how to be safe. 'Don't fight. Just go along.'"

"Your mother was taking care of you in your thoughts."

"That's weird," I said.

"You were in the midst of dangerous trauma. You accessed your mother to keep you safe in a situation beyond your control," Chris said.

My eyes widened. "That's not like those multiple personalities, is it?"

"No. This is just your way of psychologically saving yourself," he said.

"It feels kind of crazy. Is there something wrong with me?" I began to rub my hands together fiercely.

"No. I think it was your strategy for coping with what seemed impossible circumstances. Rather smart, really." Chris cocked his head and nodded.

"I have to think about this," I said. "It's pretty heavy."

"You're a strong woman, Judie."

I covered a small smile, wanting to believe him.

"I think it may be a good idea to meet twice a week for a while," Chris said. It was good news to me. A week between appointments seemed long, and there was so much to talk about and try to reason through. Lent felt so long that year.

I was quiet at dinner with Andy and pensive through the evening. *How many memories are there? Who am I? Where has this person and body been in her life? How damaged am I?* Dan was in Japan, and Andy was active with his own high school concerns. I shielded my children from my therapy disturbances. It was difficult enough for me to confront, and I didn't want them to worry about me. They weren't ready to handle the complexities of cruel adult behavior, especially at the hands of their own grandfather.

That night I couldn't get to sleep for over two hours. I awakened early the next morning and tried to go back to sleep. The dirty hotel room kept coming to mind. Finally, I got up and took out a book to read for school. I have no idea what book it was or what it was about.

Buried beneath the hotel memory was another.

Weeks after the hotel attack, Grandma Trina makes me a
special skirt for dress-up occasions. It is rose taffeta, with
hints of lavender and red, shimmering when the fabric
moves in the light. I make it swish when I can and enjoy its
changing colors as I walk. It is a circle skirt, and Mother has
me wear a white nylon blouse with it. You can almost see the
lace of my full slip under the blouse. I worry a little about
that. People might see me. Of course, I have repressed the
hotel room incident. It lingers in threads of music but not
my memory.

In ninth grade I lack grace. Tall and thin as I am, I'm aware
of my every step and movement, afraid to be awkward. "Sit
with your knees together," Mother reminds me as I sit in
the skirt like an athletic boy would. "Be a lady." I obey, but I
hate all that "lady" talk that women keep saying. *It's a man's
world.*

As a rule, kids in school don't go anywhere after supper—
not in winter. It is dark, and we don't yet have a lot of
evening school activities. I often sit on the cranberry-colored
plush couch and do my homework with half an eye on
television. Jackie Gleason, in *The Honeymooners*, reminds
me of my dad. A big bully dreamer. We often watch hour-
long shows with singers, dancers, comedians, and sketches.
My favorite is Ed Sullivan.

It is late November. The announcer calls out, "Ladies and
gentlemen, Frankie Laine!" Out comes the popular singer
with his wavy dark hair and broad chest. "Je-zze-bel," he
begins with power, drums and full orchestra behind him. I
stop diagramming sentences to watch.

He has a sexy voice. I like his songs like "Wild Goose," but I curl inside to hear songs like "That's My Desire." It feels as if people are watching me during that song.

This song, "Jezebel," says she is born a devil who lies and torments men. She is like a demon who possesses a man.

Jezebel music stirs my shame. She cheats on men. She is like Mary Magdalene at church—they say she was a temptress. I know women are expected to stay in bounds, no teasing, no sex. Jezebel breaks the rules, and I wince as the song goes on.

My gaze drifts. Kitchen sounds fade away. The living room seems empty. The dark night outside encloses everything.

I keep my eyes on the program intensely. I don't like that Frankie Laine. Too sexy. Girls aren't supposed to like sexy things.

Buried inside, playing another melody in, over, and under my reality, is my unidentified fear that I am Jezebel. *I get men to do bad things.* In Parkland. In hotels. *It's my fault.*

I go upstairs to get away from the song and be alone. I have no desk to work at, but I sit on my bed and concentrate earnestly on diagramming sentences until I blunt my buried distaste for myself.

29

SHOEMAKER

Week two of Lent. Ed called. "Dad's pretty sick. They moved him to the hospital unit of the nursing home. I just thought you ought to know."

For three years after I confronted Dad without my siblings, they accepted my withdrawal from him but maintained their places in his life. This was especially true of Ed. As Dad became weaker and experienced some dementia, Ed and Marty and their family included Dad and Stella in their family activities. I didn't feel that Sherri or Ed rejected me for my general distancing from him, and occasionally I went to family events that Dad attended. I had felt Stella's disdain ever since the apartment confrontation. Dad reflected no awareness that it had happened. Their call about the nursing home was not unexpected.

Now what? I thought. *Do I have to see him again? I don't want to go over there. But I'll feel guilty if I don't.* I ordered a pizza for Andy and me so I could squeeze in a visit to the nursing home before going to work at church.

Dad was sitting up in a wheelchair in the lobby, looking weak. I stood three feet away from him, keenly aware of how much weight he had lost over the years and how pale he looked. It was sad to see. Ed stood behind the chair, observing us.

"How are you feeling, Dad?"

"I'm getting along. Good nurses here. How're the kids?"

"They're doing fine. Danny's still in Japan, but he's good about writing. And school is good for Andy." The room was busy with visitors and an occasional staff person moving about, and yet it was as if a spotlight froze the three of us in intense light.

With familiar braggadocio he said, "They're smart ones. You tell 'em hi from me. Remember when I got them those goldfish?"

I smiled. Such giddy chaos! He bought each of the grandchildren a goldfish from the dime store one Christmas. Each fish was in a bag of water, tucked in a box under the tree. The holiday room bubbled with their delight and energy. The aftermath was less happy when the fish died after being transported home and the children were crying. Still, it was a creative idea to please the children.

"I remember that. They loved it." My voice was approving, but my body stood, wooden. I didn't feel like pleasing him, but I knew little else to do. Be nice, do your duty, and get out of here.

"Well, Dad, it's Wednesday night, and I'm due to work at church."

"Do whatever it is you're supposed to do," he said with an edge of bitterness. I never knew when he would be nasty or derisive. I offered my thanks to Ed and good-bye to Dad, unable to bring myself to even kiss him on the cheek. It would have creeped me out. I never did like being close to him.

From the nursing home I went to Wednesday-night services, where it was peaceful. My chest had felt heavy all week, and my steps were slow. Was I dragging guilt or a holdover of shame from the hotel memory? I wanted to forget it all.

The next day at school David sought me out. We sat at a lunch table mid-morning, and I drank two cups of tea as I told him the story of the hotel room.

"That's despicable," he said. In anger he threw his pile of books to the floor beside his chair.

His intensity always gave me strength, despite the whispering messages of self-hate that plagued me. *What sort of person has such an awful history? How much of this is my own fault? I'm defective. Predators must sense my weaknesses.*

I looked down. "Do you think you can hang with me through this? I have a feeling there's going to be more." I wanted to plead, but I didn't dare. I needed his support, but I wasn't sure anyone should have to listen to my sordid stories.

He didn't flinch or look away in discomfort. His dark brown eyes were steady and affirming. "I'll be here. We can talk any time."

Days later, I was talking to my friend Joan on the phone one Monday evening when my back went out. I'd had back trouble from time to time over the last several years and had to be very careful. It seemed to be related to gardening and neglected exercise. That night, the sharp pains struck me suddenly. "Joan," I said, taking a deep breath. "All of a sudden I can't move. I'm in terrible pain."

Joan was a former nurse and compassionate friend, and both she and her husband, Ken, knew my story.

"I think I need your help," I appealed. "I can hardly walk."

Within ten minutes Joan was at my house. She helped me into a tub of hot water to try to relax my muscles. After she helped me to bed, the muscles began to release, but by Tuesday morning I knew I had to stay at home from school. I sat in the rocking chair with a heating pad on, trying to do a little reading for school and rocking, rocking. My therapy appointment with Chris was the next day, and I wanted to keep it if at all possible.

At the close of the day I was slowly getting ready for bed. I was combing my hair when I heard a song going through my head. It was "The Little Shoemaker." I hadn't thought about it for years. It was a popular 1950s song with a repeated refrain, fairy tale–like and easy to sing. Strange to have it return to my mind like that.

I went immediately to the basket of sheet music alongside the piano. Careful not to twist my back, I pored through the music, some of it tattered. There it was. I used to play it in Parkland. How old was I then? Thirteen? Twelve? Without knowing why it was important, I set the music aside to bring to my therapy session the next morning.

My back strength felt tenuous as I drove to see Chris. I sighed as I told him about my trouble. "I have no idea where the pain came from. I didn't really do anything to strain my back. And I don't have time to feel sick. I'm too busy at school. It feels a little better now, but I'm not confident."

"Why don't you sit in a better chair?" he suggested, pointing to my right. As I walked to a straight, less cushioned chair, I said, "I think I have one clue about something. Maybe a memory. In the midst of all that back difficulty, I felt compelled to find this music last night. I haven't a clue as to why." I held up the bright blue music sheet.

"I want to go back there," I said. "The sheet music must mean something, or I wouldn't have wanted to find it." I closed my eyes. Before me I saw our dark upright piano, the one that replaced the old Wurlitzer. I was in Parkland. Twelve years old.

I'm playing my lesson. It's seven o'clock at night. Summer. I like this song, "The Little Shoemaker." I'm pretty good at playing it, and it's peppy. The only other person home is Dad.

"Judie Marie," he calls me from down the hall. "Come here."

"Just a minute. I'm almost done." I keep playing.

With a rush of air, suddenly there he is, right beside me. I'm surprised, and I stop playing and look the other way.

"I said, 'Come here!'" Dad's voice is strong.

I don't have much courage. I speak very quietly and keep looking away. "I don't want to."

Now he's grabbed my arm and pulls me off the round piano stool. I try to pull away, but I'm not strong enough. He's pulling me down the wood floor of the hall. My stocking feet slide, and I can't stop following him. He pushes me onto his and Mom's bed. My back is twisting to get away. I curl up real tight.

"Stop that!" He's yelling at me and reaching for something on Mom's dressing table. The perfume bottles are clinking

as they tip over. He grabs Mom's hairbrush. He's—he's
pushing it inside me. Owww! He pulls it out and slaps me
and marches out of the room. The summer world around me,
even my tears, is totally silent. I'm lying on the bed, crying.
This is what my life is like.

Now I don't know if I'm falling asleep or getting up. I
forget.

My heavy sigh filled the whole office, and I sat for a moment. "I just don't
remember anything else." Encompassed by shame over the images, I felt
as if other people had seen what he did to my body, and I wanted to hide
the event from everyone by not looking at Chris.

"Why did he do that? Why was he so mean?" My voice was still young,
and my tears fell gently. I couldn't look up.

"Your father was an angry, sick man."

"But why?" I kept my eyes on the floor. "Why was he mad at me? I
didn't do *anything* that night. I was just playing the piano."

Suddenly I looked up and waved the sheet music in the air. "I was playing this song." With all my strength I tore it in four pieces and threw it on
the floor. "I didn't do anything wrong!" I said. And I sobbed.

After a few minutes I relaxed, dabbing my face with tissues and breathing slowly as I tried to regain my composure. We talked quietly for several
minutes, Chris's voice comforting me as much as his words. Then I pulled
myself from my slouch and sat up straight.

"You know what?" I asked.

"What?"

"My back doesn't hurt anymore!" I smiled gently. "The pain went
away."

Soon after I left, weary but emptied of tension. I needed a good night's
rest.

The next day I found David in the library. We went for a walk. I told him
the story.

"It's torture," he said. "Plain and simple."

Torture had never occurred to me. It helped to hear it: I was a victim of torture. But the torturer was my own father.

The next two days seemed long. I didn't feel like studying. I went to daily worship services and sat alone in the library. Late Friday afternoon, I quietly went into the Northwestern Chapel, where a sculpture of the crucified Jesus hung. Was it me hanging there? I sat in stillness, enclosed by the dark brown brick walls. I kept wondering, *Why?*

I knew I was losing my strength. Too many memories were taunting me. I was caving in to despair and couldn't hold on to my anger. I kept up with my responsibilities at school and continued to work a thirty-hour week. My job was to produce a weekly and monthly magazine and supervise the areas of stewardship giving and social action outreach. I tried to attend all of Andy's concerts and special school events.

On the next Wednesday evening I went to church for a meeting. People milled around. Youth chased each other around the gym. A group in the library held a Bible study. I was glad to avoid them all. I wasn't up to interacting. I went into the tall, pale-brick sanctuary. The lights were dim, and I looked up at the gigantic narrow stained-glass window, where an abstract image of Jesus overlooked it all. Voices echoed in the room, and a few choir members were gathering in the tall balcony for rehearsal.

"Judie." I jumped at the unexpected voice. It was the children's choir director. "Do you know where they plan to have the kids sing on Sunday?"

"Kids are downstairs. The senior choir will be in the balcony," I said, "where I can jump off."

She gasped. I had frightened her. Did I just say that? I excused myself with a faint smile intended to discount what I had just implied and went to the church office to escape the emptiness I felt in the sanctuary—a giant cave.

As I finished writing my column for the church newsletter, I blocked out all sounds around me. But my mind was talking rapidly, disjointed sounds stuttering through my head. *Jump off the balcony? The floor is terrazzo! That's a death wish. Am I crazy?*

The next day the choir director called to set a date for lunch. I knew she was worried about me.

"I'd love to do lunch," I said. I had very little energy for taking care of myself. Thank goodness she reached out to me. I would carry on. I knew I could not stop this journey. I was compelled to remember—to know—in order to heal. I had to hold out somehow.

As an assignment for a class on suffering, I read Victor Frankl's *Man's Search for Meaning*. I identified with the story. I might have thought myself grandiose for comparing myself to Holocaust victims and survivors, but my defenses were weakening. I was, in fact, *suffering*. I suffered in self-loathing and disgust at my raw memories. I suffered as I was swallowed up by fears of what I might remember next, or whether the strange man coming toward me down the street might be another predator.

Frankl insists that every moment of life has meaning, even our pain and dying. Even in the midst of suffering, we continue to have the freedom to choose to have hope in the future. One day, driving home after a devastating therapy session, I saw a magnificent sunset reflected in the glass towers downtown. It was breathtaking.

Well, I thought, *even in the midst of this pain I am blessed with beauty. Good overcomes pain.*

30

MOTHERLESS CHILD

Karen and I had lunch and a malt together one noon. I regularly brought her up to date on my therapy. She listened but seldom probed.

"Lately I keep thinking and repeating in my mind that old nursery rhyme about 'Mother may I go out to swim.' I don't know why," I said, resting my chin on my hand. She didn't know it, so I recited the rhyme:

> Mother, may I go out to swim?
> Yes, my darling daughter.
> Hang your clothes on a hickory limb
> But don't go near the water.

"What do you think it means?" Karen asked.

"I've never been quite sure. It's as if I have permission to go, but my mother doesn't want me to really do it—*don't go near the water.* It doesn't make sense to me." I took a drink of my malt. "But I guess it is sort of like my mom. She was passive, cautious. She was proud of me, but I don't think she thought she could achieve much. She was passing hesitancy on to me by example."

"You've said she worked hard to keep things going," Karen added.

"Oh definitely. Three kids. Dad always on the road. Never enough money."

"We often talk about your dad and the secrets that were going on. What about your mother? Do you think she knew?" she said casually as she ate a French fry.

"Oh, I couldn't stand to think about *her* knowing too," I said, staring out the window at the sidewalk. Karen said no more.

I didn't forget the question. My teeth were clenched so often that week that my jaw and cheeks began to ache. I made constant mistakes at the piano, and when I washed the kitchen floor, my hands gripped the sponge with vengeance. One evening, before Andy came home from band practice, I chose a bath over a shower. I wanted to relax and let the warm water gently surround me. I slipped into the warmth easily. I wasn't aware of my thoughts, but as I washed, I gradually noticed that I was scrubbing myself. It was as if I were covered in sticky filth, virtually scraping my arms and body with the washcloth, trying to peel off my skin. *Why am I doing this?* My body was stiff and my face taut. I sighed. I was constantly discovering new feelings, habits, thoughts. It wore me out.

I put aside my washcloth and used my hands to slowly and gently create bubbles on my skin. I let myself lie back in the soothing liquid, consciously trying to let go. I added more hot water. Then more, as I was able to tolerate the added heat. I tried to breathe slowly, as Chris had often reminded me to do. I soaked for twenty minutes, and my muscles gradually let go of their tension.

I carefully rose from the tub and stepped onto the peach bath mat. The oversize towel was soft on my skin, and I intentionally stopped myself from rubbing hard to take off the water drops. I folded the towel the way Mother had always taught me, with no hem edges showing, and hung it up.

Then, standing in front of the bathroom sink, I mindlessly took a bar of soap and washed my face again. I looked up at my image in the mirror. I was covered with white suds. As if I were someone else, I said aloud, "Can you give her up?" Startled by my own voice, I stood still, staring at my face. I didn't remember what I had been thinking about, but I knew I was talking about Mom. *Can you give her up?* Hastily I rinsed off my face and dried it vigorously with a hand towel. Something was up—and the next day was my therapy appointment.

The office was especially quiet that day, and I launched into thoughts about Mother as soon as I sat down. I closed my eyes and began to remember aloud. "See, I was really close to my mom. We didn't hug much or anything, but I loved her. She tried to be a good mother. And I didn't like how Dad treated her sometimes."

One day, in Plainfield, Mom and Eva get together at Eva's house alongside the lake. Sherri has a crush on their handsome oldest son, Kevin, who's younger than me. I just finished fourth grade, and it's summer.

Eva has three boys: Kevin, Keith, and little Kyle, who's about two years old. Mom brought Sherri, Eddie, and me. I'm the oldest of all the kids.

Eva is really clever. She makes birthday cakes that look like boats or drums, and she can sew and make ornaments and all that kind of stuff. She looks really different from my mom. She's shorter and has long, red, wavy hair. She has big breasts (a word I never say out loud) because she's heavier than slim Mother. She's a very cheerful person, too.

Mother and Eva decide to go back down the road to our house to do something and leave me to be the babysitter at Eva's house. We have to stay away from the lake, but everyone can play in the house. Six kids home alone. After about half an hour, things get all upset. Eddie and Keith both want to play with the same toy airplane.

"Stop fighting," I yell at Keith and Eddie. Nobody pays any attention to me.

"You kids are supposed to behave," I say again, real strict. There are no televisions. Kyle cries until I give him a tractor toy.

Then Keith knocks over the block tower that Kevin and Sherri have been working on. Crash. Noisy blocks all over. Kevin jumps up and hits Keith.

"Stop that!" I yell.

Kyle gets scared and hides under the dining room table. Eddie sits alone in a corner.

"If you don't stop, I'm going to call my mom," I say. I go to the phone to call. It rings and rings, but no one answers. I'm gritting my teeth. This is too big a job for me.

I put the phone down loud. "Everybody sit still. I'm going to get our mothers," and I stamp out the door. The gravel road is rocky and dusty. My cheap sandals get all full of stones. In my yellow sundress I walk the block to our house. My legs are swift and my chin firm. Somebody better help me with all those kids.

The house is quiet when I enter. "Mom! Mrs. Schwarzke!"

Silence. Then I hear a shuffling noise in Mom and Dad's bedroom. I sort of tip-toe down the narrow hall to the door. It's almost closed. That's unusual. I push it open a crack and peek in.

There are Eva and Dad, in the same bed. What were they doing?

"C'mon in here with us," Dad says. He has a strange smile.

I stand still. My skin is prickly, and I wish I could run away.

"Come here. This will be fun." They are naked. My legs can't move, and my eyes look away. What am I to do?

"Now!" says Dad. I know that demanding sound. I go over to the bed, and they pull me in between them. Eva is giggling. I cover up my face, and my heart forgets. Then Dad sends me away.

I don't understand grown-ups. I go way to the other side of the house. I watch out the picture window so I can see the world.

Now Mother drives up in the noisy old Dodge. She comes in the back door.

"What are you doing here, Judie Marie?" She has two freshly butchered chickens in her hands. I remember the kids I left behind. *What will Mother think?*

I twist my skirt in my fingers. "Dad and Eva are in the bedroom," I say, slowly.

Her eyes flash. Her voice raises. "You're not supposed to know that!" She slaps my face.

Why is she mad at me? What have I done? She shakes my shoulders and marches me into the living room and pushes me onto the couch. Ow! She slaps me again. And again. My mother never acted this way before.

I'm crying now. My back is twisting to get away, and my legs curl up to cover me.

Suddenly she stops hitting me. Mother starts to cry.

"I'm sorry. I'm sorry, Judie Marie. I'm sorry." She touches my arm a little, and then she leaves the room. I'm left alone. I look around at the ceiling and the floor and out the picture window. Nothing seems real.

I look at the piano, and I hear a song in my head. "Mood Indigo." Daddy likes that song. Indigo. Purple. Depressed, passive purple. Passive Mother.

"I—I don't know what else happened," I told Chris. Suddenly tears flowed over my hands, covering my face. I sobbed for a while and then rested, taking tissues from the table beside me to put in my lap. Chris broke the long silence.

"Are you all right?" he asked softly. I was quiet.

"Yes." I dried my eyes and put the tissues in the nearby basket. I took a deep breath. I could hardly move. I had no resources left, only a hollow space in my heart. I looked up at him.

"That was the day I lost my mom."

I wept off and on the rest of the day. The next day I went to the piano and began to play "Sometimes I Feel Like a Motherless Child." The melody haunted me for weeks. *Fourth grade. Just a girl.*

Two days later I returned for therapy. "How did it go this week, Judie?" Chris had searching eyes and a comforting voice.

"Oh," I sighed. "It was pretty lonely. I didn't see that memory coming."

"Did anyone comfort you?"

"I moved Grandma Libby's picture to my dresser, where I'd notice it regularly. I suppose that was comforting myself, like a gentle patch of yellow sunlight." I began to rub my hands and wrists.

"Your self-nurturing is getting stronger," he said, nodding his head. "Did you feel angry?"

"No. Mostly sad and—I guess I felt abandoned. Left. Alone." I closed my eyes. "By my own mother."

I stared at the carpet threads. "I did cry a little," I murmured.

"Did that help?"

"I guess so." I sat for an unmeasured time, just looking at the books on the shelves and picturing the Plainfield house. "It's kinda hard, this one. This memory."

"I see that. You have great reserves, Judie. Someday you may even discover you have some anger."

"Other people have said that. But when it's about Mother, I just mostly feel sad. Mood indigo."

31

KOINONIA

My feet trudged along winter sidewalks, oblivious to the earliest signs of spring. Could everyone see? Could they tell how badly I had been treated? Were my scars visible, turning people away from me?

I cried every day. I cried in Joan's arms. I cried in the office of my dearest professor, Don Juel. I cried in the car and when no one was at home. I stole away to a study carrel in the far reaches of the library, gazed out the tall, narrow window at the hill yearning to welcome spring, and cried quietly so as not to disturb anyone.

David and I found a quiet lobby on the top floor of the library building, where there were only a few offices. The terrazzo floors echoed, but professors seldom appeared. We sat on the easy chairs, feet up on the wood coffee table, studying John's Gospel in Greek every other day, which was in itself a major challenge for me. Often I would melt into tears, remembering and telling my painful stories.

One day, Professor Satre, whom I had never officially met, left his nearby office and passed by. My cheeks were red and swollen. Tall, slender, and soft-spoken, he stopped and said, "Judie, I just want to say I love you and you've been in my prayers and you will be in my prayers." After he left, I cried even harder. How did he know? He must have observed my pain from afar. Not long after, I found a pair of symphony tickets in my mailbox, a gift from him and his wife. I hardly knew him!

Weary, I wondered how I could have so many tears. Gradually, bathed in sadness, I shed my independence and clung to those I trusted. I was afraid to be known, but I could not contain my shock and horror alone. A handful of friends knew some of my stories. I couldn't stop the memories from coming.

Both Don Juel and a seminary friend wondered, "How can anyone forget such powerful experiences for so many years?" I tensed up, balanced at the edge of a trench of doubt into which I could fall at any moment. Their hesitation gnawed at me. My heart sank beneath waves of feeling misunderstood. *Even those who care don't understand.* I longed to take them to meet Chris, who could explain the power of repressing traumatic events.

Over time, I recovered the courage to respond, "I would have gone mad if I remembered them. It wasn't safe to know. My brain protected me until I was safe."

Don nodded, looking at the narrow slot of his office window. "You are remarkable." I didn't need the praise, but I was grateful for his confidence.

Other than the strength of friendships and those who carried faith for me when I was weak, I was sustained most by the ritual of worship. I could count on the ancient liturgies and words of promise, the stories of the justice of the prophets, the prayers of the Psalms when I could muster no prayers of my own. It reminded me that the world has known my pain and struggles before.

For about eight years I had been part of a small group organized through our church that met monthly to support each other in life and faith circumstances. We were a relaxed group, laughing often and struggling together. We had been through births and deaths, worries about children, job changes, and disenchantment with churches. They all knew about my fear of deer heads because they had seen me shy away from them at group events. We called ourselves Koinonia, a Greek word for an intimate community. Close, honest friends.

Finally, in a quiet moment at a Koinonia meeting that Lent, I said, "I've been having a hard time." My hands were wringing in my lap. "I've started remembering some things that happened when I was young. Some painful things. I was hoping I could tell you about it."

My need to tell must have been obvious. They encouraged me to speak.

The room was cozy: white-trimmed French doors, a piano, and book-shelves on each side of a bay window seat. There was a fire in the fireplace, crackling. I took a deep breath as people took sips of wine and sat still, attentive in the dark winter evening.

My hands trembling, I described the origin of the deer head phobia. I paused, gathering courage, and told them about being left alone in a hotel room with a man, and three family friends terrorizing me in junior high. My voice got softer and softer. I couldn't bear to mention Mother. The entire group was silent, stunned.

My face was ashen, and no one questioned my authenticity. Somehow I spoke without crying, steeled against the invasion of the emotions of the memories. Shirley wept. Dick's hands dug into the chair arms. Jeanelle rocked fervently in a rocking chair. Gary's bent head shook back and forth in disbelief. Nancy and Neal sat unmoving, silent. I protected myself and them from too much detail, and when I grew tired, I told them it would be a good idea to move our conversation away from the intensity. Everyone sighed. We were exhausted. I answered a few of their questions, and we went to the living room for coffee and pecan pie.

The secret story was out, and my good friends understood. I wasn't alone. They hugged me close as we parted that night. I was safe with them. They promised to stand by me if I had more memories.

32

NEW ORLEANS

K oinonia's support gave me the courage and curiosity to look through Mom's document box again. I found two pictures taken in New Orleans, one of Dad and Mom having chicory coffee at a small, round, wood table and one of a mysterious-looking white hotel with filigree metal decorations on the posts by the door and an arrow pointing to second-floor windows. *I'll have to take that hotel picture to therapy*, I thought. I knew it was important.

I explained to Chris that when I had just turned fourteen my Grandpa Paul died. He and Grandma Libby were wintering near Orlando. Grandma flew home with his body and left their car behind. She couldn't drive. So Mom and Dad planned to take a train down to Florida and drive the car home, with a stop in New Orleans on the way.

"We think it would be a good experience for you to go with us, since you're just starting high school," Mom said. "You can see more of the country."

I grinned and got my homework assignments for the last week before Christmas vacation. Another train ride! A big trip to the warm South, where I'd never been. Lucky me!

We sat in facing coach seats. I slept next to Mom and in the dark night heard the conductor call, "Cairo! Cairo Illinois." In the daylight, the mountains north of Georgia were dismal. Gray. Barren winter trees. Small houses stuck here and there, with meager puffs of smoke rising from their chimneys. I'd never seen mountain people before, nor so many poor people and places.

We stayed in a broken-down hotel in Jacksonville, where men sat around the bare lobby on captain's chairs, smoking and coughing, their ashes dropping on the floor or filling metal ashtrays on small tables.

We took a bus to Claremont and a taxi from the bus terminal to the duplex where Grandpa Paul and Grandma Libby had rented an apartment. We were greeted by a friendly older couple who had packed up all of Grandma and Grandpa's possessions and put them into Grandpa's modest maroon-and-gray Plymouth for us to take home. Clothes and boxes, a few kitchen utensils, and fishing gear were stuffed into the backseat. The three of us had to sit in front on gray velour seats.

Dad wanted to go deepwater fishing, so we headed across the state toward a west-coast town called Homosassa Springs. We fished on the Gulf, and ate a shore lunch of fish and hushpuppies. Through Florida we drove on long, narrow, desolate roads with stretches of low buildings—motels, houses, small stores. The Santas propped in the middle of large yards of tough, sharp-edged grass were incongruent with my images of Christmas. Everything looked shopworn and depressing. As we traveled, I noticed gray-green curtains hanging from trees.

"What's that on those trees?" I asked.

"That's called Spanish moss," Mom said.

The mysterious, ragged strings waved in the air, pulling at healthy trees as if trying to drag them into oblivion. Hanging from a bald cypress or live oak, the moss sometimes looked like an old woman's long, matted hair. Other times it swung gently like a chiffon scarf, looped over the bending arches of stalwart trees. It was a mixed image: beauty and mystery intertwined, looming over us. At the next gasoline stop, I walked over to touch the gray, fuzzy plant. It was lightweight, with curling tendrils, some of them soft green, surviving on air and humidity and inclined to slow the growth of its host tree. Sometimes it was used as stuffing for mattresses or voodoo dolls.

We journeyed across upper Florida and through Alabama, stopping once along the chilly Gulf, where Mom and I walked barefoot in cool sand. With a bold orange sunset hanging on the horizon, we arrived at last in New Orleans.

"It was so different from home," I told Chris. "Canal Street was wide, with a boulevard in the middle. And palm trees. The tombs were on top of the ground—that was kind of spooky. The Mississippi River there was brown and huge, filled with ships and big boats. Not like here at all. Not fresh and clear. I'm not sure if we stayed one or two days. One morning we stopped at a Canal Street sidewalk coffee shop so Dad and Mom could have chicory coffee in small cups. I was tickled to get to take the picture of them sitting at a tiny table That's when I took this picture of them at their table, with our hotel in the background."

Chris reached to take the photo as I said, "When we developed the pictures, I put a black arrow on the white hotel with its louvered window shutters. And I saved it. All these years."

I paused to look at Chris. He was attentive. As he handed the picture back, I looked aside, escaping his gaze. My voice became little and unsteady.

"I'm not sure if I have anything to remember there. Maybe it was just a normal tourist stop."

As he started to respond, I continued: "We did go to an antique place. I'd never done that before. It was up wood stairs in a dark, creaky old building. I saw dust in the sunlight streaks of the room. It was filled with old lamps and tables and assorted pieces of porcelain. I didn't much like it, and then I saw a big elk head. I ducked back downstairs as fast as possible. My folks didn't catch on, and I didn't say anything. I just hung around at the bottom of the stairs, looking out at traffic. It passed by, oblivious of a young girl. I remember the sun was close to setting."

I stopped. Fear crept through me. "I think there's more. I'd better go back there." I adjusted my seat and closed my eyes. Hesitant, I began to recapture the scenes of dusk in New Orleans.

Now we're at supper at a cafe. Dad says he and Mom are going to Bourbon Street to hear jazz music. "May I go, too?"

"It's not a place for young girls, and it's expensive. You can stay in the hotel. We'll be home early," says Dad. We walk from the cafe to the hotel on that quiet street. We climb the half flight of stairs to the desk, and Dad picks up the key. I go up another half flight to the second-floor room with Mom and look around. Then they lock the door from the outside with a small key when they leave. That's to keep me safe.

I decide to change into my shorty pajamas. There's nothing to read in the room, so now I'm lying in bed with nothing to do but look at the slanting beams of streetlights coming through the shutters in the darkening room. It's noisy on the street, but the heavy air and the night shutters muffle the sound. I drift asleep.

Suddenly there's a noise—metal on metal. I sit up, on guard. What's happening?

There's a key in the lock. Mom and Dad are home already?

"Hurry up, Barbara. Get the door open." It's a man's voice, crackly and gruff. My heart starts to beat very fast.

"Hold your horses, Leo. There! It's open," says the woman. "Go on in." A short, wide man is pushing through the door. Now comes a woman with curly reddish-blonde hair. I can't see real well, but she has pierced earrings and high-heeled sandals. He's sort of bald. What am I going to do?

Barbara sits backward on the chair at the dressing table with her shiny skirt spread out and her knees showing. She turns on the little lamp with a ruffled shade. Now I can see them better. I have to figure out what to do. How can I get them out of here? Or me—where can I go? Some horns are honking outside. But I can't get to the window. And it's the second floor.

"Well, well, little lady," says Leo. "Let's take a look at you." He's pulling back the blanket, and I'm there in my pink shorty pajamas. He's reaching to pull down my pants. I kick him. Hard. Leo yelps, and Barbara says, "Get her, Leo. Get her good!"

With one motion he turns me over and pulls down my
pajamas. "Hold her arms, Barbara. Hold her down."

She grabs hold of me, and he takes her chair and cracks
it over my back. He climbs on top of me and—Now he—Oh
God! Oh the pain! I don't know what's happening to me.
He's inside me from the back. I can't stand the pain, and he
comes at me again and again. Then he yells and stops. I can't
breathe.

Barbara laughs. "That'll teach her. Let's get out of here."
She knocks over the lamp on the way to the door, and they
slam it behind them.

I'm crying. I hurt. Is there anybody who can help me?
I'm alone. I put my pajamas back on, curl up tight, and fall
asleep.

The door is opening. It's Mom and Dad. The room smells.
The lamp is on the floor, and the chair is broken. I turn away
when a beam of light shines in through the door.

Mother turns on the ceiling light. "What happened here?"
she asks. I don't speak.

She turns on my dad. "What's been going on here? Where's
that other key to the room? Who was here? What's happened
to Judie Marie?"

Dad says nothing and doesn't move.

Mom turns around, and she beats Dad on the chest.
"Where's that second room key? How could you let this
happen?"

Dad hits her across her face so hard that she falls to the
floor. He purses his lips and says, "Don't you ever hit me
again. You understand? Never." He's stalking out the door.

Everything is quiet except the traffic. Mother picks up the
lamp, turns off the overhead light, and smooths the sheet
on the bed. She doesn't say anything to me, and I am so

shocked I can't think of any words. Then she lies down on the bed with me, turns her back to me, and covers herself with half the sheet. She falls asleep. I am all alone in the darkness.

He must have sold the key to those people. Why didn't she say something and take care of me? She's not my parent. We are the same. He hurts us both. We are sisters.

I must never remember this. Never.

The office was silent. The late afternoon winter sun hung in the air like mist. I could not muster energy to move, and staring straight ahead, I was too exhausted even to cry. All I could say was, "We were sisters. She tried to help, but she just couldn't do it."

Chris sat, one arm stroking his other forearm, silent.

I asked him, "Can we wait a while to talk about this again, later?"

"Of course. You need rest. You've been immersed in so many memories and feelings that it may take us a while to work through all of them. We have time."

I paused. "I don't know if I can go home and be alone tonight. Andy's gone."

"Is there someone who can help you out?"

Immediately my thoughts turned to my close Koinonia friends Dick and Shirley. "I think I could call my friends. Maybe they'd let me stay with them tonight."

"A good idea. You can phone right from here."

In a few minutes it was all arranged. I would go to their house and have their extra bedroom. I knew I would feel safe there; it was a large but cozy home, with fluffy down quilts and carpeted floors. I would feel warm and protected.

Shirley was a fine cook, and when I arrived, dinner was ready. The children were given a special treat—to eat in the family room and watch television.

We three adults sat in the dining room. Dick and Shirley asked no questions. I sat quite motionless.

"I don't think I can talk about the memory," I said. "It's too fresh. It was awful—I was fourteen, and it was New Orleans."

We shared light conversation about mutual interests, and when I suggested I might go to bed early, they agreed. Friends, they understood. I slept well, and in the morning, breakfast was waiting. When I drove the eight blocks home, I felt restored and ready to return to my house.

When I went to bed that next night, I felt frightened at first, but Andy was back, and his presence helped me feel protected.

For the next three days I carried my memories and grief silently. I told no one about my New Orleans experience. I couldn't say it out loud, not even to David. I was easily distracted in the midst of conversations, and I hid away in the library stacks, trying to do assignments. Reading was impossible, so I scratched around for writing assignments because they would flow more naturally.

One day I had the idea to find the Southern song "Chloe." Dad loved to play that blues song. The sheet music instructed the performer, "Play in a tragic manner." It fit with how I felt: dismal and alone. I set it aside to bring to my next appointment, which felt far away.

Finally, I could go to therapy again. The office felt like comfort, safety. I was immediately ready to talk, confident Chris would understand. But I didn't want to return to open that hotel door and breathe again the septic air of that memory chamber. I focused elsewhere. Away from the pain of the assault.

Chris's brow furrowed slightly. "You've been through some very traumatic memories. How did you feel in the last couple of days?"

I hesitated. "New Orleans was a terrible surprise. It brought me down quite a bit," I said—and I noticed how I always understated pain. "It was good I spent the night with my friends. They were great. That helped me. I didn't tell a soul about it."

"Did you find any inner resources to keep you going or to give you comfort?"

I had turned to other emotional parts of me in order to manage bad situations when I could not express myself. When Mr. Herbert, the business-

man in the hotel, was encroaching on my safety, I had turned to my inner
Mother to find out how to be safe. She rose to the surface of my emotions
so that I sensed I should not resist, I should just go along with the man in
order to be safe. It was as if she took care of me. Whom did I call on from
my inner self to get strength or comfort during the pain of New Orleans?

Had Grandma Libby been there to comfort me? No. She had not.
Then, in a flash of realization, I saw myself as a college student, when
I was nicknamed Jamie. Jamie wore a bright red sweater, and she had
spunk. She didn't appear often in my psyche, but she had power. Jamie
carried my anger when I was in bad situations and could not express
myself. That self-protective part of me had been waiting quietly in the
background for years. I told Chris about how I pictured her.

I smiled and said, "You know, Jamie was furious with those awful people. She gave Leo a good kick." I smirked with satisfaction.

Chris smiled back. "You found some anger."

"Yes! I did feel some anger!" I grinned. But then I shook my head side
to side with a frown and said, "No one really comforted me, and depressed
Mother won out over Jamie inside me. Mother didn't have the strength
against Dad, and she couldn't even muster enough substance to hold me—
or even touch me. It was all gray and purple. Shame and—" I started to
weep.

I reached for a tissue. "I'm not over it yet." Then I spotted a bag I had
brought with me from home. I reached for it, saying, "Wait!"

I took out a tattered piece of music from a Dayton's bag. "You'll never
believe it. I found the old sheet music of the Southern song Dad loved to
play—the one Grandma Libby gave to me: 'Chloe.'" I handed it to him.
"Just look at that cover picture."

There she was: a singer of the 1920s, with a big bosom and short,
wavy black hair, in her fancy fur-collar dress. Behind her was a charcoal
drawing of a swamp with a distant shack, trees rising out of the murky
water. And there they were, branches draped in Spanish moss. "It's like a
drawing of my trip—a moss curtain being pulled back to reveal my life.
Gray. Shame. Despair. No wonder I've saved it all these years."

"I hope you won't run from your sadness, Judie. Let the tears flow."

I had moved my mind from the sad abandonment of New Orleans to the music. I had changed the subject and avoided my pain again.

"I know. I have to do that. Don't worry, I'll get the sadness out. I'll let myself feel the loss. I promise." Tears welled up.

Chris nodded. "You've done the hard part: you've remembered. Now you can heal by letting yourself feel how truly painful it was. We'll talk about it again, whenever you're ready."

Driving home, a quote from Isaiah rolled itself into my consciousness:

> like a lamb that is led to the slaughter,
> and like a sheep that before its shearers is silent,
> so he did not open his mouth.

I was a silent lamb in that New Orleans bedroom. Lent was not yet at an end. Would my journey soon be over?

33

DEATH AND BURIAL

For the six weeks of Lent, one memory after another had pushed its way into my consciousness, shredding complacency and confidence. Each one seemed worse than the last, and on Good Friday I felt as if I had been the one hanging on a cross. I saw Chris that day. I had no new memories. Maybe the worst was over.

"I'm worn out," I told him. "Depleted. So much at once."

"There were times when I felt like I was a midwife," he said. "You came to sessions ready to face whatever was going to surface that day. I was just there to help if you needed me."

I set my jaw firmly, and my fingers clenched. "This is Good Friday," I said. "I feel like Jesus. Despised. Rejected. Abused." In my mind I could see the large brown cross from a nearby church, the stark white body of Jesus draped over it. My voice dropped with derision. "But *even he* got to cover himself on the cross. I had to perform naked."

"Jesus was not covered either—he hung there naked," Chris corrected me.

That's right, I thought. *I'm not the only one. I'm not alone.*

Easter Sunday came, bringing warm sun and blue sky. I went to church and afterward had a glass of wine with Shirley and Dick at their holiday dinner. The smell of ham and scalloped potatoes was replenishing, and we had lemon meringue pie, just like Grandma Trina used to make. The sun and grace of Easter overcame the clouds and weight of Lent. Danny was scheduled to return from Japan in August. I would graduate soon, and my assignments were winding down. I had already accepted a position at a large, prestigious church near our cozy home. Perhaps life would settle down now.

Two weeks later I attended a national church meeting in New York for three days. It was a good example of being freed from the burdens of Lent—traveling to a new setting. When I arrived home on Saturday, Ed called. I hadn't unpacked my bags yet, but I sat down on the kitchen chair to talk a while.

"I have some hard news," he said. "Yesterday Dad passed away. We didn't call you because he was already beyond help. It didn't seem necessary for you to travel all that way." He spoke calmly, with no trace of stress.

"Thank you for not calling," I said. "It's probably for the best." I felt strangely unmoved, with a trimming of relief. Ed's voice was comforting.

"Sherri and I were there. It was peaceful, and there's nothing you could have said or done."

"What's next?"

"I'll call Aunt Mona. Stella wants the funeral on Wednesday."

Just like that. No last-minute dramatics or good-byes. He just slipped away, and I was not even aware when it happened. I was grateful. And I think everyone was relieved except Stella.

I didn't cry. I paced the house for an hour. I tried playing piano, but the songs did not flow and my fingers got twisted up. I sighed as I found my personal telephone book, picked up the phone, and called Chris.

"My dad died yesterday. I think I need to do something."

"How are you feeling?" he asked.

"I'm okay—I'm not sure how I feel."

"Do you want to come in for an appointment?" he asked.

"No. I was wondering if you and I could go to the funeral home and be alone with him for a while. I might want to say some things to him."

Chris didn't hesitate. "That might be a good idea. I can call the mortuary and make arrangements . . ."

"Do you think they'll mind if we come?" I wondered.

"I can arrange for it. They probably have had situations where families want to have private time with the deceased. People want to work things out."

I thanked him, and within ten minutes he called back to say the time was set for noon.

I was strangely calm as I readied myself to leave the next Tuesday. We met at the Colonial-style funeral home at noon. I waited in the car as Chris checked in with the staff. Then, through a private door, we entered the reviewal room. It was large, with a bay window and beige brocade drapes. The sage-green carpet absorbed our voices as we stood by the casket. A door and a long hall separated us from the offices. Everything was quiet.

I led the way. "And here is my father," I said.

The body had a small mustache. Dad was a clean-shaven person. There had been some mistake. "It doesn't look like him," I said weakly. I was unsteady as I looked at Chris, my eyes pleading for help. He looked back at me carefully, as if ascertaining my state of emotion.

Gradually I came to recognize the eyebrows and cheeks. The mustache was new, but his hair was scant now and his fierce brown eyes closed. It was Dad. Shrunken after years of alcohol and illness. But it was Dad.

I began to talk about him. "See his thick black eyebrows? They were scary. And his hands are large." Even his knuckles had black hair on them. Danger.

I turned my words to Dad. I clenched my fists.

"You did terrible things to me, Dad. You were cruel." My voice gained intensity. "You hurt me with words and yourself over and over. You were mean. You hurt Mother and all us kids. Especially me."

My voice was steady and grew louder. "You always picked on Sherri and discounted Ed." I cast on him one accusation after another. The room faded into the background as I threw my vocal spears at him. I was vaguely aware of staff members discreetly slipping out the door and later returning from lunch.

"I want you to know I remember all those times, Dad. The hotel room. The house in Parkland with your so-called friends. I remember it all. And I've told Chris all about them. And some other people too."

I steeled my look. "I hate you!"

My voice raised, nearly a shout. I pointed across the silent room. "What you did was wrong. You were terrible. I hate what happened!" I pointed toward the draped bay window. "The world can see you now, Dad. You can't hide anymore. Tonight I want you to sit over in that corner and *be ashamed* of yourself." I stared at the empty niche and pictured him on his knees, head bowed.

My voice was clear and steady as I replayed his dominating, destructive acts against me. "Remember? Remember? You were not a good father. You were a monster. You deserved to die. I hate you. I hate you!"

Only convention kept me from pushing on the casket to tip it over, as I had imagined doing to Grandma Libby's coffin. Then, in a burst of anger, I took off my narrow, navy blue belt and whipped my father's chest three times, crying, "Take that!" Worried that the marks might show on his light tan suit jacket, I stopped. He was scourged.

Finally, I was empty of rage and disappointment. "I think I'm done," I said. We waited a couple of minutes so I could wind down, as I looked around the room, taking note of the bland and heavy drapes, the prie-dieu for prayer. Dad seeped back into the corpse, no longer hearing me. Chris and I walked out the side door so no one saw us. It was two o'clock. I felt empowered and free. Dad couldn't touch me anymore.

Late that day Ramona arrived for the evening visitation. She became the hostess at the reviewal. "How good to see you again," she said to callers, a proper front. I took note that she didn't eulogize. She stayed close to Stella, who was visibly shaken. Stella hadn't eaten much and had relied on her sons and Ed to help make arrangements. She avoided me as usual.

Many friends of mine came. Some of the Zetas were there, as were a few of Dad's friends and Andy, Sherri, and Ed's families and friends. I saw only one teary-eyed person: an old friend of Dad's from South High School. I doubt he ever knew what kinds of terror Dad was guilty of.

The Koinonia group came. Each member offered sympathy and wondered if I was all right. They had never met Dad.

"Let me introduce you to my father," I told them as each walked with me to the casket. Each put an arm around my shoulder or took my hand. I was not alone. With Nancy and Neal I paused and then said, "Here lies an evil man." I had never said it before.

It was a long time before I could come to grips with people's statements that my father was evil. What is evil? A curl of smoke twisting around someone's head? Or a new image for that medieval adversary, "the devil"? It is a mighty thing to say a person is evil. Isn't evil the absence of goodness or morality? What person is fully evil? My father taught me to skate and to paint with oil paints. He delighted in my childhood fun. Of course, it was for *his* pleasure as much as for mine, but I gleaned caring from it. The good survived. Only gradually did I come to grips with the fact that my own family member was evil—lacking morality or goodness—because that reality also shames the family. And evil can be so banal, so sly, so easily excused or discounted. "Here lies an evil man." But he was my father.

I stood tall and welcomed people, in control, at ease. The monster of my childhood was not able to hurt me. I stood near the casket and carried on friendly conversations. There was little to say about Dad. It was clear that the people who knew my story knew I wasn't grieving.

Family will have altered meaning now, I thought. My brother and sister accepted me and believed my stories, but they had not heard the memories that poured out during those weeks just before he died. They preferred not to hear. I was closer to David than to my own brother, and Koinonia were my kin. I thought about all the people from church and seminary who had been there for me in the last weeks and years. They were the ones who listened and supported and encouraged me. Who held me and cried with me. They were my family.

I was glad when they buried Dad.

I felt, at last, safe. As the inexpensive gray casket slowly moved toward the open grave, the crowd following behind it, I stood off to the side, erect in my lilac suit. I wondered how the mourners really felt. What did they know of this man who gave me life yet continually chipped away at my soul? Did anyone know—or want to know?

The funeral service had been in a handsome brick church that echoed every sound. I sat with David in the middle of the small congregation. As we entered, a Visitation nun approached me and said, "You know we must forgive and try to understand." I'd never seen her in my life. Dad had converted a couple of years earlier to please Stella. When the priest announced that communion was only for Catholics, I went forward anyway. No one was going to tell me whether I could have communion with God.

The procession gathered around the casket at our Hallstrom-Thorsen plots, marked by a large, rectangular, gray granite monument, in the prestigious Southside cemetery. The spring day was sunny and cool, trees barely leafing out and the ground wet from early rains. People went through the motions of the rite and began to walk toward their cars. As Stella moved to leave, I went over and said, "I'm sorry." I sympathetically touched her frail arm, and she glared at me, saying nothing.

I told the rest of my family, "Go on without me; I have to go back to seminary," as they left for the reception at Ed's. No one coaxed me to come with them, and nothing was said. They knew I would feel uneasy among them. The last thing I wanted to do was pretend that we were a normal grieving family.

After everyone had driven away, I approached the funeral director. "May I watch?" He agreed, and David and I stood close by the deep hole, watching as they eased the gray box down and then maneuvered the huge cement slab cover, lowering it slowly over the vault until it clanged into place. Sealed. Shut. He could never get out. I sighed.

"May I throw in the first dirt?" I asked. The director obliged. I picked up a mixture of wet dirt and clay, an ugly brown color, in my bare hand. A broken piece dropped onto my taupe high heels. Vigorously, I cast it on top of the vault. *Splat!* I grabbed more. *Splat!* Again. Again. Mud thrown on the remains of my father, as in a country outhouse. I said nothing.

The gravediggers lingered cautiously at a distance, behind the trees of the spacious, well-kept cemetery. I didn't care what they saw or what they thought. I just threw mud and anger until I was tired and satisfied.

I walked a few feet over to my mother's flat marker, lifting the fake grass to see it. *Jeanne Thorsen.* "You didn't do your job, Mom," I said sadly, and I turned away. I chose a few day lilies and white roses from among those at the graveside and walked to the car.

David and I took the flowers to my house. I changed into comfortable clothes, and we went for a malt. Then I went to class, as announced, and gave my assigned report for the day. I was forty-four years old.

34

SURROGATE

A year passed. Dan had completed his first year of college, and Andy would soon be a high school senior. My work at the big church was demanding but filled with new learning. After the funeral, I had a few therapy appointments and was recovering from the intensity of Dad's death and the Lenten memories. I walked around the lake from time to time to relax.

One summer day the air was hot and humid, and the lake was very low. We had waited for rain for ten days. The grass turned yellow and brown in spots, and its fresh scent disappeared into dry air. I looked for traces of dew in the morning, reassurance that the plants could take in at least a minimum of lifesaving water. There was only a hint of moisture on the blades, already at risk of being evaporated by the early morning sun and lost again to the soil.

By noon I felt a change in the air. It was heavy, and clouds were developing into an impenetrable gray cover. There was an ominous silence. My whole body grew tense. Internally, my arms pushed against boulders of air, piled one upon another, weighing my spirits and body down. Trapped in low barometric pressure, I wanted to scream, *Set me free, rain! Please break this tension. I cannot tolerate it anymore. Rain!*

Then, at four o'clock, the rains came. Hard. Driving. The drops splashed on the pavement, forming streams, running along the curbs and sidewalk, spilling over onto the thirsty grass. I took a deep breath and walked outside.

Cleansing rain released my body from its prison. My hands and shoulders relaxed. My face was no longer taut. The air was crisp, the smell of wet grass sweet. Drops of rain, resting on the slender blades, captured rainbows with the gradual return of sun.

I drew in air again, closing my eyes. Even on an urban street I smelled the fragrance of clover. The world was quiet and relaxed.

Then, like the weight of air before rain, I began to stir inside, knowing something was wrong. A memory was coming. *Will it ever end?*

I told myself that perhaps I didn't need to remember. Dad was dead. I was safe. But the argument didn't hold. I needed to know. I heard the Chordettes in my head, singing "Mr. Sandman." I called Chris.

I settled uneasily into my chair.

"I know I'm close to remembering something," I told Chris. I paused and dropped my voice. "I want it to be over. I dread knowing."

I shifted my stocking feet and rubbed them across the floor over and over, unable to ignite the flame. "I've got to go back there. I have to face it. We lived in the old farmhouse then. I hear the Chordettes singing in my mind." I closed my eyes and began to talk slowly, hesitating.

> I'm fifteen. Dad is traveling. There's a man staying at our house. Dad hired him, and he's living here while he refinishes our basement. It will have birch-paneled walls covering the coarse rock in one large and one small room, and there will be tile floors and white fiberboard ceilings. It will take him six weeks.
>
> My math assignment is hard. I sit on the living room couch and close my eyes so I can concentrate on the problems and avoid the television noise. It's early winter, so it's dark before five, and I have a floor lamp beside me so I can see to do my work. I'm sitting close to where the chimney passes through the room so I can feel warm. Years ago there was a black metal heat grate in the middle of the room where the air blew up from the basement. These days we have a forced-

air furnace, and Mom covered the grate with an area rug.
Sheri and Eddie are on the floor across the room from me,
watching some cartoon program. They don't have homework
at their young age.

I'm feeling hungry as the smell of meatloaf supper drifts
into the living room. From the kitchen I can hear Mom and
Stan, the carpenter, talking. He has a sort of whiny voice.
My dad has a name for Stan: the Frenchman. Stan has a lot
of wavy gray hair and a long face with fat cheeks. He's old,
maybe sixty. He's been living with us for weeks already,
sleeping in Eddie's room. He's doing a nice job, but he's sort
of a boring person. I avoid him.

Mom's tired after working at the telephone switchboard at
the office all day. As usual, Stan has been hanging around,
watching her fix dinner and talking. He rattles on in his
annoying monotone voice. She told me she gets tired of
listening to him. It's a long time to have an extra person in
the house. I can hear Mom filling the coffeepot with rushing
warm water. I'm sure she doesn't feel like entertaining a
guest after a long day at work. The old farmhouse kitchen is
toasty warm, but the end of the breakfast bar where Stan is
waiting is cluttered with papers, and everyone has left their
wet boots in the entrance by the back door.

"Sherri, haven't you finished setting the table yet?" Mother
implores.

I look up from my homework as Sherri gradually gets up,
her eyes still fixed on the television program as she slowly
walks out of the room. The silverware rattles, and she sets
the plates around the round oak dining table. Within five
minutes she's back in front of the set.

"Sherri? What about the drinking glasses? And two coffee
cups?" Mother's voice is impatient. "Never mind, I'll do it
myself." Mom loudly sets the glasses on the table. I turn back

to my homework. Algebra is still hard for me since I changed schools.

Mom's calling me this time. "Judie Marie, can you come here for a minute?" Her voice is more gentle, the way she usually talks. I tuck my pencil into my open book with a sigh and stack it with my papers on the seat of the davenport. I didn't change clothes after school, so I smooth out my skirt before I get up. The kids are still glued to the television, which catches my attention for a moment. I leave the light on and walk through the dining room toward the kitchen. Last summer Mom and Great Aunt Ida put new wallpaper in the dining room. It feels as if we are finally improving the old house, and Mom loves it.

I stand in the wide opening leading to the kitchen. The big room is bright. The breakfast bar overlooks the stove and counters; behind its tall chairs are the doors to the basement, the closet, and the staircase up to our bedrooms. The ceiling is high. Mom is still wearing her brown polka-dot work dress and low heels, covered with a half apron that she embroidered when we were at the resort where her company let us vacation for a week the previous summer. She opens the oven door and slides out the baked potatoes, using hot pads for protection. She takes one of the long, sharp metal skewers that she uses to tie up a turkey and stabs the potatoes to test them—steam hisses into the room. Mom doesn't look at me, but I see Stan across the room near the basement and closet doors, standing there, smiling.

"You need to go upstairs with Stan," Mom says. Her voice is unemotional and detached. She is busy with the open oven, looking down as the heat escapes into the room. Out of the corner of my eye I see Stan move from the shadows toward the stairs to our second floor, and I take a small, involuntary step back into the dining room, back toward my waiting math assignment.

"Go ahead now," Mom tells me in a coaxing, quiet voice as she turns away to do some dishes in the sink.

I'm trying to think of reasons why Mom would say I should go upstairs with Stan. He doesn't do any carpentry up there, and it's just three bedrooms and a bathroom on that floor. My legs are weak, and I feel shaky inside. The room seems suddenly dim and cold as I stand, unmoving.

"Judie Marie." That's her expectation voice. She clinks the dishes in the sink as the water runs for rinsing, her back turned to me.

I start very slowly toward the stairs, hardly noting the pile of boots near the door. Stan moves to the side, as if to usher me ahead of him at the first stair. I twist a little to the left to avoid his touch. I'm looking down at my white Keds as I lift my foot onto the first stair. I take another step, then another. Each lift of my leg feels heavy, and I feel Stan behind me, too close. The cartoon music from the living room fades and disappears.

We go to Eddie's bedroom, where Stan sleeps. It's a small room, and the mahogany double bed takes up most of the room, except for a tall, dark bookcase. The room is painted dull yellow, and the light is dim.

Stan sweeps his hand forward to point me toward the bed. He is smiling. "Here is a good spot for us. Climb onto your brother's bed."

My brother. This is his room. There are his guitar and his ribbons from the all-school field day last spring. He won the dash. Neither Mom nor Dad came to the field day, but Eddie was so proud of his blue ribbon.

Now I feel Stan's hands on my waist, steering me toward the bed. I put my knee on the mattress and slowly get on top of the gold rib cord bedspread. The light dims even more, until I can hardly see the blue ribbon. I wish I didn't have a skirt on. Stan reaches to move me so that I'm lying down, and I turn my face away from him and toward the wall. I'm so close to the wall I can feel its coolness near my face. The bed squeaks, and he crawls over beside me. *I wonder if Eddie can win again this spring. Everyone was happy when he showed off his ribbon.*

Mom is starting to make a lot of noise in the kitchen. Pots and pans are banging together, and I hear the kitchen radio playing. Stan moves my skirt up and strips down my panties as I hold my breath. He zips his pants open. His hands are big and clumsy, even for a carpenter. Suddenly I feel something touching my legs—it's him. It's moving and touches my skin. I shiver all over. Oh God! I'm trapped!

He turns me so his face is right in front of mine. I squeeze my eyes closed tight—I can't stand his looks. I don't remember that this has happened to me before. He's pushing in. I'm afraid I'll get sick all over the bed. I see our school colors on the pennant on the wall by the dresser—purple and white. I hear Mother, in my heart, telling me, *Don't fight. Just go along when you are in danger.* I won't hear his grunting noises; I will just hear the kitchen noises and the radio playing WCCO. *I won't remember this.*

I opened my eyes and took a drink of water. I paused and looked at Chris. "That was so ugly."

"Stay with the moment for a while, Judie. What are you feeling?"

"I don't know. Disgusted, I guess. What an awful thing to do," I said.

"Notice how *you* feel. Not just about Stan. How do *you* feel about what happened to you?" Chris's voice was gently urging me. "How about *your* emotions?"

I couldn't feel any emotions—no anger or fear or disgust. I was afraid to know what I truly felt. My feelings were drifting away, displaced by my questions. "What makes a man do something like that? Doesn't he have any feelings for somebody else?" I was protecting myself from the depth

of the pain and transferring over to my intellect. It was my habit, sidestep-
ping the pain by analyzing.

"Try again, Judie. How did you feel when he was coming at you and
assaulting you?"

My throat choked tight, and stinging tears hurt my eyes. "I felt lost. No
one cared. I was a piece of . . . shit."

Chris paused, as if to let me steady myself. I had allowed my feelings as
far out as I could for that day. I was afraid of falling apart.

Chris spoke. "Some people—like Stan—don't have empathy. And some
men don't respect the feelings or dignity of women. They use women."

We talked a while longer as my tattered emotions tried to reassemble
themselves. Then I headed home, saying confidently, "I'll see you next
week."

"Try to stay with your feelings. Let yourself go into those painful spaces," Chris said. "It will help you heal."

Andy needed a ride to band practice that afternoon, so I tucked my emotions away and involved myself in a discussion of his activities at school.
I hoped Andy would never have such ugly youthful memories to plumb.

During the week that followed, I felt distracted and on edge at work. I
didn't tell anyone about the assault. I could scarcely believe what had happened to me that night in our own home. With a stranger. Then, toward
the end of the week, just before I went to therapy, I began to wonder, *What
about Mother?*

I was relieved to return to the safety of Chris's presence. "I didn't say
much about my mom last week, did I?"

"Not much. What did you feel and think during the week?" he asked.

I started to cry immediately. "I love my mother. I can hardly stand to
think about her deserting me like that. Letting that creepy man do that
to me—no, not just *letting him. Sending* me upstairs with him! She *knew*
what lay ahead for me." A mask of tragedy spread over my face, my cheeks
and mouth bending downward, my eyes nearly closing, as thick heavy
tears of loss rolled down.

"You felt close to your mother." Chris's voice was sympathetic.

"She played with me when I was small. She used to say she waited to do her ironing at night so she could play with us during the day." I rubbed the arms of the chair, pressing hard against the wood. "She had a gentle voice, you know. And she didn't have a lot of self-confidence. I used to feel sort of sorry for her. Dad was a jerk, and she tried to please people, and we never had enough money. The smallest things would please her, like that display rack for her spoon collection that she bought for the dining room. It started to make the house look like a real nice house, decorated and everything." I caught my breath and blew my nose. Chris was silent.

"She was a good person . . ." I nodded as I said it, but then I paused.

In a harsh voice, I continued. "But she *wasn't* a good person. She hit me that time when Eva came to be with Dad, and she gave up in New Orleans. Gave up! I had to struggle on, and she gave up! I was the one who went upstairs with Stan!" A guttural scream gathered as I called out, *"She made me take her place!"*

I sobbed, my body shaking. Then I ran to Chris, kneeled, and put my face in my folded arms on his knees, sobbing. He didn't push me away but gently touched my head, patting my hair. I cried and cried, and he gave me a tissue. Finally, I rose slowly and returned to my chair. In her weakness, my mother had abandoned me. But in that moment of reality, I had met the pain of my truth, and I survived.

35

BETRAYAL

It was three weeks later. For two therapy appointments I had cried and tried to reason out the evening when Stan ruined me.

"You are not ruined. He assaulted you, but you are a whole, good person," Chris asserted. I was slow to believe him. I felt like a dirty rag.

The next appointment I had a nagging feeling, like barbed wire raking over my whole body. "I think there's more to tell about Stan," I said reluctantly. I took off my shoes, and I felt Chris covering a deep sigh.

"When the rec room was finished, Stan left for Ohio. Six weeks went by. I got a B+ on my math test, and Eddie started playing hockey. As always, we had Sunday dinners at Grandma Libby's house. Mom bought a copper chafing dish for the center of the round table. I was tired of winter, and February was cloudy."

I closed my eyes. Something was coming back.

It's Monday afternoon. I'm sitting at the breakfast bar, doing some spelling words for English. I hear Mom come home from work, and cold air splashes into the kitchen as she closes the heavy back door. She slips out of her boots and sets them on the boot tray as I push my papers aside. She is still in her old gray storm coat with its big fuzzy collar. She walks across the room to the kitchen counter and puts down a small bag of groceries. My heart is hammering as she stands there, not noticing me.

"Mom."

"Oh, I didn't see you."

I try not to mumble. But I have to say something. I have to tell . . .

"I have a problem."

She pauses, then walks over behind me to hang up her coat in the closet with the rifles. "What kind of problem?"

The room feels as if it's caving in, and I stiffen up. Those rifles are behind me. My mouth is dry.

"I didn't get my period."

Mom stands still for a moment, looking out the side window. The room is silent. The tall chair where I sit feels unstable, rocky.

"Are you sure?"

"Positive."

She sits down beside me, looking straight ahead at the stove. "How late?"

"Over two weeks." Desperation floods my brain. "Mom, I'm always right on time. I'm *sure*." I cross closed fists over my chest, my eyes looking down, my voice barely audible: "It was Stan."

I glance a little to my left at her, but Mother isn't looking my way. She sits, sodden and silent as after a downpour.

"Mom?"

"Let me think about it."

I can't wait. "Mom. What'll I do? Where can I go? Is there some place I could stay for . . . until . . . Where can I go?" I'm panicky and scared. It's as if electricity is filling the room.

My voice rises. "Maybe I could go to the Carpenter farm for a while."

Her words are curt. "Judie Marie, I just have to think about it. We'll figure out something."

My mind repeats, *We'll figure out something.* I long to believe her words are a reassuring promise, but her silence chokes my hope. *Just give her time to think of a solution.*

I turn from the bar and slowly retreat up to my bedroom. The echoing stairway leads to the dark brown tiles of a hallway wide with emptiness. Sherri isn't home, so I sit alone on the bed in our room, immovable. The late-day traffic on the wet street outside the window passes to destinations unknown. I lean to the side, fall onto my pillow, and cry. Where can I go until summer? Where can I hide?

It's Wednesday now, and Dad is coming home today. I got only a C on my history test this week, and Mother and I said nothing more about my future. The days are cloudy, and the sidewalks are messy with melting snow. My Keds got wet when I walked home from school—I had to tip-toe along the edge of a big puddle—so I put them on the oven door to dry when I get home. While the shoes are drying, I make myself a snack of graham crackers in a bowl with milk—comfort food. I just hope Mom doesn't say anything about my situation to Dad when he gets home. He might get mad at me. Maybe Mom and I can figure out a solution before we tell him.

I take my bowl to the sink when I hear him coming onto the back porch. I catch my breath and bite my lower lip. He opens the back door, letting the cold air in, suitcase in hand. He has left his sample cases in the car. "Home again," he calls to the house.

I take my now-dry shoes off the oven door and turn off the stove. "Hi, Dad." I look up at him. He's starting to get a little more bald these days, and he's still a lot taller than me. I'm up to Mom now at five-seven, but he's six-two and strong, about 210 pounds. He expects me to go to college, and when I get Bs in school, he says I should aim for As. I know for a fact he never finished his first year of college and didn't do very well in classes in high school either.

"How was school this week?" he asks me.

"Just regular," I reply in a disinterested tone. I slip into my shoes. "My feet got wet on the way home from school."

"You have to be more careful." Dad is always teaching us something—tips for driving, how to make dumplings, where to shop for the "best" meat. He starts upstairs with his simulated oxblood leather suitcase. I remember how, when I was little, I used to love to find all the little hotel soaps in his luggage after he returned home. The soaps were just the right size for my small hands. Right now I need something to be busy with when he comes back downstairs. I'll go down to the basement and iron a skirt to wear to school tomorrow.

"Go get my sample cases and put them on the back porch," he says. I figure by the time I do that and iron my skirt, Mom should be home, and I won't have to talk much to Dad.

We have supper at the round oak table, but no one says much. Dad corrects Sherri's English and reminds Eddie to say thank you to Mom for a good dinner. The acorn squash is good, and since Dad is home, we had a bigger meal of chuck roast and potatoes and carrots. Sometimes when he's gone we just have some eggs and bacon or maybe a hot dish. Dad doesn't like hot dishes much. The kids go into the living room to watch television while I help clear away the dishes. As soon as possible I get busy doing homework, and at about eight o'clock Dad dishes up ice cream for everyone to eat in front of the TV. Even Mom comes in for some ice cream. When I finish my homework, I watch one program and then go to bed early, when the kids do. So far nothing has been said about my problem, but I lie awake for a while, wondering what Mom and Dad are talking about downstairs. Will she tell him? Won't she? The lights from passing cars flash across the ceiling of Sherri's and my room—light, dark, light, dark.

The next day is Thursday. I leave early for school because I have an extra choir rehearsal, so I don't talk to Mom, and Dad is sleeping in after his long road trip. I am distracted by my classwork during the morning. I watch the kids in the lunch room, and everybody seems carefree. They don't know what it's like to have a serious decision to make. I can't tell any of my Girl Scout friends. They like me, but they would be appalled. What would all the kids think of me if they knew?

After school Eddie has Cub Scouts in the grade school gym. Sherri has gone for an overnight to her friend Alice's. I'm surprised when Mother comes home early from work. She hardly ever does that, but with Dad home she probably got off early for the weekend. I'm upstairs in my room with the door closed, half-changed from my school clothes, so I'm wearing my slip. I'm startled when Mom comes into my bedroom. "I need to have you come to Eddie's room." She turns and walks down the hallway.

At last the silence is broken. I take a big sigh. Probably she has a plan. I start to follow her toward Eddie's room, but then I freeze—I hear Dad cough his thick cigarette cough. He's up here; he's in Eddie's room. My mind races. Maybe they've come up with an idea about what we can do. Maybe I could go to somebody's house in the country. Or Milwaukee. I'll go into the room to find out what they've planned. I walk across the hall.

Going back into Eddie's room brings bad feelings. His ribbons are still there, and the room is as dull as ever. The light is dim, and I hear some noisy sparrows scolding in the window under the eaves.

Dad is sitting on the side of the bed, and Mom sits at the foot, her face turned away from me, her hands in her lap. "Did you want me?" I ask, looking at Mom. My voice is very weak, and I feel my abdomen cramping.

Dad sounds annoyed. "I want you to lie down on that bed, that's what I want," Mother says nothing. I reach to support myself on the door jamb.

He points at the bed and starts to move in my direction. "Lie down."

He's mad at me all right. I promptly move to the bed and kneel on the mattress, slowly collapsing onto the surface where a large bath towel is spread.

"Now go ahead and do it," Dad orders Mother. For a moment I can hear nothing, nothing. Just a menacing silence. Then waves of silent screams fill my head.

I can see Mother reaching down to take something from a basket on the floor. It's her knitting basket, and she takes out one of her metal needles, about nine inches long and pointed at both ends. Instantly I pull my knees toward my shoulders and turn away.

"Try to hold still," she says gently as she moves my slip upward and starts to pull my legs straight. I resist, but fear of pain eases my muscles, and I let go.

"Mom!" is all I can say, my voice trailing into a pit of betrayal, keeping wary eyes on Dad, who stands near the closet door, watching.

She spreads my legs. My body goes rigid. I try to wriggle away, and Dad moves in my direction as she holds my ankle firmly. *My God, I'm alone. Who will save me? Am I going to faint?* I open my mouth, but my voice is mute.

She pulls down my underwear, and I see her right hand holding the long needle moving toward me. I close my eyes and block out the pain, the excruciating pain of invasion. I gasp. Whatever happens, I won't make a sound. I won't let them hear me scream. I almost faint from the agony and weakness.

Now she is finished and pulls away from me. I kick at her—my foot lands hard on her arm as she moves away. How can you do this to me?

My thoughts scream. *Mother, I promise you: I will live, and you will die!*

Dad says nothing and leaves the room. I hear his heavy step on the stairs to the kitchen. Mother moves over and gently helps me sit up on the edge of the bed. I'm bleeding. "We need to take you to the bathroom," she says. "We'll run some warm bathwater." She goes to the bathroom to start the water and returns with an old towel.

I am immensely tired and weak. I can only take small steps, and I lean on Mom as she helps me walk into the bathroom. I sit on the closed toilet seat, folded over, as she runs warm water into the tub, and then she helps me get in. I look at her, questions in my eyes, but we do not speak. The water is both comforting and painful. A while later, Mom dries me carefully and helps me into pajamas and a pad. Then she leads me to my bed, and I carefully sit, then lie down.

"Try to sleep," she tells me. She turns out the overhead light as twilight begins to fill the room. I do not hear the family at dinner; I sleep until I hear Sherri enter in the dark and get ready for bed. She moves quietly so that she doesn't disturb me.

The next day when I get up Sherri asks, "Are you done with your flu?"

"Yes," I say and get ready to go to school. I feel sore and stiff, but I block it all from my mind. It's too much pain to remember and still be a cheerful girl. I forget it.

The office was completely quiet. I slowly regained my sense of presence. I began to cry gently.

"No wonder I didn't want to remember," I said in a broken voice.

All my supports were gone from beneath me. I had friends and sons. I had successes and honors. But I had no parents anymore.

"I had no mother," I said gently. "No mother at all."

I looked up. Tears filled Chris's eyes.

36

EXPLOSION

I felt weak driving home and for days afterward. I couldn't shake the terror and crushing disappointment. I was used to managing my father's violations, but this—this took hold of me by the ankles and cast me, splayed, onto rock-hard ground.

For the first few days I had phantom pain in my uterus. My mind returned to the old farmhouse: the dark brown vinyl tiles upstairs and the small, crowded bedroom where my brother slept, dimly lit. I revisited the bathroom tucked under the eaves, with a large mirror above the sink that Dad had bought and overlaid on the small medicine chest. I didn't want to look into any mirror. I was weighed down by the reality of the deeds and struggled to believe that perhaps it wasn't true.

It was true.

I debriefed with Chris three times. First, in despair: "She never loved me at all. She didn't care." I wept without hope, my brain swirling with grief. Still, I felt her arms gently guiding me into the warm water.

"It's so confusing! She hurt me and then comforted me," I wept.

Then I was furious! "Mother, how could you do that? Your own child! You didn't stand up for me. You let—no, you *did* that terrible thing. And you carried on as if it hadn't happened. No wonder you died young!" I found a photo of her and tore it into bits, and then I stamped on them.

Before the third time, I came home from work, weary. I dragged my feet as I climbed the stairs to my bedroom. The bedroom windows were covered with white sheers and tie-back curtains in a green forest print.

The mint-green walls were fresh and relaxing. The room was quiet and private, a woodland.

Sitting on the bed was my doll in her navy blue dress, pigtails, and lace collar. I'd been caring for her for years—taking care of myself through her image. Today I was exhausted as I moved her over to a side chair. "You sit over here now, Judie Marie. I'll move you back later." I adjusted her braids gently and then lay down on top of the kelly-green rib cord bedspread.

Lying there, I couldn't close my eyes. The white ceiling fan was still, but I felt like my agitated head was whirring round and round.

The image of my gentle mother filled my mind. She who had tended me when I was sick and home from school. Mother, who had been our primary parent in long, lonely times. How could it be? *How could you have done that to me?* Pain suddenly stabbed through my abdomen, and I rolled into a fetal position, pulling the bedspread into chaotic wrinkles. I cried quietly, hoping I might go to sleep.

Suddenly I was consumed with an overwhelming energy. In fury, I searched for a weapon. I bounded from the bed, tripping over my shoes on the floor, and went to the side closet. I dug behind the clothes hanging there for my covered, oversize tennis racket—something to hit with. I jerked it out with all my strength, and shoes and boxes tumbled about the closet floor. Then I stamped over to the bed.

"Mother! Why did you do that? How *could* you?" I beat the bed with the tennis racket, plunging it into the covers and mattress with all my power.

"I was helpless!" I yelled. Again I struck the bed. "You were an adult!" Finally, tears released. *Wham! Wham!*

"That Stan was a pig! How could you let him do that?" I gagged.

"You abandoned me—sent me upstairs at dinnertime. Left me in New Orleans. Punished *me* for discovering Dad and Eva! And now this." I beat the bed with each word. "I—could've—died!

"Why couldn't I go to the farm or something? Hide myself?"

Then the whole room shrunk into my brother's small bedroom and suffocated me. I was trapped, in memory, with my parents in the room.

Wham! The racket struck the bed. I cried out, "Pain! It hurt so much! Didn't you *know that?*" Red anger flashed throughout the bedroom.

Again and again and again I hit the bed, sometimes growling, sometimes crying out, "Angry! I'm furious! Take this!" *Wham!*

Was it five minutes? Three? Ten? Whatever the duration, I finally dropped the racket and fell forward onto the bed in sobs. "How could you? Why didn't . . . why didn't you take care of me?" I pleaded. I wrapped myself in the bedspread and cried until I fell asleep.

An hour later I woke up and slowly got off the bed. I told my doll, "I'm sorry, Judie Marie. I'm sorry you had to see all that. I'm all right now. And so are you." I straightened the spread and put her in her usual spot on the pillow. Then I went downstairs in my stocking feet, fixed a light supper, and, after a hot bath, went back to bed.

When I shared the tennis racket event with Chris, I brought an old 78-rpm record of "It Had to Be You."

"This was Mother's favorite song. She hummed it all the time. Do you know the words?" I asked.

"Probably you'll have to remind me," he said, sounding a bit apologetic.

I straightened up in the chair and said, "Well, it starts out like a lot of love songs, 'blue' and 'true' and all that. But then it begins to change.

"The singer says she's not attracted to the men who are never mean or bossy or cross. She loves this man despite his faults and even if he makes her feel blue or sad."

I began to trace the maroon center of the record roughly with my finger. Then I grabbed the record and shook it at Chris.

"What kind of thinking is that?" I demanded. "Happy to be sad? Glad to feel hurt as long as it's by him?"

He nodded in response.

"So the song says that when someone continually hurts you, and you love him even more, it's a sign that your love for him is true." I stared at Chris. "She *chose him* over me. She *chose* him!"

I took the record in both hands and smashed it into the carpet. Pieces shattered all over the room—on the desk, at my feet, as far away as the door.

"Oh!" I gasped. "I'm sorry! I've made a mess." I leaned forward to clean up the pieces, but Chris raised a hand.

"Wait. Wait for a moment. Let yourself be angry."

"But—" I stammered.

"You have taught yourself to bury your anger. Let that power out of you. Let it fly! You have good reason to be angry."

"But I've made a mess of your office," I said.

"Finding and releasing your anger is more important. I'll pick it up later."

I shook my head back and forth. "I'm not used to doing this."

"I know," he said. "You've been the recipient of anger, but like all human beings you have your own feelings—fury, anger, disgust, fear, joy. All of those feelings are part of you. You've separated feelings from each other in order to maintain control of dangerous situations, but you are entitled to your anger."

I sat for a moment, looking at his bookshelves but not seeing them. The words repeated in my mind: *You have your own feelings.* It was as if someone had opened a window shade and let sun into the room.

"I have feelings too," I murmured.

"Yes, and you deserve to feel them without apology."

It was true! In a way I had never known before, I could breathe fully, blocking nothing, not measuring the reaction of others or judging my feelings as good or bad. Free! Alive!

"Nearly fifty years old and I've never known that," I mused. "Thank you."

"You're growing and changing every day. You're a strong woman, Judie."

I smiled faintly, weary of anger expressed and new lessons for life. "I guess I'd better go. But I'd like to clean up—"

"No," he said. "You have done nothing wrong. You don't have to clean up anything."

Still hesitant, I rose and started toward the door.

"Thank you. I'm really quite amazed by all this," I said. Chris smiled. My fists tightened. "And I still say, she *chose* him over me."

To this very day there is a tall glass bottle with a royal blue cap in my linen closet. I saved it after Mom died. I liked the smell of the Nivea lotion, and she sighed with pleasure when Grandma Trina rubbed it over her back, arms, and legs. The oil has separated and gone to the top of the nicely crafted bottle, and occasionally I open it to smell the sweet, smooth fragrance of its contents.

I held in tension for years the competing experiences of Mother. She brought me roses the night of the class play and helped me buy my formal for the 1956 junior–senior prom, which cost all of twelve dollars. Yet I had the more buried remembrances of being robbed of my dignity and pregnancy by that very same person. I had repressed the painful memories in order to sustain my life, but now I had to face her duplicity.

How does that happen? How could she be both persons? What was at stake?

A few months after raging with the tennis racket, I attended a party in my old high school neighborhood. Our next-door neighbors, the Halvorsons, were there. I hadn't seen them in years and was happy to reconnect. I sat beside Paula, the mother of the family.

Cautiously, I mentioned that there had been abuse in our home. "Dad didn't treat us very well, you know," I said, and vaguely described how he had browbeaten Sherri and Ed and molested me.

Paula was a practical and pleasant person, a strawberry blonde who had taken time to talk with me when I was in high school and college.

"I had no idea. I feel terrible that we didn't realize what was going on," she said.

I was quick to say, "You tried to help, even without knowing. Remember how, after Mom died, you helped Sherri with homework three days a week after school?"

Paula nodded.

"I knew I would have been safe at your house if I needed to come."

I reflected on how a friend of the Halvorsons' daughter, Pat, had stayed with them during her senior year when her own family was unstable. The sweet, modest stucco home was a haven.

Paula paused, her eyes sincere. "You know, one of your mother's friends—I don't know her name—told me that your mother refused to let your father come in the hospital room when she was dying. She wanted only a friend. The woman told me she thought your mother was angry with your dad and rejecting him."

My eyes opened wide, and I caught a surprised breath. "Really?"

Pat, listening nearby, added, "I think your Grandma Libby was in tremendous denial. To her, your dad was like a prince. Maybe that made things harder for your mom."

Their words were unexpected and jarring. "Do you think you can remember which friend it was who stayed with Mom when she died?" I asked.

Nearly thirty years had passed. Neither of them knew who it had been or even what she had looked like.

Our mothers are so deeply woven into us that we cannot separate our selves from them. Mother carried herself stiffly; so do her daughters. Sherri and I do not relax our arms at our sides but hold them stiff, often with the right arm bent in front of us, hand dropped at the wrist and hanging loose. We aren't comfortable with our bodies. Who might be looking at us?

We learn who we are from mothers. Mine welcomed her father into our home when we first moved there so he could build us a staircase. He chewed "snoose" and spit into a coffee can, saying, "Everything is copacetic," whatever that meant. Mom was polite and indulgent with this man who had abandoned his family and never carried his weight. *I guess men are like that*, I reasoned. *Women have to adapt to their ways.*

How grateful I was for the women who held me and listened and *believed* me. Karen and Joan and Koinonia friends. I struggled with the slap in the face that was women who found ways to deny or forget my pain, who overlooked my fears and pretended that life is fair or that (if you pray enough) bad things either don't happen or go away, leaving me clinging to a feeble branch of a birch tree blowing in the wind.

It all began to form a picture of how we women forsake ourselves in order to have safety or avoid shame or be "loved." I am one of them: cautious with my own anger as I exclaim with admiration to those women who speak their truth, "Did you really say that out loud?" Little by little, I grow more confident to do the same. Still, it is the ones who embraced my pain and led me through the wilderness whom I cherish, even though others let me down.

At Eric's first congregation there were some very distinguished women, often monied and with proper skills of entertaining and decorating. I watched them, eager to learn how to best appoint a home. Edna was one of those. She had a large house that always showcased special seasonal touches: a pheasant-feather wreath in fall, fresh forsythia in a vase in the spring. I spent twenty dollars—an inordinate amount of money for us—on wood candlesticks for the mantel of our first rental home, just to match hers. A member of the congregation gave each pastor's wife a beautiful table centerpiece in my favorite colors of blue and silver. I kept it for years and years.

These were things my mother would not have known much about. She worked to match colors and make do with small amounts of money, but she wasn't sophisticated. When I inherited special household decorations she purchased, I carried them from home to home, even after they were worn. The tarnished copper chafing dish—wasn't it still nice? *It was Mom's.* I still have glass highball swizzle sticks that I've never used, and her Fiestaware soup bowl and pitcher. I keep them in an attempt to catch a glimpse of her in happy moments, profoundly aware that I also felt abandoned, and I cling to the fragments of her love, however scattered they are.

In the years that have followed, I have come to be at peace with Mother's weakness. She had been bruised with depression and worn down by hopelessness. She wasn't capable of being all that we dreamed a good mother would be. But she was proud when I directed the choir, and she played in the snow with me when I was small. She did the best she could, and then she died.

Let her go.

37

CRIMES

The quiet days of autumn calmed me as I tried to put into perspective my memories and feelings about Mother and Dad. In winter I saw Chris when I was haunted by the images of Stan in our farmhouse kitchen, but my usual February malaise did not come. Spring awakened the earth, and I looked for ways to feel renewed, especially outdoors. Mowed grass and damp ground were sweet, and the fragile new growth on the late-blooming locust tree caught my attention. In a few weeks it would be a lacy shade over the backyard. I breathed deep, content.

I checked the transplanted rhizomes of the deep purple irises that we had brought from the parsonage when we moved to the city. They were a bit weak, needing some richer soil to flourish. But the tiny shoots of the clematis were pushing up, looking for something to cling to. I wound them around the white trellis that leaned on the house, satisfied to give them an anchor. Quite soon I could plant the annuals along the fence and in the front by the windows. I loved the yard work, the flowers.

Then I heard a whisper in my mind. It was my voice saying, *You'll never have a good relationship with a man. It's never going to happen. You'll always be alone.*

It had happened before. When Roberta Flack sang "Jesse." When I watched the kindergartners perform in the school program and ached as they grew into older children. The feeling crept across my chest and came to rest like a stone in my throat. Loss.

I don't know how to be with a man. I'm afraid of them. I desire their company and long for their support, but I'll never be desirable in their eyes. Dad didn't love me, and I've been tainted by all those ugly moments, those wicked men, those women who didn't protest and help. I am alone, and I always will be.

I rose slowly from beside the flower bed and made my way to the back door. The yellow kitchen felt cool and clean. I took off my muddy shoes and walked slowly, pondering, into the living room.

The silence of the empty room was deafening. The records alongside the phonograph drew my attention, and I sat on the floor to go through the stack of vinyl. I slipped *Johnny Mathis Hits* out of its cover and put it on the turntable.

I'll never be like the women men are attracted to. I can't walk in that saucy way that Jan does, swinging my hips. She told me men like that, but I just can't do it. I don't dare.

I have so much baggage; no one will want to take a chance on me. Probably ministry is the best choice. Men are cautious around women clergy; they think we're not sexual or that we judge others or are like big sisters. They'll leave me alone. That's maybe what's supposed to happen. Being alone.

I collapsed on the carpet into my folded arms and wept. The spring air grew heavy and close. *It will never happen. I can't overcome my past.*

Two days later I went out to the backyard, where lilies of the valley grew along the foundation of the house, alongside wild violets. The fragrance of the lilies and the subdued, fragile beauty of the violets were my favorite confirmation of spring. They grew wild against the dark earth. Birds splashed in the birdbath, and the air was mellow.

I gathered enough flowers to fill three empty pill-bottle vases. The purple and white blossoms, encircled in green leaves, were a sweet bouquet. As I did each spring, I wanted to deliver one each to Don Juel at school and an elderly neighbor and keep one for myself. I set them on the kitchen table and began arranging them. Sunlight from the south window warmed the yellow room.

My thoughts returned to the Big House with its hill of wild violets, and I heard the music of "Peg o' My Heart" by the Harmonicats. It had been popular in 1947, when we lived in that mysterious house by the lake. As

I began to hum the song, my mind took a sharp left turn: Dad standing, blocking the kitchen door so I couldn't squeeze past him.

"What was *wrong* with Dad?" I said aloud to no one. "What made him like that?"

Alcohol had been my solution to the question for years. The way he wavered, arriving home from the Cozy Bar. The way he crashed down onto an easy chair, almost tipping over, when he was intoxicated. His sneaking out for drinks or inviting drinking buddies home for a beer. *Why did I ever believe he would stop?* I wondered.

In the middle of putting flowers into the small bottles, I stopped. I heard nothing but a ringing in my ears. I dropped the fragrant bouquet onto the kitchen table and looked up to the ceiling in wonder, as if some spirit were there ready to hear me.

"He was never drunk!" I said. I sat down. I went back over the years. The only time Dad was drinking during sexual abuse was on the Northside, when Mom came home and he left me alone. He was never drunk when he assaulted me. Not at any of the houses. Not with Eva, not with Vern and Earl. All through my high school years he didn't drink. Not at the hotel or New Orleans. Not anywhere. Not ever. Alcohol *wasn't* the cause of the attacks. Maybe, in fact, it was the remedy, the way he forgot.

I delivered one of the vases to Don Juel. I told him what I had realized. His slim, expressive face, framed by black hair, stretched and contorted as he said, "That's monstrous."

I straightened up, surprised. "Why was Dad's *not* being drunk monstrous?"

"Because," my loyal friend said, "he knew what he was doing."

"That makes it worse," I said. Tears filled my eyes, And I tried to distract myself by looking at his dark wood shelves full of books. "He must have hated me."

"That may not be true," Don reassured me. "But he was a sick man."

As I drove back home that afternoon, traffic jammed ahead of me and I took a wrong turn in a familiar neighborhood. I was confused. My mind called out, *On purpose! He did it on purpose. Where does that leave me?*

I called to make an appointment with Chris.

I walked into the therapy office resolutely and chose a different chair from the usual one.

"I figured out something," I said. "My dad seldom assaulted me when he was drinking. He was sober."

Chris looked intensely at me. "You're sure?"

"Absolutely. I've thought through all of my memories so far. Except for the Northside, when nothing happened because Mom came home, he was always sober. All the years from junior high through high school he didn't drink at all."

"I'm surprised. But it's possible."

"What in the world was wrong with him?" I asked. "How do you describe his behavior?"

Chris shook his head slowly, looking at the floor. "It's not that I don't know, but there are so many things."

I looked around at his framed degrees and certifications. "It sure would help me to know a cause. To have some sort of label. I know you can't just categorize people. But there must be something I can hang onto. I've been walking around lately, thinking he hated me, and it's an awful feeling."

"Your dad was an alcoholic and a narcissist."

I nodded my head. That made sense. "You, you, you!" I had yelled on the day I confronted the poster of him. It was always about him and his need to be important.

"He was also a sociopath."

"A what?"

"A sociopath. It's a complex diagnosis, but some of the characteristics are a grandiose sense of self and superficial charm and glibness. As I've listened to you describe your dad, I've heard his incapacity for love and his lack of shame or remorse or even guilt."

I sat for a moment, looking at his tidy desk. "He had no sense of commitment or predictability, did he? Just a phony bragger."

Chris continued, "When a sociopath feels exposed for having no ego, no self, he or she will do anything to regain a sense of self, to fill his emptiness, to prove he or she exists."

"It was like he had to swallow up my mom and everyone else to fill his emptiness." I pressed my fingers into my cheeks. "And he lied. He arranged all those terrible assaults on purpose and lied to us all." I shook my head. I couldn't emotionally absorb all I had heard, but I imprinted it on my mind.

Then I added, "I wonder if he remembered what happened?"

"We will never know. But he was clearly able to plan and execute his crimes."

"Crimes?"

"It was a crime what he did to you. It was violent assault. He made illegal arrangements."

I shuddered. "You know, sometimes I just can't even believe it all happened."

"I know. It's outside our normal behaviors and lives. And you repressed for so long that it's hard to recover its reality."

I hastened to say, with a sad sigh, "It's true, though. I'd like to shout the name of every one of those nasty men to the world. And my dad didn't really love any of us, either. He expected to be waited on. He *used* everyone."

"Does it help to give a name to the personality disorders?"

I took a deep breath. "It does. It helps me get a handle on stuff. It doesn't change anything, of course."

"You've handled all this with grace and strength," he said, looking directly at me.

I looked away, caught myself avoiding direct communication, and looked back at him. "I do feel like I'm getting better."

"There are many people in the world who aren't capable of doing what you've done."

"Really?"

"Many. They carry their buried memories or even their remembered events for years and years without getting free. Some never tell anyone."

"That's sad. I'm grateful."

"Your gratitude is how I know you're strong." He smiled.
I returned his smile and said softly, "Thank you so much."

38

AFTER DAD

If we live long enough, we may discern how the fabric of our lives was woven. A person, with us at an early time in life, disappears, only to return to add color to the pattern in another moment of life. One thread is woven with another. Experiences create slubs in otherwise fine threads. The fabric's design forms over time, and on rare occasion we see it all— the whole story. So it was with me. In the years following Dad's death, strands of past experiences wove themselves into a fabric of understanding. One moment overlapped a remnant from another time, and a new design emerged. I collected and saved those new understandings as they opened my life to fresh awareness.

I began to realize that just as memories do not return chronologically, they also never go away. After time and talking, a person thrown about in a tornado feels the dread of another storm subside. But the memory of the trauma stays. We are changed.

The morning of Danny's birth, I awakened at ten in the morning. I had started contractions. Due date! Right on time. After checking with the doctor's office, I called Eric.

Excited and focused, I said, "It's time to go to the hospital."

"I'm supposed to do the closing of the children's program. Can I come after that? I can be there within an hour."

My brow furrowed, but I agreed. *Should I insist on an immediate response?* An hour later he picked me up. We drove through downtown as my contractions came about every five minutes. We talked about how we would inform our parents and reviewed our carefully laid plans for the hours ahead. When we pulled in under the sheltered entrance of the hospital about noon, the weather was eighty degrees and rising. Eric dropped me off, and I walked across the lobby to the check-in desk.

The people at the desk did not notice me until I pointed out that I was in labor. Immediately I was thrust into a wheelchair in my red paisley cotton dress, and an attendant pushed it into an elevator full of curious people who stared at me, perhaps terrified I would deliver on the spot.

Eric joined me after registering me at the admissions office. We followed well-taught procedures of breathing and coaching. The process seemed natural and not unusually painful. I lay looking out a window at the hot summer world. Between contractions I gazed at that scene, a low hospital addition surrounded by trees and grass, and contemplated that the world out there had no idea what a momentous thing was happening to us.

After more than an hour, the nurse said kindly, "You have a big baby. Things are going slowly. We're going to have to break your water in order for you to deliver."

I looked at Eric, unsure of what would come next.

She reached for some sort of instrument from the shelf behind her. I strained to see it, but I was distracted by another nurse adjusting my hospital gown. "Spread your legs a little more, Judie."

I did as I was told but stiffened. I looked around the room, surveying the white walls and the nearby washroom, everything smelling of antiseptic. A thread of terror came over me, beginning with my throat and moving into my stomach and arms.

"This will only take a moment," the first nurse said. Tense, I watched her coming toward me with a long, needle-like instrument. She had a kindly face, but I stared intently at her arm and the glove on her hand, moving toward me. I took a deep breath and turned my head away.

Then I panicked.

"No!" I resisted and twisted away.

"Hold still, Judie," they cautioned gently. Eric squeezed my hand.

Eyes wide, I wanted to kick at someone—hard! I was terrified.

"There," she said. "All done."

There was nothing to it really. No pain. Just my pure terror. I was embarrassed to have been so resistant and afraid.

It was years before past and present connected. I had seen a large needle coming at me once before, when I was fifteen and helpless. The image was embedded in my memory, and it emerged eleven years later in that hospital room, releasing my terror once again. Fortunately, this time people cared for me.

In similar fashion, during a time when I was working on unearthing a series of memories, I heard, "What did they take?" A group of work colleagues were gathered at two of the large round tables in the Sunday school room. One of the secretaries had been robbed the night before while she was gone from her condo.

"Not much, really," the woman said. "I think someone must have scared them off."

We were a church staff of thirty-five, a mixture of support staff and leaders, attractive young women, busy working mothers, middle-aged and wizened older men. It was my first assignment after seminary graduation. Coffee times at ten and three were sometimes raucous, always crowded. I got my cup of tea and approached the tables. It was a year after Dad died, and I had adapted to my new role as pastor. I listened to the group.

"Did they get your jewelry?"

"Fortunately I don't have much jewelry, or money either," said the secretary, a natural blonde with crystal-blue eyes. "Mostly they just messed up my drawers, searching." Everyone winced.

"I feel . . ." She paused. "So violated."

It was an unexpected jolt to my composure. *Violated*, I thought. *You don't* know *violated*.

Of course, I understood her use of the word and her feelings. Someone had ransacked her room. But *violated* was something I knew most intimately. These were days when I hated my life and none of them knew. I straightened my spine and set my jaw. To them I looked accomplished and strong: the first woman pastor at the largest Lutheran church in America. No doubt it appeared that I had an easy life. I couldn't muster sympathy for anyone that day. I was self-absorbed. I left as soon as I could without drawing attention to myself.

Back in my office, I muttered to myself, "Violated, indeed. Try going to a hotel with a strange man. Try fighting off your father when you're in junior high." I sat heavily in my desk chair and reached for a pencil.

You don't know *violated,* I thought. The pencil broke in my hands.

I looked out the window at pine trees and the creek. I thought about my days at seminary when the tempest of memories spilled over. In those days I had caught myself walking by that same creek, closer to home, and wondering whether I would die young. Had I been on the verge of giving up?

Certainly the spate of memories had shaken how I looked at life. I was keenly aware of abuse issues. Soon after my ordination, when I was new at the congregation, I visited a friend in Boston for a week and took some time to tour the city alone one day. In a fall of blue skies and unseasonably warm temperatures, the day was sunny. In a pedestrian shopping area downtown, people in college T-shirts and cut-offs were walking, shopping, and admiring the colorful leaves that unfolded around us like a circular fan. I sat for a moment on a bent wood bench, taking in the activity in contentment.

A young girl walked by. She was tall and shapely, with long blonde hair, wearing a very tight and short white miniskirt. Her blue top was skin tight and cut low. I stared at her as she walked up the cobblestone street, as I'm sure others did. She wore high-heeled sandals and an ankle bracelet. She uneasily glanced behind herself now and then.

Five yards behind her walked a man: young, with a thin, dark beard, carrying a large ring of keys in his hand. He swung the keys carelessly, watching the girl—or was she a woman?—as she nervously progressed down the brown pavers. I was overcome with anxiety. I looked more carefully at her face, her stunning, worried face, as she glanced back at the man every few steps. My breath grew weak, and I felt queasy. A street-walker. A prostitute and her pimp. It shook me to my core, and my cheeks fell in sympathy and fear. I knew that look on her face. She was trapped. And scared.

I couldn't take my eyes off her, riveted by the unspoken story in her long-legged saunter. Then she was lost in the crowd, and I leaned forward on the bench to hide my tears. There was no one to help her. How often had she been violated?

I had learned that girls who have been sexually abused often learn that being cared for requires them to allow violation. "Do you like me, Dad-dy?" When the child is hungry for love, attention feels good in any form, from any adult. If sexual gratification is a requirement for love, a girl can grow up craving attention and sometimes become skillful at attracting men, even at the expense of breaking boundaries. Or she might grow up angry with men or unwilling to trust them. What was the streetwalker's story?

A week before the robbery of the secretary's home, I had time to read the newspaper before I left for work. One headline caught my immediate attention: "Johns Caught by Undercover Women Police Officers." That was a switch. The news was usually about "bad" women being arrest-ed for prostitution and the men getting away scot-free. I straightened the newspaper in my hands and paused to think. I rationalized, maybe being a prostitute isn't necessarily bad. It can be a good thing. You make men happy by doing that.

My eyes opened wide, and I flattened the newspaper into my lap. What in the world was I thinking? That being a prostitute is a caring service to men? Why would I think something like that? I crushed the paper in my hands.

Sitting in my church office, I realized I had thought of myself as a ser-vant of men. Jezebel. It was one way to ease the pain of being violated. I longed to feel clean and healed from my traumas. To believe it wasn't my fault. That the violation was the work of others, not me.

I stared out the window at the pine boughs, where blue jays squawked with worry, protecting their nest from potential predators. A purple film seemed to shade the windows. Would I ever be truly well? Would it ever make sense? Would the strands at the ragged edges ever weave together?

In the early days after Dad died, some people were aware that I wasn't grieving. A church woman who knew Dad had been a cruel person asked whether I had forgiven him. (I never did like her.) Her faith was paper thin, and she pinched it into spitballs to throw at people who thought differently than she.

"If he's forgivable, that's God's job," I said. I didn't carry bitterness toward him. Or disabling anger. All I knew was I had never felt safe in his presence, and some of that guardedness remained even after he died. I continued therapy—though less often—to maintain my healing.

In some cases, I found that I had unwittingly created my own healing. After the shame of exposure on a couch and the fierce pain of the attic incident, I'd had to repress my memories, but still I sought a companion or a model to give me hope. I had always found inspiration in biographies about national leaders when they were children. Perhaps I could be like them someday.

No book had captivated me as much as *Caddie Woodlawn*, the story of a pioneer Wisconsin girl. In Wisconsin, my fourth grade teacher read the book to our class after lunch each day. When my family left Wisconsin and moved to the Northside, I longed for something familiar and a quiet place where I felt safe. I found it in the library only four blocks from home, a tall red sandstone building with a turret and curved windows. My shoes clicked gently as I walked over to the east corner, where upper-elementary books were shelved alongside a large fireplace. And there she was! Caddie! I checked out the book again and again.

In sixth grade I wrote to Carol Ryrie Brink, the author of Caddie's story and Caddie's granddaughter. My eyes opened wide when she sent me a personal reply with her picture on it, handwritten with a fountain pen. I save it in my documents box even now.

Bewildered as I sometimes was after we left Wisconsin, Caddie gave me hope. *If only I might have a good father and be a free, strong, brave girl.* Caddie stood up to unrighteous adults. She cared for those who were left

behind. She fought the school bully. While my life was oppressed by igno-
rance and anger, she was a model of independence. Through Caddie, I
read myself into another reality.

After Dad died, I found a copy of the book, with its original sketches,
and read it again. Even as an adult I was engaged by the true stories of this
young girl. So, on a fall day, I drove two hours to the preservation site near
Durand, Wisconsin, where Caddie had lived.

The country road wound among rivers and farm fields and stories.
I entered the preservation park on a rough gravel road that crunched
beneath my tires. I was as close to Caddie as the ground and trees around
me.

Just beyond stood a huge white sign, perhaps ten feet wide, explaining
who Caddie had been. I read it carefully.

> On this site during the Civil War Caroline Augusta
> Woodhouse, known throughout the world as "Caddie
> Woodlawn," experienced the excitement of growing
> up in pioneer Wisconsin. Her tomboy adventures with
> her two red-headed brothers, and her fearless trust in
> the Indians who lived nearby, were faithfully recorded
> by her granddaughter Carol Ryrie Brink in her book
> *Caddie Woodlawn* and in its sequel, *Magical Melons*.
>
> In 1935 *Caddie Woodlawn* received the coveted
> Newbery Award Medal as "The most distinguished
> children's book of the year."

The words of the sign blurred as I burst into tears. Kind Wisconsin oaks by
the park entrance were sentinels, protecting me. Their leaves and branches looked wavy as grateful tears flooded my eyes. "Thank you, Caddie, for
helping me survive," I said. Another strand of life was woven into place in
my story. Caddie had survived. So had I.

39

PROTECTION

The sun shone, and temperatures were warm. I put on a light jacket and went for a walk around Lake Harriet. From the bird sanctuary came the sounds of singers of spring. I breathed deep as I walked. I had come to think of it as my lake: familiar, welcoming, waiting for summer sailors and band concerts, and safe.

Relaxed in the uplifting beauty of flowering trees in early spring, I stopped at a park bench to rest. Looking out over the lake, I pondered that I had been a pastor for nearly seven years. Andy was traveling in Hungary. Dan was married and teaching, living in New Jersey. Then I cocked my head to the right and thought, *Why, it's spring! I hardly noticed February!* No depression. No creeping cynicism or self-doubt, no days of beating myself up with defeated attitudes.

A woman with her dog passed by, and we nodded. Her dog was about the same size as Mindee, our brown terrier of almost twenty pounds. She had been a sweet dog, often left inside all day because our schedules were busy, and thrilled when we came home, where she waited at the back door, her tail and whole body wagging wildly. Her loss was still fresh.

Just the previous week I had taken Mindee for a walk. She pranced along on her white feet and sniffed fences and hedges with her black nose. We meandered up and down blocks and turned toward home through a paved alley a block away. The garages were well constructed and flanked by flower beds showing the first signs of rebirth. The lilac bushes were blooming; the air was fragrant.

Suddenly from a backyard tore a barking black shepherd-rottweiler. He was after Mindee. He skidded to a stop on the sandy pavement, and I rose to her defense. I stepped between them and beat at the eighty-pound aggressor with the end of Mindee's lightweight red leash. It was a whirl of vicious attack, sand, and concrete.

"Stop!" I yelled. Then I realized I also was in danger and ceased beating the dog. In a flash he grabbed Mindee's neck, shook her right out of the leash, and carried her into his backyard beyond the fence.

"Help!" I screamed. "Stop! Let her go!" I pursued them toward the yard, and as I reached the entrance I was joined by a tall, handsome, dark-haired young man who had been driving past with his wife. They were on the way to a movie, and, hearing my calls for help through the open window, he had dashed from their car to answer.

"We heard you yelling. Let me help!" Tears staining my face, I pointed into the yard.

There he found Mindee where the monster dog had dropped her. The man picked her up, without any sign of resistance from the big dog, and we stepped back into the alleyway just as a car drove up.

"Here's my wife," the man said. "We'll drive you to the emergency vet."

The owner of the enemy dog came to the door. "We're going for help," I shouted to him. He had no time to respond. In moments we were in the car; I held Mindee close, wrapped in their car blanket, eyes open and motionless, but breathing. The stranger took the wheel, and his wife climbed into the backseat and leaned forward to comfort us.

"The vet is open on Saturdays," she said.

As the car sped over to the freeway, we introduced ourselves and discovered we lived two blocks apart. I was shaky, comforting Mindee with soft words and petting her head. In ten minutes we were at our destination, leaving a trail of gravel dust behind us as the car stopped and the man and I raced inside. His wife was allergic to cats, so she couldn't come in.

Behind us, she called, "I'll drive over to tell my parents what's going on. They're waiting for us at the movie theater. It's right across the highway from here."

The veterinarian met us in the front office. He was about forty years old, wearing a traditional white coat, with a gentle way about him. He peered through his glasses, and his brow wrinkled as he nodded his head. He took Mindee in his arms and set her on the counter and examined her carefully. Seeing my anxious face, he said, "I can assure you, she doesn't feel any pain. Her neck is broken. That's how rottweilers attack enemies."

"Is there anything we can do?" I asked.

"I'm afraid not," he said.

I turned to the young man. He put an arm around my shoulders and said, "I'm sorry."

As tears rolled down my cheeks, and in the presence of a kind stranger, the veterinarian put down our pet of twelve years by injection. Mindee never moved, her eyes open in trust.

"She's gone," he said.

"Already?" I murmured.

In a stupor, I signed papers and wrote a check. The clinic would take care of burial.

"Thank you," I said to the doctor, whose face was filled with sympathy. We walked out and found the man's wife waiting for us in the car. I couldn't think of much to say, so I asked about them. They were waiting to adopt a child.

The couple drove me home, and I walked into the house in a daze. The whole world seemed hushed, as if everyone were watching me. No happy dog came to the door to greet me. She was gone. My tears trailed across the threshold into the living room.

I poured a glass of water in the kitchen and stared mindlessly out the back window at our fenced, empty yard.

The phone rang, startling me. It was a neighbor worried for his children. He expressed sympathy but suggested something must be done about the other dog. I was too stunned to say much, but I agreed that he could talk to the owners. He and others promptly took action to see that the attack dog would also be put down.

Still weak and numb, I lay down on the couch and replayed the events. I couldn't sleep.

Gradually there rose in me an unexpected wave of confidence and relief. Mindee was gone. But someone had come to assist me. There was rescue from violence and darkness. Unlike many other times when I was attacked, this time I hadn't been alone. Someone—a stranger—cared.

And I had yelled for help! I had screamed in the midst of danger. I wasn't silent anymore, as I'd had to be in my childhood. I had defeated Dad once again.

Several years later, another broken thread rejoined the whole. I was hurting. Little by little my left knee had deteriorated. It became a challenge to climb stairs, even just the height of a curb. I walked less and less and developed a strange gait that protected my left leg and back from pain. After consultation with a good surgeon, I had a knee replacement.

After the surgery, I had high expectations of being out and about soon. I had heard stories of people capable of walking around the lake after a month's time—no doubt I would be doing so as well. It would be early summer, when I enjoyed being outdoors. It was my usual head-down-in-a-storm approach. Faithfully I did my exercises at the rehab center, but confidence and exercise weren't enough to stretch my constricted muscles back to where they belonged. Despite good work in the physical therapy gym, movement meant pain, and I was discouraged. When I headed home after sixteen days in rehab, I was certainly not ready to walk outdoors. For the first few days, Ed's wife, Marty, brought me meals and offered her company and assistance.

I sank into a mild depression reminiscent of my days in therapy.

Getting around was complicated and awkward. Each day was cloudy, and I longed for sunshine. My muscles resisted the exercises. I was weepy. My whole world felt hopeless, and I couldn't think of how to help myself feel better.

I tried to maintain a friendly, positive disposition. I knew I had to get some help. I went to my physician and sat in her office, crying. I could do nothing else. She immediately prescribed a mild antidepressant. Gradual-ly that low spirit disappeared.

Still, I made very slow progress on regaining muscle strength and heal-ing. Bending my leg or lifting it to climb stairs was very difficult.

My physical therapist, Sarah, encouraged me and helped me build con-fidence. She also gave considerable thought to my situation and conclud-ed that electrical stimulation would coax my tight muscles to release and recover. For twenty minutes each session, small bursts of electricity jolted my muscles, loosening them so I could be flexible again.

"Some people have this problem," Sarah said with a compassionate smile. "I call those muscles 'hedgehogs.' They curl up against a painful enemy and won't let go."

Of course! I thought. *She's right. My muscles have learned to curl up and protect themselves from invasion.* It was an old habit, learned while I was still young and in danger. My body and soul turned inward to protect me.

I had a flash of me running to the closet above the Wauwatosa stairway to hide, scrambling among the shoeboxes and a folded wood laundry rack and sitting very still, trying not to breathe. Hiding. Daddy gave up look-ing. My muscles curled up against invasion.

It was like that for years. My past invaded my present. A tangle of memories would be triggered by an event or a comment. Some led me back to therapy. Others just rang a bell, like a tavern pinball machine as each ball finds its own hole in which to drop. Over and over I realized, *So that's why I felt that way! That goes back to when I was young.* Thread by thread I wove a fabric of understanding and liberation.

40

SELF-DOUBT

It was election time. Upwards of a thousand people had gathered in the gym auditorium of Gustavus Adolphus College to choose a new bishop to lead the Minneapolis Area Synod.

These were familiar halls, for I had spent a beautiful hoarfrost winter semester there, as the interim chaplain of the college, just two years earlier, months after Mindee's death. Over half of those crowding the gym were laypeople, representing some 150 synod congregations. A constant murmur moved across the crowd as people greeted old friends or chatted over a cup of coffee or bottle of water in the back. But when it came time for nominations and speeches and forums, people hurried to take their places. Tension rose, and all eyes were on the front platform. Quiet prevailed.

A group of urban pastors from both Minneapolis and St. Paul had asked me if I would allow them to put my name forward for Minneapolis bishop as a way to champion urban ministry needs. I agreed that I could take that risk, knowing it was unlikely to go further.

On Friday morning, the screens up front revealed the names of around forty nominees, some "favorite sons" of their congregations, others well known for their leadership of large congregations, some popular for their interest in the synod as a whole. As the names appeared on the list in order of votes received, I discovered my name in the top ten. The urban pastors had successfully coalesced, and I would soon be giving a three-minute speech. In anticipation of the unlikely, I had memorized a short message. My mouth went dry.

Do I look all right? I had worn my favorite, comfortable sapphire-blue suit with a small vase, holding live lilies of the valley on the lapel. *Will what I prepared make sense?* I was going to focus on the future and on collegial leadership. I was a good speaker, I knew that. *But a thousand people?* We drew numbers, and I was among the first three to speak. At the end of the speeches, five names appeared on the screens. I was a finalist!

Friends and members of the congregations came to wish me well. I basked in their affirmation until I realized this could turn into more than I planned for. My competitive juices began to flow, accompanied by a slight tremor in my whole countenance. *What if . . .*

Things began to take shape in the afternoon open forum. The four men with me on the dais were accomplished leaders, all of them senior pastors and one the incumbent bishop. The audience submitted questions, and they weren't easy. "Where do you stand on gay/lesbian rights?" "How do you think the synod can be more effective?" "How does the contrast of city and suburb affect this unusually large synod?" I spoke to that last question immediately.

Near the end, a more personal question: "What is your greatest difficulty or weakness, and how do you handle it?" The audience was quiet as each pastor spoke of vulnerability. I knew what I would say. What about the others? Each man spoke in deflected ways. "My wife tells me . . ." "Probably people would say that . . ." It looked to me as if the men involved had trouble acknowledging their own weaknesses. Did they suppose they should always look strong and capable? Especially in an election?

My turn. I spoke with ease. "My greatest weakness is self-doubt. I second-guess my decisions, and I wonder if I'm capable of meeting a challenge. The way I manage that is by having friends and colleagues around me who can keep my thinking level. I've been part of a small group of men and women for over fifteen years. I can tell them the truth, and they help me get perspective on ideas and actions. I suppose the self-doubt never goes away, but I have good support to get through it."

After this hour of intense thinking, people voted for their candidate. I joined my friend Shirley in the visitor section of the bleachers.

"You were wonderful," she said.

As one might expect, I was doubting. "I don't know about that question about our weaknesses. I probably blew it. Isn't a leader supposed to look strong?"

"No," she asserted. "That was a perfect answer. *Everyone* understands self-doubt. They'll all identify with you!"

I smiled.

She went on. "Do you see who's sitting over here?"

There, to my surprise, was Andy. She had brought him down to hear the speeches that afternoon. He grinned at me and in his understated way said, "Great job, Mom." Tears welled in my eyes. (A day later, after the whole event had ended, I would receive a voicemail message from him: "The assembly was thrilling. I could feel the Spirit in the whole place.")

Still waiting for the results of the voting, I left Andy to make my way to my place on the assembly floor with our congregation delegates. I was immersed in congratulations and support.

"May I have your attention," the vice president of the assembly called. "No one has reached the necessary 50 percent of votes yet. We have three candidates remaining." They were the incumbent bishop, a senior pastor close to retirement, and *me*. With an amazed murmur, the assembly applauded. The rest would wait until the next day—Saturday. I walked over to the magnificent chapel with its modern vaulted walls and sat down, stunned. I hadn't planned on this outcome. Was I up to the job? I leaned my arms and head on the pew ahead of me and wept.

That night, I went upstairs to the room where I was staying, leaving my hosts and many other friends to celebrate downstairs. I began to write a short speech. In the rooms below, the phone rang again and again with congratulations from across the country. Had I known, I would have been shocked.

Sleep came slowly that night and was interrupted by wakeful periods and a cluttered mind. In the morning I went to the college cafeteria, where a kind urban pastor friend listened to me prattle on with nervous excitement. He wisely did not advise or direct. He listened.

Then the hour of final speeches came. There were three of us, and I drew number one. Each of us spoke briefly. Would anyone reach 50 percent? The numbers were flashed on the board. Two top candidates remained: the incumbent and me.

The outcome lay outside my input now. I had said my piece and offered my vision. After another vote, the bishop had 52 percent and I had 48 percent. Twenty-five votes separated us.

After celebrating the bishop's victory, I was called to the stage to cheers and applause. I saw a friend on the sidelines in tears. I was thrilled. We had not yet elected a woman as bishop, but we had a good start.

I was exhilarated. I had taken on an unexpected challenge, and, without winning, I had achieved my own victory. I had spoken my truth and confessed my own self-doubt. Friends and colleagues rose to support me, lifting me past my tears and reluctance. I had taken hold of life and *lived* it fully. I did not fail. I had once been a bruised reed, but I did not break.

41

THE DEER HEAD

A s years passed, I weathered changes. Danny survived Hodgkin's disease, a form of cancer. I ate too much chocolate that year but got through. Andy graduated from Harvard and spent a year in Budapest. I traveled to Africa and Europe, and spent a semester at Harvard on a fellowship. Life was full as I entered my sixties, healthy with the exception of detached retinas.

At sixty-eight, I moved cautiously on the stairs, following my five-year-old grand-nephew Jake as he scooted down the stairs in his stocking feet as fast as he could without falling, chatting all the way. I smiled at Jake's enthusiasm. We had left the big birthday party upstairs when I asked him to show me the remodeling his father, Scott, had done in the basement. Scott was Ed's oldest child. As I carefully made my way down the stairs, I just barely heard Jake proclaim, "My daddy got it in Montana."

Oh. My feet stopped. Silence fell over the stairway. I felt weak all over. Scott loved to hunt with his dad. There had been comments about a recent successful hunt. There must be a deer head down there. I had never mastered my phobia.

Jake was jumping up and down, waiting for me at the foot of the stairs. I couldn't turn around and disappoint him. With dread I slowly continued. *I can handle this. It won't last forever. I just have to figure out where the deer head is so I won't be too shocked.*

As I reached the base of the stairs, Jake ran across the room, feet flying. He climbed on the hearth's foot-high white brick border and proudly gave a big hug to his daddy's deer head, which hung at adult eye level. I felt sick, but I smiled. Jake looked so happy. I stared at him as he did something I could not imagine myself ever doing.

As each of Ed's sons and grandsons reached puberty, Ed took them on a bonding and coming-of-age trip. To my relief, Ed never had a head stuffed and hung on the wall. Scott, on the other hand, was less close to my pain, and when he shot the twelve-point buck with nearly interlocking antlers, he proudly had it made into a trophy for their basement family room.

"Show me the laundry room remodeling, Jake," I said. Jake hurried over to show me the new tile floors and fresh cabinets.

"Very nice," I said. "Your daddy did a good job." Then we turned to go upstairs. I made a point of looking straight ahead as we passed by the deer head again on the way to the stairs. I couldn't tolerate it looking at me. I couldn't wait to get away from it.

I rejoined the party. "I'm so sorry," Scott said as he came over to me in the living room. "That wasn't supposed to happen."

"Thanks," I said, grateful for his consideration. "Jake didn't realize—I asked him to show me the laundry room." Scott gave me a half squeeze and rejoined the crowd.

Shame rises up from deep smoldering coals. I couldn't "grow up" about deer heads and trophies. I hid my fear, hoping not to be discovered, but I scanned the walls of recreation rooms and dance halls and even movie theaters, hoping to not be surprised by dark animal eyes staring at me.

I decided then and there I wanted to beat this thing. *If a five-year-old can be at ease with a hunting trophy, so can I.* Jake was small, but he knew he was safe. Surely I could be like him.

I called Chris. Years had passed since my spate of memories and the trauma I had overcome, and I no longer went to him for regular therapy. Now he shared with me a new technique called EMDR: eye movement desensitization and reprocessing.

"What it means is that the traumatic memories that are captured in the limbic portion of the brain can be desensitized and reprocessed so that the trauma disappears," he explained. "I'm not trained to do it, but I know someone who is."

I met the EMDR therapist, Pam, a small woman with a flair for interesting, flowing clothes. As is customary, we reviewed my sordid past and the thread of personal successes woven into the story.

"I think I can help you with that," Pam said. "Your traumas have been kept vivid in a part of your brain, but after twenty years of study we now know it can be relieved. Would you like to try?"

I took a deep breath, shaking my head from side to side. "I've got to give it a try. Nothing else has worked."

"What have you tried before?"

I explained that forcing myself to be around or even to touch deer heads had not solved the terror. Not even the Thunderbird confrontations.

"Often exposure methods don't work," she said. "This may be better."

I went home and read about EMDR, then called Pam for an appointment. We worked together for around six months. First we conversed about my traumas. Then Pam set up a two-foot rod that showed a moving line of green dots, the line first moving left and then returning to the right. She handed me two quarter-size pads. After I reviewed a memory aloud, concentrating fully, I watched the dots move as the pads created a gentle buzzing electrical sensation in my hands. Back and forth my eyes moved. Back and forth. Some days, through a headset, I listened to tones that sounded in sync with the lights. Back, *beep*. Forth, *beep*. Back, *beep*. Forth, *beep*. My mind gradually desensitized itself to those jolts of terror I experienced when I saw the animals. Bit by bit, I was reprocessing the pain until I could handle it again.

To discern whether it had been effective, I needed a way to test my progress. I found some time to talk privately with Scott's wife, Jennifer. Though we are a generation apart, we have always communicated well, and she understood my fears. I explained my EMDR therapy and said, "I'd like to come over and test out whether I can truly feel safe and normal around Scott's deer head. Without saying anything to anyone else, how about if I arrange a little family party where I can come over and find out if I can feel safe? Would you be willing to help me do that?"

"Of course! That's a great idea," she said, smiling. We made a plan for after Christmas.

It took place on a very cold, clear January night. We called it our After-Christmas Party, since we had been too busy to get together in December. My body was tense as I drove the four miles to their nice suburban house. I brought an ice cream party cake.

Jake was excited to show me their new Ping-Pong table. Two of the children missed out, but Ed and Marty came. Only Jennifer knew what was up. Dread sneaked in like a ghost. *Will my whole body quake as usual when I see the deer? Will the children discover my fear and think me foolish? What if I reflexively turn away and have to go elsewhere? What will everyone think of me?*

I chattered nervously as I went downstairs behind Jennifer. After the last stair I took a deep breath and forced myself to look to the right, straight at the deer.

Nothing. I felt nothing. No fear. No jolt of surprise. No anxiety. There was simply a deer hanging there, and it seemed as if I had interrupted its grazing in a meadow and it had turned to welcome me calmly. A friend.

I gave Jennifer a secret smile and turned away to relax my body. Then I joined Jake and Scott by the Ping-Pong table. A few moments later, I returned to the spot where the deer head and I could look at each other. I had no feelings of terror or even upset. The EMDR had worked!

After a few moments of visiting with Marty and Jennifer, I remembered that no one else had any idea that this had been a major test for me. Everyone was busy with activities and conversation. The deer head was simply decoration. I went to Ed and said, "Tell me about the deer." My stomach quavered with three-year-old fear.

"Oh sure," he said. "This one is a special deer. See how its antlers nearly touch in front? That's very rare. And there are twelve points. Very unusual." His comments seemed to me to be routine. He had no idea how important it was to me.

I spoke at last. "It's a darker brown than most. And sort of smooth. In a way it's sort of handsome." *Did I say that? I am an adult speaking, not a child.*

Ed smiled, and we walked over for some ice cream cake.

I knew for the first time, in my whole being, that the deer over the fireplace was dead. Those eyes weren't real or menacing. The deer couldn't think or plan to chase after me. For the first time in over sixty-five years, deer were my companions in the world, not my enemies.

The family went on with the party, playing Ping-Pong and Wii. But the evening had depleted me. I had no energy for small talk, and I felt like being alone. I said special thanks to Jennifer and left early, my brother accompanying me to the car on a calm, still night. The stars were brilliant, the moon full. As always, Ed wished me well. "Drive carefully," he said. He kissed my cheek. "Good to see you."

As I started toward home, I felt as if I had taken my first bike ride alone. I breathed deep and smiled. *How was I able to do that?* I turned away from their quiet neighborhood onto the highway. The sky was dark and calm. Watching the road ahead, my eyes misted. I succeeded because in that setting I had felt safe. I was loved. My family wanted the best for me. I had found Home.

42

TIME TO HEAL

The rows of the garden center were orderly but showed signs of weariness as summer came to a close. The skies were cloudy, and the remaining plants were dried out or overgrown in pots. Planting season was long past. It was time to move on.

Over seventy years old now, I was planning to return to the homes near Milwaukee where I had lived until I was ten. By age forty I had already visited each one to verify the accuracy of my memories from childhood. At each house I took my graph-paper house plans so that I could compare them with what I found when I stepped inside. It was satisfying: my child self had seen and remembered well.

I no longer needed to confirm my memories. I had wrestled with them again and again for fifteen years until, at last, I broke out with a fever of anger and tears and then began to bury them, one by one. Enough.

But what of the houses those memories occupied? Were they still poisoned by past terrors lurking in the walls? Was there a way I could cleanse the homes and release the bulky baggage that I had hauled through life into adulthood? Native Americans might correct the spirits of living spaces by smudging with burning sage wands. But I could not imagine entering those houses, now the haven of strangers, for such a ritual, refreshing and renewing as it might be. *Do you mind if I come into your house and burn sage to smudge out the negative memories here?* No, that would never work.

I decided to bring symbols of healing to my houses of trauma. I spent two hours online, searching for the meanings behind herbs and flowers.

Now, on a cloudy Friday afternoon, I walked the garden center's paths slowly, searching. First I saw aloe. Of course—the healer. I could cut the thin succulent stem and spread the moist balm on the hand of a toddler, burned over a stove's flame as a punishment for crying. I put a very small plant in my cart.

I went to the herb aisle. Rosemary branches, like soft pine needles on a stem, held a healing balm. I put the plant into my cart and reached for fragrant sage, the symbol of wisdom and immortality. Sage smelled like my Grandma Trina, who loved cooking and nourished me with gentle hands and kindness. It was scraggly but still fragrant enough to clear my sinuses.

A few steps farther and dill weed stretched out of its pot on long skinny stems, ready for canning time in the fall. Mother canned tomatoes and pickles at the Plainfield house. I breathed in the gentle scent, knowing I would need it at Plainfield because it is said to give power over evil.

Raindrops began to fall. I hurried to the peonies, favorites of Grandma Libby. How peculiar: they were named after the god of healing but were also an expression of both indignation and shame. I wasn't about to purchase a whole plant that had no blossoms and couldn't survive on my condo porch. So I looked side to side and surreptitiously pulled off dried petals and leaves, stuffing them into my jacket pocket. Then I headed inside to purchase my antidotes to fear.

Now, how to use them? At the craft store I found packages of two-by-three-inch white organza pouches, intended for jewelry or party favors. Each bag had a white ribbon drawstring. Those would do fine.

The next day I sat at the kitchen table with my herbs and flowers. I broke off pieces of each plant and put them in piles. Then, carefully, I put a portion from every pile into each organza bag and pulled the ribbon drawstrings tight. I made eight little bags, all smelling mostly like sage, and tucked them into a manila envelope for safekeeping.

My plan was to drive my granddaughter and her mother to Madison. The trip was calm and pleasant, with full sun and good roads. We arrived before dinner, and I left them with a welcoming family who had four daughters. They were going to have a good time.

Staying in a Madison hotel by myself was the first challenge. I had not yet overcome my self-conscious fear of being alone in a hotel, watched by strangers. New Orleans and the Curtis Hotel hovered over me. I was hungry, so I delayed settling into the hotel until after dinner. Then a crowd of students arrived in the lobby, easing my fears. *Nobody is going to pay attention to a seventy-five-year-old woman.* I went to my room and turned on my television set, aware that I had no fear. The hotel ghosts of my past were gone. In the morning, I knew that I was no more noticeable than anyone else in the breakfast room. I ate my waffle and headed for Milwaukee, eighty miles away.

The freeway from Madison to Milwaukee was constructed after the demolition of the railroad tracks that had bordered the back of our property at the Big House. The route east is trimmed with towns and lakes as it passes through rich glacial farm country. Many have American Indian names: Mukwonago, Oconomowoc, Waukesha, Pewaukee, and Milwaukee itself. The mid-August day was pleasantly warm. As I drove into the city, I saw familiar sites: the Miller brewery, the spacious waterfront. I realized the city had a lot of Old World architecture, unlike younger Minneapolis and St. Paul. I had my map beside me and headed for Shorewood, the once-substantial northern suburb.

I knew what the stucco Shorewood house looked like, sitting atop a small hill on the corner. Sandy and I had been welcomed by its current resident. I'd found it on a satellite picture map recently and recognized it immediately. But that day I had no intention of asking if I could go into the house. I wanted to say good-bye. Good-bye to the stained-glass windows in the living room and the pain of my small hand held over the stove flames.

I drove past the house, taking notice of the half dozen stairs carved into the front slope. *I can put the herb pouch in the grass if I sit on those stairs. I think I can look unobtrusive if I stop to tie my shoe.* I parked at the end of the block and, a bag of herbs tucked into my pocket, walked back to our first rental home and sat on the second stair. As I sat down, I grabbed hold of its inexpensive wrought-iron railing, which wobbled. I landed askew. *Did anyone see me do that?* I tied my shoes, something I could scarcely do when we lived there and I was four. Then I tucked the bag of herbs along the edge of the stairs, rose to look at the house—the shadow image of me, a small, dark-haired girl, gradually fading—and walked back to my car.

I drove around the block once, twice, looking at the neighborhood's assortment of brick and wood family homes in Craftsman, French Country, Tudor, and Dutch Colonial styles. I returned down the side street that passed our garage. It was not the old, shadowy garage of my childhood. It was double width, with a deck on top. At the corner, I turned left and drove away toward a busy thoroughfare. *Good-bye, House. I don't have to carry you in my heart anymore. I'm an adult now.*

I had traveled downtown Wisconsin Avenue with childlike wonder for decades. It was our connection between the city and the countryside to the west where we had lived. I had been intrigued by the large Tripoli Shrine Center, with its onion dome and colorful tiles. Two concrete camels rested on pedestals along the front stairs—*Look, Mom! The camels!* This day, a gray fog rose around me, seeping out from the mortar of nearby brick apartment houses, stealing my breath as my psyche slipped back to childlike vulnerability, and I turned the corner away from the camels.

Earl used to live near here. I'm not safe here. I had visited his downtown apartment once in the 1970s. I searched the street names as I drove past vacant stores and streets lined with cars. His block had been disrupted by highway renovations. *Today I choose not to search for his building. Earl is dead, long ago. Get out of my life, Earl.*

I headed west to Wauwatosa, a suburb where we had rented a double bungalow. The route began among small city businesses and old stores, homes close to the curb, and cement parking lots. It opened into increasing green spaces with trees and homes trimmed in Lannon stone. Vliet Street morphed into Milwaukee Avenue, and soon trees lined streets bearing names like Martha Washington Drive. With surprise I looked up, and there was the street I'd lived on during the polio-scare years.

Mother's voice echoed. *You're in kindergarten now. You must always tell the truth.* The names of playmates who walked with me to school passed through my memory: Judy, Mary Jo, Sheila, Susie, Barbara, Carol. One of their yards used to have clusters of brilliant zinnias. Most of the homes were wood. And then, there it was: a tall white house with two entrances. I slowed down to take a good look. We had lived on the left side. I'd visited there once as an adult, and it had looked just as I remembered. In the bungalow next door had lived a little girl who had genuine ballet toe shoes, and her daddy wore Old Spice from white bottles that we used to play house.

Now, as I slowed my car across the street, I saw that the living room window was open about six inches. The walk split into a Y as it approached the two entrances, and a nice garden had been planted in the space between them. *That's where I can put the healing herbs, if no one is looking.* The street seemed deserted.

I stopped the car and tucked a pouch into my hand, out of sight. *Who might see me? If I go into the yard, will they be suspicious?* I put on a confident air and walked up the sidewalk toward the flowers. When I reached into the garden, I grabbed a lavender aster and held it up as if I were examining it. As I touched its stem, I dropped the organza pouch. *Done! It will not be easily discovered.* I smiled to myself. I walked boldly back to the car. *If anyone questions me, I'll tell them a white lie.*

I couldn't resist one more ride around the block where we used to chant, "Step on a crack and break your mother's back," so I traveled down Milwaukee Avenue toward the village of Wauwatosa. I took the angled turn toward the shopping area and found a small French cafe where I could treat myself to lunch. I wanted to nourish my child self, now grown. Close by were the train tracks of the old Hiawatha Line, now Amtrak, which had carried me many times between Milwaukee and the Twin Cities. Often I had stretched my neck to catch a glimpse of quaint Wauwatosa. After a pleasant meal, I drove past my elementary school, which was across the street from the Lutheran church we had attended. It now had two pastors; one was a woman.

That sunny afternoon I retraced the railroad tracks that had become the I-94 freeway from Milwaukee to Madison to Minneapolis. I headed to the lake country west of Milwaukee. I had two more houses to visit.

My first stop was a small, upscale lake community called Delafield. I wanted to experience it anew, so I stopped for gas and drove through the area. When I was small, I had yearned to win a Kewpie doll with sparkles, preferably Snow White, at the annual firemen's carnival. Now the area is Firemen's Park, a green space with picnic tables and playground equipment.

The narrow road from Delafield wound alongside the freeway until it reached an area where Dad used to hang out. "Skid row" a friend had once called the strip of land between two lakes where people could land their boats and slake their thirst at one of the many taverns. Nearby was the channel where Dad had taken me to skate for the first time. The bridge between the two lakes was still there, running parallel to the freeway. I crossed it and drove past the Spanish-style home belonging to what we had called a "rich" family. Directly across the road had been a line of small houses, crowded with poor people; they had been destroyed to make way for the interstate.

The side road led me to a shallow beach on the south lake and, to the north, the open gravel area where the Big House had once stood. Time for a healing of the land.

I drove up beside the hill where we had once tried to plant tulips. I scarcely heard the passing freeway traffic above as I brought out a pouch of herbs and tossed it into the weeds and grasses of the hillside. *Good-bye to the loneliness. Good-bye to Dad's blurry eyes. Good-bye to an old run-down lake house. Give all of it new life with these plants.*

The hardest mission for the day remained. Plainfield—that makeshift home we constructed from an old cottage, with two picture windows that looked out on a lonely world—held power over me. What had people seen when they looked into those huge windows? What had we hidden there? A little girl lying naked on a couch? Adults exposing their bodies in sensuality and their pain in rage? I did not want to see inside the windows anymore.

I drove my small SUV toward the lake, where a large farm section had once stood, now encircled by a road and divided into lots. One nearby house looked tidy and white. At eight years old I had watched a man build it out of brown and black planks of used lumber on the weekends. I drove toward the bend in the road. I could see the lake lots on my left and, on my right, the house we had built and ruined.

Drat! As I reached the bend I saw a truck and trailer maneuvering back and forth into a lake-lot driveway. *What in the world should I do?* I paused the car, watching, and wondered how I could get my healing packet into the shrubbery near our old house without anyone noticing. Finally, the truck was secured in its place. *I'd better move ahead so they don't pay attention to me.*

I drove around the entire subdivision and back into the former farmland division. Once again I turned the bend and stiffened. Someone was across the road from our old house, mowing his backyard. *Now what? He might see me.*

I drove a short way farther. I couldn't go into the driveway toward our house. I would be too conspicuous, and the owners might be home. But I had to get that dill into the yard and bushes somehow. "Dill represents power over evil."

I stopped the car, a plan forming in my mind. *I'll pretend to be getting something from the trunk.* I picked up the pouch and pressed the button to open the back hatch. Then I climbed out and walked around in front of the car, keeping it between me and the man who was mowing. As I walked toward the back of the car, I tossed the pouch into the bushes. *Too close to the road! Do it again.* I picked it up and tossed it farther, hoping the man mowing the lawn wouldn't see.

Then I walked to the back of the SUV, lifted the hatch, and fussed with some supplies inside, looking busy. I looked at the yard around the house and heard the squeal of a butchered pig in my memory. Then I reached up high and slammed the trunk door. Closed. It was closed tight. Silence.

Dad, you shamed me and scared me. Mom, you put your own pain onto me. House, you do not have to carry those ugly memories anymore. I free you to be a happy family home.

And I drove away, headed to Minnesota and home.

I thought that finding places to tuck the healing pouches at our Minneapolis homes would be less emotional. I drove to the farmhouse and Parkland bungalow, feeling less conspicuous, probably because I had been in those neighborhoods more often and recently. Seeing no signs of life at the farmhouse, I parked in the alley and found a spot alongside a fence where the herb packet would not be soon discovered, if ever. It felt cleansing.

There. Now the home, basement and all, can be renewed and healed. I am free.

On a Sunday afternoon I headed for Parkland. I drove among the post-war tract homes, looking at Belle's house and places where I had once babysat, remembering how we would call Mother at work when we got home from school. Apprehension clung to me, intensifying the closer I came to the double bungalow. The specter of three men hung over me, dimming my confidence. My brain was clouded. I had better scout out the territory first, to feel safe. I looked at the window where the shade had been closed except for four inches that gave me hope of liberation. *Who had been in the house across the street that brutal day? Would they ever have dreamed that the house was filled with violence and broken dreams and pain?*

I drove around the block and headed down the alley. Then I noticed it: the house had been improved! New siding. A wicker chair and a table with flowers on it stood near the back door. A garage had been built on the site, and behind it was a full, healthy vegetable garden. Alongside the garden were other garages that hid me from the neighbors' view. Unobserved, I walked over to the tomato plants and dropped the symbols of healing in their white pouch onto the soil. The filth and dirt of my past experience had become rich, good soil where nature flourished.

It's over. I'm clean. The abusers were dead in the ground, and new life was alive in me.

EPILOGUE

A HOLY TIME

On a warm summer evening in June, I gathered with old friends from Lutheran churches across the nation. I saw the friend who, three decades earlier, had encouraged me to go to seminary and was my boss during those years of working part-time, raising sons, attending seminary—and heavy-duty therapy.

"I'm sorry if I was difficult to work with during those days when my life was so mixed up," I said to him.

He looked at me with his calm, dark brown eyes and said, "It was a holy time." His words were pure grace to me, filled with forgiveness and understanding.

A holy time: when life is full and intense with awareness of the enormity of what is happening. When we are in touch with the Spirit of life and death. When we discover what it is to confront evil and to survive. When one is deeply moved by pain and trauma and, at the same time, immensely grateful for being cared for and loved. He was absolutely right. It was a holy time.

"You are standing on holy ground." Moses experienced it when he heard a voice from a burning bush and was called to free his oppressed people. Mary knew it when she accepted her role as the one who would be called blessed for generations to come. Each of us experiences it as we say good-bye to one who is dying or feel tears spill over as a baby enters the world. Holy times.

In writing this memoir, I have had countless moments of insight and new awareness. As hard as it was to revisit some of my memories, I was also touched to recall a kind friend or a gentle moment when someone reassured me or took care of my body or my weak spirit. In the midst of telling this story, three writer friends watched me come to terms with ugliness and encouraged me to keep going. Bridgit, Romelle, Toni, and I met in a writing class, and over a period of eight years we bonded as friends and especially as cheerleaders. Writing can be a lonely task, but they kept me engaged and surrounded me with patient teaching. Thanks always to them.

My therapists included a kind man of faith, Justus "J" Olson, who was trained in psychology and constantly affirming of me. Char Follette and Brian Willette also listened and led me to new understandings. Bill Percy was there when I went through the most jarring psychological times: he was steady, competent, always available, and expert in the field of abuse. He has taught many students and now is an author of novels himself. Thanks, Bill.

I have teachers and editors to thank: Mary Carroll Moore, Ashley Brooks, Elizabeth Jarrett Andrew (who helped me find the "heartbeat of the book"), and Beth Wright, who was a competent editor, coach, teacher, confidence-builder. Students from Loft Literary Center classes were helpful, and Mary Knutson was a frequent companion in that process. My life experience tells me that all of us need support in our endeavors. Going it alone is an empty process and not nearly as beneficial as being in community.

As my memories unfolded and I grew stronger, many friends stood alongside me, listening, helping me make sense of the experience, and giving me courage. I could never name them all here, but I am deeply grateful to them. Friends are essential in my life.

Nagging questions remain about the meaning of my experiences. How can a parent hurt a child? Is the person forgivable? Is my own spiritual well-being dependent on how or whether I forgive someone else? Was

Mother a "bad" person? How can people overlook or deny events? I wrestle with those questions from time to time, but ultimately I have learned to live with ambiguity. There is so much we do not know or understand, and much that we will never know for sure. Our drive to be *certain* about the meaning of life is understandable but futile. If anything, I am suspicious about certainty. In seminary I took great energy from a dialectic or paradox, a premise that has opposites, both of which are true.

Rather, I am in wonder that, on the whole, I trust people. Even some of those who ultimately betrayed me also at times offered me love and, in some cases, security. Somehow, that is what lasted: the knowledge that life can be good and I can nourish others and contribute to a better world. I somehow expect the best from people and the future, even when wringing my hands over life's ordinary complications. I fight with edges of depression and fear of strangers at times, but I live life full-heartedly. I think that's what people call faith.

This is my story, my memories of what happened. I have changed the names of my family and of predators, neighbors, and others who might prefer to be anonymous. The locations and chronology of events are sometimes adapted. I cannot know which memories of mine might intersect with those of others, especially my family members, since we lived such private, secret lives even while we shared the same home. I have made no attempts to guess about what happened to them and only reported what I recall. Memoir is always imperfect. We don't always remember what color clothing we wore at a given time or whether the day was midsummer or fall. We do remember the traumas, the emotions of the experiences, and I have tried to portray those accurately here.

I carry away some important themes. First, I am safe. In many ways it was my husband and his family who gave me enough security to dare to look into my youthful days. I could not have written these memories had I not been freed from fear and suspicion. Of course, we all are afraid or doubtful at times, but I am grateful that on the whole I now feel safe.

I'll always be grateful to my husband for the fun times we had, the values we shared in caring for the world and its people, and the immense love we shared with and for our sons. I'm thankful for his forgiveness and kindness and acceptance of me. He was a good dad.

I believe that life is rich with experiences, both good and unpleasant, and when we face them, we come to know ourselves and find meaning in life. I am perhaps most disappointed in those who are afraid to know the truth, who work tenaciously to avoid being aware of hard things. It is in *knowing* difficulties that we discover how wonderful life can be and how strong we and all humanity are. And we must *know* the truth so the truth can make us free. After all, if we do not know what is happening, we cannot help those who need us.

The heritage of faith has undergirded me all my life. I am a progressive thinker in terms of theology, cautious of misuses of Scripture and narrow thinking. But when all else seems to fail, I find comfort and strength in the history of ages of believers—people who rose against injustice and hate in order to preserve a created, good earth and its beings.

Finally, I hope for us all to be watchful. My sensitivities to abusive behavior are well tuned because of my experiences. However, even as I choose to trust, I do not avoid the reality that there is evil in the world and we must be ready to expose it in order to save others. God is good and acts through us.